THE BENTLEY COLLECTION GUIDE

published by j.phillip, inc.

Eighth Edition
2000 – 2001

a **j.phillip**
INCORPORATED
publication

★ Acknowledgments ★ 

This Eighth Edition of The Bentley Collection Guide is dedicated to all who love and enjoy collecting Longaberger Products®. We are so thankful to all who have helped contribute basket information, market values, and baskets for photography purposes. It is because of all of you that this Guide continues to be the most comprehensive and accurate listing of Longaberger Products® available. We were also thrilled for the third year in a row to have so many great entries into our annual Nationwide Photo Search Contest. Our job keeps getting harder with so many creative pictures to review. We hope that you will enjoy the ones we have chosen to share and that they will inspire you to find new ways to use and display your baskets.

Please understand . . .

This Guide is published by J. Phillip Inc. and is in no way affiliated with, authorized, endorsed or licensed by The Longaberger Company®. The Longaberger Company in no way sets, reviews, approves or determines the secondary market prices published in this Guide. Longaberger Baskets®, Longaberger Pottery®, J.W. Collection® and other basket names are trademarks registered and owned by The Longaberger Company and J. Phillip, Inc. has no interest therein.

Photographs by:
Andrew Korcok, *Lighthouse* Photo Services
Terry Thurston, *Morning Light* Photography

Copyright© 2000 by J. Phillip, Incorporated
• P.O. Box 2245 • Westerville, OH 43086 •
• (800) 837-4394 • (614) 855-8507 •
• Email: info@bentleyguide.com • Website: www.bentleyguide.com •

ISBN 0-9646280-5-8
ISSN 1082-4790

 Table of Contents 

★ Basket Fun Facts ★

Index

ear Collector,
Welcome to the Eighth Edition of The Bentley Collection Guide®.

Many exciting changes have taken place in The Bentley Guide since the Seventh Edition. This new book is filled with over 100 new photos along with all new sneak-peeks into the homes of our Third Annual Nationwide Photo Search Winners. If you would like your home to be showcased in next year's Guide, see page 134 for details on how you could be chosen **and** receive your next year's Bentley FREE!

Along with these new pictures, the Bentley Guide also continues to grow with the addition of *three new collections*. Last year, The Longaberger Company® renewed their commitment to the American Cancer Society through the Horizon of Hope baskets. With this renewal, The Company declared *Horizon of Hope* as its own collection; therefore, you will no longer find these special baskets in the *Feature Collection*.

Another exciting addition came to Longaberger fans during the Christmas season with the new *Tree-Trimming Collection*, promised to bring many adorable miniature baskets to adorn your Christmas trees. This new collection starts on page 195.

And perhaps the most exciting addition to The Bentley Guide this year, is the long-awaited *J.W. Original Collection*, starting on page 139. While we are still in "research mode" for these rare and unique baskets, we have compiled the information we have been able to gather thus far along with some *wonderful* photographs of a few *J.W. Originals* in the market. If you have information about *J.W. Originals*, we would love to hear what you have learned.

The objective of this Guide is to provide a comprehensive and accurate listing of all baskets and products that have been produced by The Longaberger Company® of Dresden, Ohio. Although we are not affiliated with the company, our goal is to promote and further the collectibility of Longaberger Products®. Therefore, with each new Edition, we make improvements and additions to the Guide to provide more information and detail of the products.

As always, please keep in mind that the current market values listed in this book and in the Collector's Checklist should be used *only as a guide*. They are not intended to set prices, which vary from one section of the country to another. Secondary market prices vary greatly and are affected by many things, such as condition and demand. To better represent your specific market, we encourage you to report your results to us regularly.

We hope that you enjoy this Eighth Edition. The Fun Facts, the photos of personal collections, and the improvements in information are all for you, the Collector. Through the Bentley Collection Guide, we hope to bring you many hours of happy collecting!

History of The Longaberger Company®

In the early 1900's, in the small Ohio town of Dresden, John Wendell "J.W." Longaberger developed a love for hand-woven baskets. As a teenager, J.W. joined his father, Daddy John, at the Dresden Basket Company as a full-time basket weaver to help support the family. In 1927, J.W. married Bonnie Jean Gist and together they had 12 children. In order to support his large family, J.W. worked at the Dresden Paper Mill during the day, but continued to make baskets at night. In 1973, J.W. and his fifth child, Dave, began to teach others how to weave baskets. Although J.W. died that year, the quality and attention to detail that he wove into his baskets were kept alive, by Dave, through The Longaberger Company®. On March 17, 1999, Dave Longaberger passed away after a battle with cancer. His vision for The Longaberger Company continues through his daughters, Tami and Rachel.

Each basket is hand-woven, using hardwood maple splints. Since 1978, once a basket is completed, it is dated and signed by the weaver. In 1982, the practice of burning The Longaberger® name and logo into the bottom of each basket began, guaranteeing its authenticity.

The company started selling through home parties in 1979. In 1981, the company had 100 consultants and delivery of baskets took approximately 8-12 weeks. Back then, the consultants delivered the orders to each hostess *personally*. Many changes have taken place since this humble beginning. Within the past year, The Longaberger Company® has added over 13,000 Sales Consultants. They now employ more than 8,000 people and have approximately 65,000 independent Sales Consultants throughout all 50 states. In 1999, The Company generated $850 Million in Sales. Over the next 4-5 years, they are targeting to double where they were at in July 1999, bringing them to $1.5 Billion in sales, 10,000 Employees and 100,000 Consultants!

Along with its growing popularity among collectors, The Longaberger Company® has also been recognized nationally for its dedication to quality and commitment to excellence by many major sources. The U.S. Department of the Interior awarded the "Take Pride in America" Award to The Longaberger Company® in 1991 while Inc.® magazine recognized the company with their "Socially Responsible Entrepreneur" Award in 1992.

The Longaberger Company® has come a long way from the garage that once housed Dave's dream over 25 years ago. We encourage you to visit Dresden, Ohio to fully catch the history and commitment behind his entrepreneurial vision. If you are interested in touring the Dresden area, call the Dresden Village Association at 1-800-315-1809 or The Longaberger Company® directly at 740-322-5000.

Inc. is a registered trademark of Goldhirsh Group, Inc.

Interest in collecting Longaberger Baskets® and Pottery® has increased in recent years due to their increasing value, both inherently and monetarily. It no longer is surprising to see a collector basket double in value in only one year. Due to this interest, there is a need for reliable and accurate information about the value and identification of Longaberger Baskets® and Pottery®. As more Longaberger® products are produced, keeping this information updated is essential.

The purpose of The Bentley Collection Guide™ is:

- To provide a reference tool to Secondary Market Dealers, Consultants, Collectors, Investors and Enthusiasts.

This is accomplished by:

- Providing *actual* selling (market) prices – not just "asking" prices.

- Lending credibility to Longaberger Products® as true collectibles.

- Providing a complete, up-to-date compilation of Longaberger Products®, including individual pictures of products for identification purposes.

- Providing a "Quick Find" Index that acts as a cross-reference of baskets made from the same form.

- Providing valuable information on how to identify and appraise Longaberger Products®.

There are many applications for this Guide, including:

- An essential educational manual for new, as well as experienced Consultants.

- A great training tool for Consultants on the history of Longaberger® products.

- A sales tool for Consultants to show customers that Longaberger® products have indeed increased in value.

- A price guide for those wanting to buy, sell, or trade baskets on the Secondary Market.

- An inventory checklist to record and price all of one's baskets.

- A reference tool for valuing one's baskets for insurance purposes.

- Identifying one's baskets and evaluating their condition.

Where to find Longaberger Baskets®

New Longaberger Baskets® can be obtained only through Sales Consultants, usually at a basket home show. The baskets are ordered from a Wish List™ containing products currently available directly from The Longaberger Company®. If you are interested in ordering a current line basket, but do not know a Consultant, contact The Longaberger Company® at (800) 966-0374 to be directed to a Consultant in your area.

Collector and specialty baskets are available only for a limited time throughout the year. For example, the 1992 Christmas Collection Season's Greeting™ Basket was offered only from September through December of 1992. After this, the basket was no longer available from Longaberger®.

Older Longaberger Products® can be obtained only on the Secondary Market, which is made up of people wanting to buy and sell these older products. These items are available from a number of sources. The directory on the next page is a listing of the various services we have found to be available for collectors to buy and sell their products.

Please understand . . .
The Directory of Secondary Market Resources on the next couple of pages is for **informational purposes only** and constitutes neither an endorsement nor a recommendation. The publisher does not assume any responsibility with regard to the selection, performance, or use of these services. All understandings, agreements, or warranties, if any, take place directly between the services and the prospective users. This listing of secondary market resources is based on information available at the time of publication and J. Phillip, Inc. makes no warranties as to the completeness or accuracy.

To help our customers better evaluate the services that are listed on the next pages, we have devised a system to inform our customers of the length of our relationship with each service.

The number of 'βs' listed to the right of each name stands for the number of years that we have been in contact with the service.

It is not a rating system

We do not charge these services to be listed in this publication. The only requirement is that they have been in business for at least a year and consistently report their market results every month to us for at least a year. When dealing with any of these services, we do encourage you to let us know of your experience as we do wish to continue providing you with quality information about the secondary market.

Directory of Secondary Market Resources

Auctioneers: Auctions have been becoming a very popular way to buy or sell baskets within the last few years. Baskets can be purchased through the bidding process or can be put up for auction on a consignment basis. Each auctioneer has different terms and commission rates.

The Rebel Yell Auction Company [β]

Brent Witt, Auctioneer (VAAR#1762)
(540) 966-4656
Web: www.rebelyellauctions.com

84 School Drive
Troutville, VA 24175
Email: brentwitt@rbnet.com

Dealers There are many dealers in the market that specialize in buying, selling or trading Longaberger Products®. This type of source is often preferred for collectors who have a need to acquire or liquidate items very quickly.

Baskets Galore & More [β β β β β β β β]

Ask for Emily
(740) 754-1143
or (740) 453-8586

#3 Lacy Alley
Dresden, OH 43821
Web: www.y–city.net/users/emily/index.htm
Email: emily@y–city.net

Bay-Side Baskets [β]

Greg & Cathy Burr
(740) 754-1193
fax: (740) 754-2377

315 Main Street
Dresden, OH 43821
Email: bayside@bright.net

Greg Michael [β β β β β β β β]

(219) 686-2615
or (219) 967-4442
fax: (219) 686-9100

P.O. Box 7
Camden, IN 46917
Email: gpmmgtco@netusa1.net

Lighthouse Antiques [β]

Bette & John Emry
(317) 736-5800
fax: (317) 736-6070

62 West Jefferson Street
Franklin, IN 46131-2311
Web: www.lighthouseantiques.com
Email: john169jeff@worldnet.att.net

Newsletters Most newsletters are designed to bring basket lovers together through articles of interest. Many have the primary focus of providing a place for collectors to advertise items to buy, sell or trade. Often information regarding events for collectors is also included.

The Basket Collector's Gazette [β β β β β β β β]

Ask for Suzy
(970) 641-5838 (MDT)
fax: (970) 641-2624

PO Box 100
Pitkin, CO 81241-0100
Web: www.basketlover.com
Email: suzy@basketlover.com

continued next page

Newspapers The following source has sections dedicated to advertising baskets to buy, sell, or trade. Most also have feature articles concerning The Longaberger Company® and other subjects of interest. It is not necessary to subscribe in order to advertise; however, some offer free space with a subscription.

Dresden Transcript [β β β β β β β β]

(740) 754-1608
<u>fax</u>: (740) 754-1609

PO Box 105
Dresden, OH 43821-0105

Online / Internet Here are some areas on the information super-highway that you may also find helpful.

American Online (AOL) Posting Board:

<u>Keyword</u>: Collecting -> Other Collectibles -> Longaberger

The Bentley Collection
1-800-837-4394

<u>Web</u>: www.bentleyguide.com
<u>Email</u>: info@bentleyguide.com

The Basket Broker [β]
Frances Shifflett
(423) 947-6726

7533 Glastonbury Road
Knoxville, TN 37931-1845
<u>Web</u>: www.thebasketbroker.com
<u>Email</u>: seroba@aol.com

Basket City USA® [β]
Christine Hendershot
(419) 229-1285

2285 June Drive
Lima, OH 45805
<u>Web</u>: www.basketcityusa.com
<u>Email</u>: christine@basketcityusa.com

The Basket Gallery [β β β]
formerly listed here as Joe's Basket Gallery
Ask for Cheryl
(816) 537-4919

<u>Web</u>: www.sky.net/~jdeshon/forsale.html
<u>Email</u>: jdeshon@sky.net

The Basket House [β β]
Ask for Wendy
(540) 438-1977
<u>fax</u>: (540) 438-8187

<u>Web</u>: www.baskethouse.com
<u>Email</u>: info@baskethouse.com

The Longaberger Company
<u>Web</u>: www.Longaberger.com

For other internet sites, use your *search engines* and type in the word *Longaberger*. This will connect you to a variety of different locations.

About the Current Market Values

The prices provided in this Guide are Secondary Market values obtained from various sources, such as Dealers, Auctioneers, Collectors and Consultants.

The values shown are the *average* and the *highest* reported "selling price" for that particular basket, not the "asking" price. By providing the "selling" price of the baskets, the most accurate and reliable value is given for each basket. However, several points must be understood in relation to this pricing Guide:

(1) It is the intent of this Guide to gather all pricing data up to the last possible moment before the Guide is published. However, some prices may have changed due to the time it takes to publish and send this Guide. This is one reason for offering an update to this annual collector's guide; to keep the value of Longaberger® products continually up-to-date.

(2) The market values shown are not absolute. Increased demand in some areas may result in higher prices for particular baskets. It is also impossible to be aware of every sales transaction; therefore the market values listed may not be the absolute highest selling price during that particular period of time. We encourage you to help us represent your market even more accurately by reporting to us all transactions that you participate in throughout the year.

(3) Although some transactions reported to us may include shipping costs from seller to buyer, the prices reported in this Guide **do not include shipping and handling costs.** Even though shipping is often a part of a transaction, it is a cost of participating in the market and should not be considered part of a basket's value. However, you may need to consider this additional cost when insuring your collection because most insurance agencies will only cover <u>up to</u> the insured value listed, regardless if there are additional costs incurred to replace the item.

(4) The range of values that are listed throughout the Guide reflect the range of activity that is occurring in the Secondary Market. The *Average Value* is determined by taking a straight average of the values reported and confirmed for an item during a specific period. The *High Value* is the highest value within the range of values reported. If a transaction is reported which we consider to be much higher than other results, we do not consider this to be a true reflection of the market and therefore will not report on it until more transactions in this area are reported. It is important to note that this definition of High is different from the one used in the Fourth Edition Guide, but is the same definition used in all other editions.

Although this Guide and Collector's Checklist reflect what J. Phillip, Inc. considers to be current market values, J. Phillip, Inc. in no way warrants the prices listed therein. The publisher assumes no responsibility for any losses that might be incurred as a result of consulting this Guide.

The Bentley Collection Guide® is the most accurate and most reliable reference tool available for valuing Longaberger Products®.

★ Using this Guide ★

Finding your way through the Guide . . .

All collector series and specialty baskets are listed categorically in the first part of this publication. The order of the categories is alphabetical and can be found in the Table of Contents. Regular Line baskets are not listed in the Guide, but are listed in the *Collector's Checklist* for inventory purposes. We do not include pictures of Regular Line baskets because we do not consider them a part of the secondary market since they are still available directly from the company. It is a good idea to keep a copy of a current Wish List™ with your Guide to have pictures of these baskets on hand.

The dimensions, form number and quantities produced are now listed directly under the picture. If it is not photographed, most of this information can be found in the *Quick Find*.

Reading the notations in the Guide . . .

Each basket in the Guide is listed by its year and name(s). Special characteristics may also be listed, such as "swinging handles" (sw/h), "stationary handles" (st/h), "no handles" (no/h), "inverted bottom", etc. If the basket was originally sold with accessories, the following notations will distinguish which accessories were available: Protector: (**P**); Liner: (**L**); Lid: (**Lid**); Divider: (**Div**).

If a basket was available as a Combo, the parenthesis that follows this notation will distinguish which items were originally a part of the Combo price. When many accessories were offered with a basket, the term "Full Set" has been created to reflect this combination selling in the market. The initials in parenthesis that follow will identify what we are considering a Full Set to include.

Applying the range of values to your collection . . .

After the description of the item, an original price, if available, is listed. The next two columns list the range of values from the current market. Before applying these values to your collection, it is important to fully understand how we are determining the Average and the High values throughout the Guide. These definitions can be found on page 8.

We consider the *High Value* to represent a basket in excellent condition while the *Average Value* better represents a more average product; however, without having seen each individual product, it is inappropriate for us to judge the condition of items reported to us. We encourage each collector to evaluate the condition of their individual collection before determining its market value. Refer to page 14 to better assess the condition of your collection.

When insuring your collection, the best option is to individually determine the unique value for each piece of your collection based on its demand, condition and other characteristics. If time is an issue, the *High Value* represents the potential of the collectible, thus should be used as the potential replacement cost.

★ Using this Guide ★

Quick Find Index . . .
On page 209, there is a cross-reference index of baskets listed alphabetically by name, not collection. For example, *J.W. Corn*® is listed under *Corn* and then lists *J.W. Collection*® as a collection that this basket was available in. It will also list the other collections that have featured the Corn basket. This tool is great when wondering which collections a particular basket is available in or if the collector knows what the shape or form is, but is unsure of which collection it belongs. This index was specifically designed to be more helpful during auctions where a lot of information is needed quickly and when very little details of the item are made available to the collector. See page 209 for more information on how to use this section effectively.

Dimensional Search . . .
This next section is a reference tool that will help when trying to identify a basket by its dimensions. The baskets are divided into four size categories (square, rectangular, round, oval) and the dimensions are then listed in numerical order under each appropriate heading. The first page of this section lists specific steps to take when using this great tool to help identify items in your collection.

Collector's Checklist . . .
The supplemental booklet that came with your Guide is an inventory checklist. The collector edition and specialty baskets are listed in the same manner as in the Guide. Regular Line baskets are listed alphabetically within the year they were offered.

This checklist enables you to indicate the quantity of baskets you may have, as well as your original cost. If a current market value has been reported, it is already printed on the checklist. The values listed are clarified by the following notations: C (Combos), B (basket only), L (basket sold with liner), P (basket sold with protector), or F (full set). If any accessories were purchased with the baskets, such as liners or protectors, they can be noted in the description column. Any unique characteristics of the baskets should also be listed, such as special order color weave found in many earlier baskets.

When using the Checklist for insurance purposes, we do give permission to make <u>one</u> copy for your Insurance agent or to place in a safety deposit box. Additional copies are not permitted unless expressed written permission is given by J.Phillip, Inc.

A Word About Insurance

As your basket collection grows, you need to consider how best to cover it with insurance. A relatively small collection is usually not a problem under the normal homeowner's policy; however, any collection can be viewed as more than just a hobby if it reaches a size or falls into a category where the insurance company views it as more than "items normal and incidental to a normal household." A hobby can be viewed as a business, even though you have never sold one basket, simply because the potential to "some day" make money from it exists.

The best person to consult with on this is your insurance agent. He may initially recommend "scheduling" your individual baskets onto your policy, which simply means they are insured separately under a floater from the items listed as "unscheduled personal property" in your policy. If you don't schedule your baskets, at least make sure you have a "replacement cost endorsement" so that you will not have depreciation taken that you cannot recoup after a loss.

If you are an associate, you will need to have a separate business policy since your homeowner's has a limit on the amount they pay for business property. Your agent will be able to advise on the best package for covering your business risk. He also can explain some liability coverages. In today's "lawsuit happy world", even casual statements about "potential resale possibilities" or product durability can come back to haunt salespeople at some future date. Many have secured "professional liability" coverage to provide for defending themselves in court.

If you ever would suffer a smoke or fire loss, do not clean the baskets with normal household cleaners. Smoke has toxic chemicals that not only soil a basket, but interact with it chemically. It needs to be cleaned professionally, the sooner the better. After 24 hours, the damage begins to get substantially worse. Your insurance adjuster will not be upset if you have accrued some "reasonable expenses" to protect your baskets from further damage before he is able to inspect the loss. You will have saved him the cost of replacing them or at least improved their salvage value somewhat, even if they will not clean completely. Again, your agent can advise on who to call since he knows cleaning contractors who specialize in fire and smoke damage restoration.

Finally, as you should do with all your valuables, take photographs/videos in duplicate of each basket; identify it by noting type, age, unique characteristics, condition, original cost and current market value. Then keep a set of the photos/video at a location other than your house. Give the duplicates to your agent to keep in your file. Like any object, baskets get damaged and destroyed so you need to protect yourself from that potential loss, and insurance is a good start.

Richard Gordon, Jr.
Insurance Adjustor

The first step in identifying a Longaberger Basket® is to look on the bottom of the basket for the Longaberger® logo, which is burned into the basket. There have been five different logos used by the company since 1982:

Longaberger Stamp Progression:

Original stamp. First used in 1982 on the Grandad's Sleigh, but broke in 1983. Prior to 1982, no stamp was used.

This stamp was a temporary replacement in 1983 and was used on several hundred baskets until it was replaced by a permanent one.

This was the third stamp, which started to be used in 1983. The company wanted the baskets to have Dresden, Ohio on them, so it was replaced in 1989.

This stamp was only used for approximately one year, from 1989 to 1990. It was replaced with the fifth stamp.

This stamp was used from 1990 and is still being used currently.

However, if a basket does not have a logo, that does not mean it isn't a Longaberger Basket®. In this case, the basket was probably made before 1982. In addition, the weaver of the basket will usually initial the basket and date it. This practice began in 1978, when the company began selling the baskets through the home-party plan.

These are the three markings that help identify the authenticity of a Longaberger Basket®:

- **Longaberger Stamp – starting in 1982**
- **Date – starting in 1978**
- **Weaver's initials – also starting in 1978**

However, there are baskets produced by the company that may be missing any number of these markings, including all three. If your basket is missing any of these markings, we suggest having the basket authenticated directly by The Longaberger Company®. If you are not able to take it to

(continued on page 13)

(continued from page 12)

Dresden yourself, contact your Consultant and they may be able to help you make arrangements or give you instructions on how to ship it to the company for authentication.

In addition, baskets woven by J.W. himself, most likely will not have any markings on them. If you believe that a basket is an original J.W. basket (a basket hand-woven by J.W. himself), you will need to have it verified by one of the Longaberger family members. These baskets would have been made during the 1930s through the 1970s (before The Longaberger Company® began operations) and do have some identifying "trademarks" on them that were commonly found on J.W.'s work. This year, we have created a collection especially for these baskets. See page 140 for more information about J.W. Originals.

The value of a basket will depend on several things:

• Is the basket part of a collection series or retired from the Regular Line?

Baskets which were part of a series, or were featured only for a short time, will generally increase in value faster than baskets still found in the Regular Line. A *collection series* is a series of baskets produced either on a yearly basis or for a limited time. There are different trends occurring in the market all the time that will make different collections more "sought after". In the past year, some of the more popular series have been:

- Horizon of Hope – page 103
- All-American – page 15
- Easter Signature – page 55
- Collectors Club – page 39

• What year was the basket woven? Is the stain dark or is it light?

Baskets that were a part of the Regular Line, but later retired, tend to have higher values then those still in the Regular Line. However, older (darker stained) Regular Line baskets are beginning to become more popular. We continue to see that collectors are starting to recognize the added value that these older baskets have due to their age as well as to the fact that they have a stain that is no longer available. If the older baskets have been maintained in good condition, they generally should be worth more than newer baskets for the following reasons: (1) There were fewer made each year, (2) older baskets have a darker stain, which

(continued on page 14)

Identifying and Valuing your Baskets

(continued from page 13)

was discontinued in 1986, and (3) these baskets could be customized stained or unstained, with colored weaving and a variety of handles. These options are rarely offered anymore through the company.

• What is the condition of the basket?

The condition of a basket will significantly affect its value. A basket in "excellent" condition is worth much more than the same basket in "poor" condition. Determining the condition can be difficult to do and ultimately will need to be agreed upon by the buyer and seller. Keep in mind that these baskets are all handmade; thus some inconsistencies in weave or staining are natural to the process and add to the uniqueness of the product. See page 52 for information on what The Company considers to be "normal and acceptable" condition.

There are some characteristics, however, that should be considered not "natural" and may affect the value. Anything within the owner's control, such as, obvious heavy wear, broken handles, missing or cracked splints, or ink stained liners are just a few conditions that could lower the value of the basket.

• Is the basket signed by a family member?

Generally, baskets signed by members of the Longaberger® family can increase a basket's value, especially if the signature is either Dave's or Grandma Bonnie's. A collector can have their basket signed by taking it to Dresden or meeting up with the family at a Collectors Club™ event. In either case, it is getting more and more difficult to get signatures. The family has really been cutting back due to many infringements of privacy that have occurred in the past year or two.

Jerry Longaberger can still be found pretty easily in Dresden and is usually very happy to provide a signature. A few of the other family members can be located at the Longaberger Homestead. Wendy (#2), Jerry (#3), Larry (#4), Mary (#7), Judy (#8), Carmen (#11) and Jeff (#12) can be found at the J.W. Workshop, Monday through Saturday. See page 46 later in the Guide for more information on the family members as well as pictures of actual signatures.

The value that a signature adds also depends on the circumstance surrounding the signature. For example, signatures on Bee™ baskets, Tour® baskets, Employee or Incentive baskets are more common because family members are more attainable during the Bee, in Dresden or to an employee. This does not mean that signatures on these baskets have no additional value, it just means that these signatures were theoretically easier to obtain.

Nathan & Janet Benzing
Fairmount, Illinois

Janet's first basket was a Kiddie Purse she received as a young girl. Since then, her collection and baskets have gotten much larger. Collecting is now a family affair as she even has her Mother involved making liners to go with her own decor.

Features:
Red & Blue Weave and Trim.

MARKET VALUES

Photo	Description			Original	Avg.	High
A.	1987	Medium Berry™		19.95	**122**	155
B.	1987	Large Picnic™		64.95	**255**	365
C.	1988	Cake™		39.95	**155**	225
D.	1988	Small Picnic™		65.95	**144**	215
E.	1989	Stitching™		25.95	**106**	160
F.	1989	Quilting™		46.95	**140**	210
G.	1990	Small Spoon™		23.95	**93**	135
H.	1990	Medium Spoon™		27.95	**100**	140
I.	1990	Mini Waste™		35.95	**132**	180
J.	1990	Small Waste™		45.95	**138**	210
K.	1991	Two-Quart™		36.95	**110**	150
		Combo (**L**)		39.95	**117**	155
L.	1992	Small Market™		39.95	**100**	140
		with **Protector**		48.90	**109**	150
		with **Liner**		56.90	**109**	150
		Combo (**P/L**)		54.95	**114**	158

The first year for the All-American Series® was 1988, not 1987. The 1987 Medium Berry and Large Picnic were actually called the "Baskets and Stripes Forever" baskets. In 1988, the All-American Collection® was introduced and these baskets were then considered a part of this series.

A. 1987 Medium Berry

7.5^L x 7.5^W x 3.5^H

Form No: 1400-ABRS
No. Sold:

E. 1989 Stitching

7RD x 3^H

Form No: 5400-ABRS
No. Sold:

I. 1990 Mini Waste

7.5^L x 7.5^W x 10^H

Form No: 12000-OBRS
No. Sold:

Third in All-Around Basket Series

B. 1987 Large Picnic

17^L x 14^W x 11^H

Form No: 300-HBRS
No. Sold:

Hostess only

C. 1988 Cake

12^L x 12^W x 6^H

Form No: 100-GBRS
No. Sold:

Divider shelf also came with the basket.

D. 1988 Small Picnic

12^L x 12^W x 6^H

Form No: 100-HBRS
No. Sold:

Hostess only

F. 1989 Quilting

12RD x 5.75^H

Form No: 54000-ABRS
No. Sold:

Hostess only

G. 1990 Small Spoon

5.5^L x 5.5^W x 6^H

Form No: 10000-OBRS
No. Sold:

First in All-Around Basket Series

H. 1990 Medium Spoon

6.5^L x 6.5^W x 8^H

Form No: 11000-OBRS
No. Sold:

Second in All-Around Basket Series

J. 1990 Small Waste

9.5^L x 9.5^W x 12^H

Form No: 1800-OBRS
No. Sold:

*Hostess only.
Fourth in All-Around Basket Series.*

K. 1991 Two-Quart

9.5^L x 5^W x 9.5^H

Form No: 1000-CBRS
No. Sold:

First year for accessories.

L. 1992 Small Market

15^L x 9.5^W x 5.5^H

Form No: 10707
No. Sold:

Features:

From 1987 – 1997, this collection was promoted in June. Starting in 1998, it was promoted through April.

M.   1993 Liberty

$11.5^L \times 5^W \times 3^H$

Form No: 14541
No. Sold:

Q.   1997 Patriot

$7^L \times 5^W \times 3.5^H$

Form No: 10651
No. Sold:

MARKET VALUES

Photo		Description	Original	Avg.	High
M.	1993	Liberty™	29.95	70	95
		with Protector	33.90	70	95
		with Liner	37.90	70	95
		Combo (P/L)	36.95	75	100
N.	1994	Candle™	34.95	70	85
		with Protector	39.90	77	85
		with Liner	47.90	77	91
		Combo (P/L)	42.95	85	115
O.	1995	Carry-Along™	34.95	70	90
		with Protector	39.90	75	90
		with Liner	48.90	75	90
		Combo (P/L)	44.95	79	100
O.	1995	Flag Tie-On	6.95	17	20
P.	1996	Summertime™	34.95	60	65
		with Protector	39.90	60	65
		with Liner	47.90	60	65
		Combo (P/L)	44.95	65	100
P.	1996	Small Flag Tie-On	5.95	13	15
Q.	1997	Patriot™	32.95	55	70
		with Protector	36.90	56	80
		with Liner	44.90	56	80
		Combo (P/L)	44.95	60	89
		Full Set (C/Lid)	59.90	62	90
R.	1998	Pie™	55.00	75	105
		with Protector	64.00	80	110
		with Liner	77.00	83	110
		Combo (P/L)	72.00	85	133
		Full Set (C/Lid)	115.00	130	140
R.	1998	Pie Tie-On	8.00	8	10
S.	1999	Blue Ribbon Bread™	39.00	54	70
		with Protector	44.00	55	75
		with Liner	55.00	55	75
		Combo (P/L)	49.00	56	80
S.	1999	Oval Tie-On	8.00	9	10
T.	2000	Sparkler™	48.00	—	—
		with Protector	58.00	—	—
		with Liner	66.00	—	—
		Combo (P/L)	67.00	—	—
T.	2000	Century Tie-On	8.00	—	—
	2000	Hostess Star-Spangled Serving Tray[np]	98.00	—	—
		with Protector	119.00	—	—
		with Liner	126.00	—	—
		Combo (P/L)	139.00	—	—

18   [np] = Not Pictured

N. 1994 Candle

9^L x 5^W x 5^H

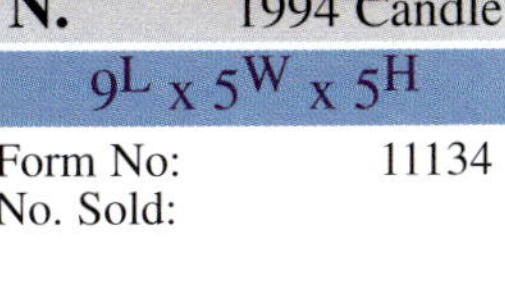

Form No: 11134
No. Sold:

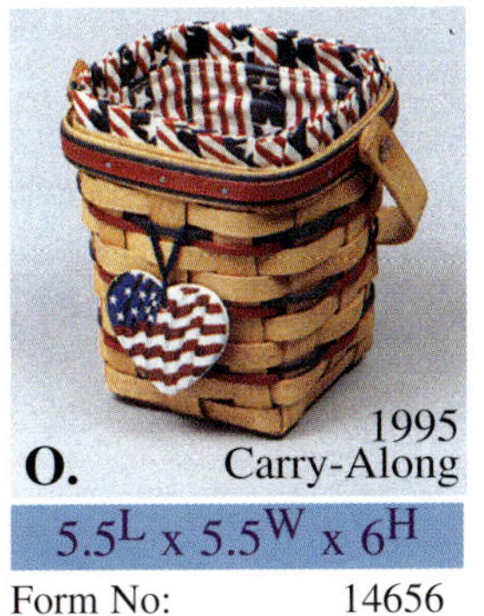

O. 1995 Carry-Along

5.5^L x 5.5^W x 6^H

Form No: 14656
Tie-On: 31551
No. Sold:

Tie-On sold separately

P. 1996 Summertime

7.75^L x 4.5^W x 2.25^{FH} x 4.5^{BH}

Form No: 18911
Tie-On: 32891
No. Sold: 146,951

*Both regular and divid-
ed protector offered.
Tie-On sold separately.*

R. 1998 Pie

12^L x 12^W x 4^H

Form No: 12289
Tie-On: 31950
No. Sold:

*Pie Plate was retired after
April 2000. See Pottery
on page 156 for details.*

S. 1999 Blue Ribbon Bread

10.5^L x 8.75^W x 4^H

Form No: 14346
Tie-On: 36218
No. Sold:

Tie-On sold separately

T. 2000 Sparkler

11^L x 8^W x 5.5^H

Form No: 18694
Tie-On: 35483
No. Sold:

Tie-On sold separately

Fabric Fun Fact

The year 2000 brought an end to the popular Star-Spangled Stripes™ fabric in the All-American Collection®. This exclusive fabric was first introduced in 1994, however, it was not exclusively offered for the feature baskets. Liners for the Serving Tray, Cracker, Small and Large Picnic, Bread and Oregano baskets were also available. Place Mats, Napkins, Garters, and Handle Ties were just a few other accessories created in the fabric to complete the patriotic fanfare.

CONGRATULATIONS!

Nationwide Photo Search Winners
2000 – 2001

FIRST PLACE WINNER
Received $100 worth of Bentley products

Kristin Anderson – Mackinaw, IL
see page 193

Here are our other Eighth Edition Winners
Received their Eighth Edition Bentley Guide *FREE!*

Gretta Adams	Grayson, KY	page 53
Marsha Artis	Portsmouth, OH	page 185
Janet & Nathan Benzing	Fairmount, IL	page 15
Lois Bergman	Rantoul, IL	page 163
Connie Boring	Columbus, OH	page 87
Theresa Drake	Lockport, IL	page 155
Tina Fitzpatrick	Oronogo, MO	page 21
Janet Gardner	Gallipolis, OH	page 47
Donna Gilbert	Enola, PA	page 73
Susan Grasso	Sellersville, PA	page 39
Jean Greiner	Bellevile, IL	page 197
Paula Hawkins	Union Grove, AL	page 161
Peggy Herb	Halifax, PA	page 175
Judy Holt	Manassas, VA	page 143
Denise Johnson	Santa Ynez, CA	page 179
Julie Kokoszka	Issaquah, WA	page 205
Tricia Kutz	Alburtis, PA	page 33
Lisa Lahmon	Mount Vernon, OH	page 147
Ruth Libey	Angola, IN	page 195
Angela Lundgren	Los Angeles, CA	page 103
Kimberly Malkiewicz	Valrico, FL	page 91
Nancy McMahon	Convington, IN	page 61
Sarah Mueller	Tecumseh, NE	page 151
Carolyn Powell	Hurlock, MD	page 27
Elaine Renner	Eaton, OH	page 189
J.Dianne Ricker	Chester Gap, VA	page 135
Susan Ryan	Pickerington, OH	page 139
Elizabeth Sanders	Crown Point, IN	page 111
Rita Scaggs	Raceland, KY	page 107
LeAnn Starner	Dover, PA	page 97
Suzanne Tobin	Williamsport, OH	page 93
Purdue Troy	Kokomo, IN	page 69
Karen Weller	Seymour, IN	page 55

See page 134 for information on how to be a part of our Nationwide Search for our Ninth Edition Guide.

Bee Baskets™

Tina Fitzpatrick
Oronogo, Missouri

Tina has about 50 baskets in her collection. This snapshot here is a sampling of her collection, which centers around baskets with red accents.

Features:

Only available to those who attend the Basket Bee. Starting in 1990, tagged with Bee Theme. Basket form and accent colors vary each year.

MARKET VALUES

Photo	Description	Original	Avg.	High
	1988 Bee Decorated Basket Contest			
A.	Small Peg	N/C	—	—
	Medium Peg[np]	N/C	—	—
	Large Peg[np]	N/C	—	—
B.	1988 Large Bee Basket™		145	165
	1988 Medium Bee Basket™		100	100
C.	1989 Bee Basket™		145	180
D.	1990 Bee Basket™	19.90	69	100
E.	1991 Bee Basket™	19.91	82	165 ✍
F.	1992 Bee Basket™	20.00	89	155 ✍
G.	1993 Bee Basket™	25.00	100	125
	with **Protector**		106	130
	with **Liner**		106	130
	Combo (**P/L**)		115	150
G.	1993 Tote	N/C	13	15
H.	1994 Bee Basket™	25.00	167	270 ✍
	with **Protector**		167	270
	with **Liner**		180	270
	Combo (**P/L**)		208	300 ✍
H.	1994 Tote	N/C	16	23
H.	1994 Bee Tie-On™		—	—

[np] = Not Pictured
✍ = With Signatures

About The Bee™ . . .

This celebration of baskets is not for the faint of heart. "Longaberger Homestead Days" are usually held the last day of each Bee™. On these days, vendors from all over the country set up tables throughout Dresden and the town is flooded with enthusiasts from all states. The 2000 Bee™ will be held on 7/26–7/29, 7/30–8/2, and 8/2–8/5 and is called the "Un-BEE-lievable" Bee™.

Hope to see you there!

The Basket Bee™ is t annual convention usually in August, tl The Company hosts Columbus, Ohio fc their Consultants. T first year for "The Bee" was 1981. No "The Bee" has grow to three convention each consisting of three days of speake and seminars and o day to visit Dresde

B. 1988

14^L x 7.75^W x 5.25^H

Form No: 3600-AO
No. Sold:

No Tag. Stained over Medium AND Large Easter baskets. Available with Blue, Green, Lilac, or Pink weaving.

E. 1991

8.5^L x 8.5^W x 5^H

Form No: 1500-
No. Sold:

Teal and burgundy weave. Theme: "Imagine the Possibilities"

1985 (Potpourri)

5^L x 5^W x 2.5^H

1986 (Forget-Me-Not)

5RD x 4.5^H

The 1985 and 1986 Bee Baskets shown above were not officially given out by The Longaberger Company®. These baskets were Booking Baskets tagged by a Director for her consultants. The first Bee Basket sponsored by the company was in 1988, in which Large and Medium Easter baskets were stained over.

A. Decorated 1988 Small Peg

5^L x 5^W x 4.5^H

Form No: 14000-AO
No. Sold:

Med. Peg: 5.5^L x 5.5^W x 6^H
Lg. Peg: 6.5^L x 6.5^W x 8^H

C. 1989

8.75^L x 4.75^W x 6.5^H

Form No: 5600-BRST
No. Sold:

Christmas Memory, including Christmas tag. Only difference is wooden bottom

1989 wooden bottom

C.

Bee Theme burned into bottom. Theme: "Weave Your American Dream"

D. 1990

7RD x 6.5^H

Form No: 3900-AO
No. Sold:

Dusty rose and blue weave. Theme: "Together We're on the Move".

F. 1992

14^L x 9^W x 4.5^H

Form No: 12335
No. Sold:

Burgundy, teal and golden rod weave. Theme: "Discover the Vision"

Totes:

G. 1993

13^L x 8^W x 5^H

Form No: 13501
No. Sold:

Pink and teal weave. Theme: "Making it Happen Together" First year for accessories.

Totes:

H. 1994

6.5^L x 6.5^W x 8^H

Form No: unknown
No. Sold:

Rose pink and purple weave. Theme: "Celebrate Your Success".

23

Features:

The Bee™ is usually held during the first week of August. The 2000 Bee is 7/26–7/29, 7/30–8/2, 8/2–8/5.

MARKET VALUES

Photo	Description		Original	Avg.	High
I.	1995	Bee Basket™	25.00	**190**	**250**
		with **P**rotector	29.95	**190**	**250**
		with **L**iner	37.95	**190**	**250**
		Combo **(P/L)**	42.90	**190**	**275**
I.	1995	Tote	N/C	**32**	**40**
I.	1995	Bee Tie-On™		**—**	**—**
J.	1996	Bee Basket™	25.00	**90**	**205**
		with **P**rotector	29.95	**96**	**205**
		with **L**iner	37.95	**105**	**225**
		Combo **(P/L)**	42.90	**138**	**290** ✎
	1996	Tote	N/C	**17**	**25**
J.	1996	Bee Tie-On™		**16**	**20**
K.	1997	Bee Basket™	27.95	**85**	**135**
		with **P**rotector	32.90	**89**	**150**
		with **L**iner	40.90	**89**	**150**
		Combo **(P/L)**	45.85	**95**	**175** ✎
K.	1997	Tote	N/C	**26**	**28**
K.	1997	Bee Tie-On™	7.00	**10**	**19**
L.	1998	Bee Basket™	25.00	**75**	**80**
		with **P**rotector	29.00	**83**	**90**
		with **L**iner	37.00	**85**	**99**
		Combo **(P/L)**	41.00	**99**	**110**
L.	1998	Tote	N/C	**27**	**40**
L.	1998	Bee Tie-On™	7.00	**—**	**—**
M.	1999	Bee Basket™	29.00	**81**	**100**
		with **P**rotector	33.00	**81**	**100**
		with **L**iner	41.00	**81**	**100**
		Combo **(P/L)**	45.00	**85**	**110**
M.	1999	Tote	N/C	**34**	**52**
M.	1999	Bee Tie-On™	7.00	**—**	**—**

✎ = With Signatures

Tote:

I. 1995

10^L x 6^W x 4^H

Form No: unknown
No. Sold:

Purple and green weave. Theme: "It Begins with a Dream" Accessories sold separately.

M. 1999

7^L x 3.5^W x 4.75^H

Form No: unknown
No. Sold:

Green, Rose, Blue and Purple weave. Theme: "Building Tomorrow Together". Accessories sold separately.

8.5^L x 8.5^W x 5^H

Form No: unknown
No. Sold:

Gold, red and blue weave. Theme: "Light the Fire Within" Accessories sold separately.

5.5^L x 5.5^W x 6^H

Form No: unknown
No. Sold: ≈ 24,000

Red, blue and green weave. Theme: "Bringing America Home". Accessories sold separately.

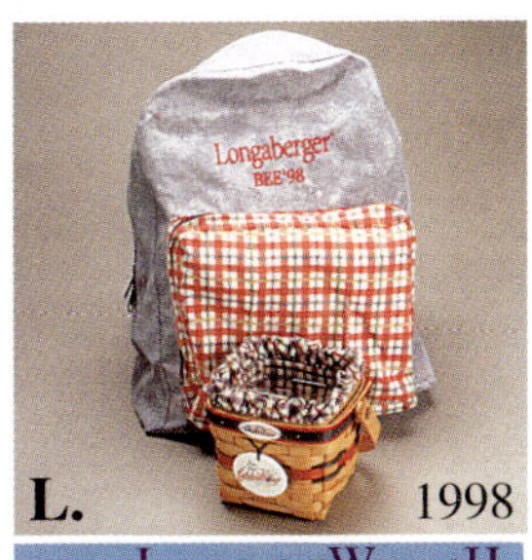

5.25^L x 5.25^W x 4^H

Form No: unknown
No. Sold:

Red and blue weave. Theme: "Join Our Celebration". Accessories sold separately.

Remembering Dave...

Since Dave Longaberger's passing on March 17, 1999, Consultants and Collectors, along with many family and friends, have searched for a special way to express their appreciation for the person who had inspired them for so many years.

The Dresden Transcript, the local newspaper, published a column for 10 months in each paper entitled "Remembering Dave. . ." where people wrote in special memories they wanted to share. In another tribute, on April 22, 1999, a tree was planted at the local Tri-Valley High School in his memory.

But, perhaps the most special tribute has been the one made for all his collectors to enjoy for years to come. Woven by his weavers and dedicated by his daughters, every feature of the Founder's Basket is linked to Dave. It is a tribute in which everyone can participate (see page 86).

2000 Dave Longaberger
Founder's Basket

Basket Fun Fact

The Spirit of Longaberger™

This annual award is possibly the most prestigious award that The Longaberger Company® gives. It is an award to recognize the "Achievements of The Heart".

There are eight different criterion set for the award and each candidate is nominated by their peers. Nominations are usually accepted until the end of May and the award is given to one person at each Bee™. There have only been 20 presented since its inception in 1994.

Areas of Achievement:

- *a sense of family*

- *sharing, caring and helping others*

- *treating others the way they want to be treated*

- *humor, the ability to laugh at one's self*

- *the pursuit of excellence*

- *a commitment to education, recreation and community beyond what is typically expected*

- *a concern for the environment*

- *an active pursuit of human endeavors aimed at stimulating a better quality of life*

Carolyn Powell
Hurlock, Maryland

Carolyn has been collecting since 1984. Her first show was over $1000! In her collection of almost 400 baskets, she feels that the one that gets the most use is her 1984 Hamper™.

MARKET VALUES

Photo	Description		Original	Avg.	High
A.	1980	Sunburst	3.95	**140**	**165**
	19XX-84	Small Spoon [WL]	—	**49**	**55**
		5" Measuring [WL]	—	**30**	**35**
		Button [WL]	6.43	**58**	**65**
B.	1984-90	Candle™	—	**45**	**76**
C.	1985-90	Potpourri™	3.00	**45**	**95**
D.	1986-87	Forget-Me-Not™	—	**60**	**90**
E.	1988	Sugar and Spice™	—	**62**	**95**
F.	1988-90	Keepsake™	16.95*	**52**	**85**
G.	1990-92	Ivy™	**	**52**	**80**
		with **P**rotector	2.95	**54**	**90**
H.	1990-92	Laurel™	**	**52**	**70**
		with **P**rotector	2.95	**55**	**80**
I.	1990-92	Rosemary™	**	**57**	**78**
		with **P**rotector	2.95	**58**	**90**
J.	1992-94	Sweet Basil™	22.95*	**42**	**65**
		with **P**rotector	25.90	**46**	**65**
		with **L**iner	31.90	**46**	**65**
		Combo **(P/L)**	34.85	**52**	**70**
K.	1992-95	Potpourri Sachet	11.95*	**13**	**20**
L.	1992-96	Ambrosia™	22.95*	**42**	**60**
		with **P**rotector	25.90	**44**	**60**
		with **L**iner	31.90	**44**	**60**
		Combo **(P/L)**	34.85	**51**	**65**

*Basket Value, not cost.

**Free, with 2+ bookings

[WL] = Wish List™. It is similar to what is available today. Pictures can be found in a current Wish List™. See the Quick Find for dimensions and form numbers.

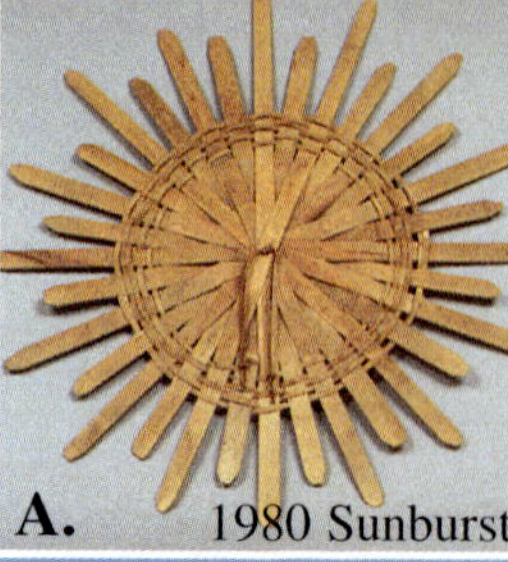

A.　1980 Sunburst

22" diameter

Form No:　　　7000-O
No. Sold:

E.　·　Sugar and Spice　1988

5.75^L x 3.75^W x 3^H

Form No:　　　45000-AO
No. Sold:

I.　1990-92　Rosemary

5.75^L x 3.75^W x 3^H

Form No:　　　45000-JOS
No. Sold:

3/8" Weave. Free to Hostesses with 2+ Bookings.

B. 1984-90 Candle

9^L x 5^W x 5^H

Form No: 1100-AO
No. Sold:

C. 1985-90 Potpourri

5^L x 5^W x 2.5^H

Form No: 13000-AO
No. Sold:

Free to Hostesses with show sales greater than $150.

D. 1986-87 Forget-Me-Not

5RD x 4.5^H

Form No: 3800-AO
No. Sold:

Free to Hostesses with show sales greater than $150.

F. 1988-90 Keepsake

5.75^L x 3.75^W x 3^H

Form No: 45000-IO
No. Sold:

G. 1990-92 Ivy

5.5^L x 5.5^W x 2.5^H

Form No: 13100-JOS
No. Sold:

3/8" Weave. Free to Hostesses with 2+ Bookings.

H. 1990-92 Laurel

5.5RD x 3.75^H

Form No: 17000-JOS
No. Sold:

3/8" Weave. Free to Hostesses with 2+ Bookings.

J. 1992-94 Sweet Basil

5^L x 5^W x 2.5^H

Form No: 10146
No. Sold:

3/8" Weave. Free to Hostesses with 2+ Bookings.

K. 1992-95 Sachet

N/A

Form No: 209581
No. Sold:

Free with 1 Booking.

L. 1992-96 Ambrosia

5.5^L x 4^W x 4^H

Form No: 10120
No. Sold:

3/8" Weave. Free to Hostesses with 2+ Bookings.

Features:

Prior to 1990: 1/2" weave
After 1990: 3/8" weave

MARKET VALUES

Photo	Description	Original	Avg.	High
M.	1992-99 Lavender™	22.95*	32	53
	with **P**rotector	25.90	38	50
	with **L**iner	31.90	40	50
	Combo (**P/L**)	34.85	45	75 ✍
N.	1995-98 Thyme™	25.95*	34	45
	with **P**rotector	28.90	40	45
	with **L**iner	35.90	40	45
	Combo (**P/L**)	38.85	46	65
O.	1996-00 Spoon Rest	18.95*	22	25
P.	1998-00 Spoon Rest, Holly	20.00*	25	32
Q.	1999 Candy Corn™ Votives	20.00*	26	30

* Basket Value, not cost.
✍ = With Signatures

M. 1992-99 Lavender
8^L x 4^W x 2^H

Form No: 10138
No. Sold:

Q. 1999 Candy Corn Votives
3RD x 2^H

Form No: 37508
No. Sold:

Set of 2. Offered in August 1999 FREE with two or more bookings. Not available for purchase.

What happened to the All-American Votives?

When the All-American® Votives were first introduced in 1999, it was not clear if they would return, or not. During the 2000 campaign, not only did they return, but The Company has promised that they will be seen again in 2001. Since they are items that continue to be offered, much like the Booking items in the Regular Line, they have been pulled from this collection until they are discontinued and can only be found on the secondary market.

N. 1995-98 Thyme

4.5RD x 3^H

Form No: 19003
No. Sold:

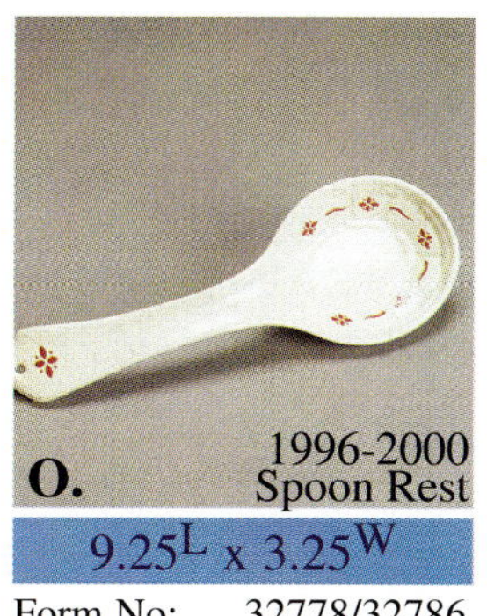

O. 1996-2000 Spoon Rest

9.25^L x 3.25^W

Form No: 32778/32786
32794/33651

Available in blue, green, red and ivory.

P. 1998-2000 Holly Spoon Rest

9.25^L x 3.25^W

Form No: 33472
No. Sold:

Fun Fact

The Longaberger Company has been growing in leaps and bounds! They continue to target new audiences, while catering to their current loyal collectors.

Starting November 15, 1999, The Company broke new ground with the introduction of sales flyers and Wish Lists™ being printed in both Spanish and Japanese.

Our beloved Longaberger Products are now available in three different languages!

Aren't you Dyeing to Know?

Many Collectors prefer the baskets "with color". But most do not know what is involved with making those colors possible. The complete process takes place at Longaberger's Hartville plant.

The splints will spend between 40 minutes to 2 hours in a vat. The entire dyeing process can take 3-4 hours, per batch.

A strip of weaving is first dyed to the exact color and then used to check every batch. After a couple of days, a new sample is made to protect against fading.

Freshly clipped weaving uses more dye, so the weaving has to be dried first. It is then placed into a vat which holds 37 gallons of very hot water. The employees are trained to watch several vats at a time and to carefully test for the exact color. Each batch is dried for 4-5 seconds under a heat gun to check the color, which can change once it is dry.

Once the color is judged to be perfect, the bundle of weaves is rinsed. Often it takes more than one rinse to remove all of the excess dye. Next, comes a salt bath which sets the color. The amount of salt added to the water depends on the color. The weaves will stay in the salt bath until the "bleed off" is faint. Finally it is rinsed again. At this stage, the remaining water from this final rinse should not have any color in it.

The weaves are then allowed to drain to remove excess water and then shipped to the weaving facilities.

The Classic Stain and Whitewash finishes are applied after the basket is completely woven. This staining process helps to protect the color of the dye even further. Handles or "ears" are not attached to your basket until after the staining process.

Christmas Collection®

Tricia Kutz
Alburtis, Pennsylvania

While this beautiful staircase is a great place to show off Tricia's Christmas baskets, it also illustrates her creative way she uses her Glad Tidings™ baskets. Each family member has their own basket as their Christmas stocking, which are hung on the staircase with obvious care.

Features:
Red or Green Weave and Trim.
Commemorative Brass Tag.

MARKET VALUES

Photo	Description		Original	Avg.	High
A.	1981	Candle™	14.95	**737**	**950**
B.	1982	Grandad's Sleigh™	19.95	**790**	**950**
C.	1983	Bell™	22.95	**690**	**915**
D.	1984	Holly™	24.95	**325**	**475** ✎
E.	1985	Cookie™	24.95	**200**	**340**
		with Liner	33.95	**243**	**350**
F.	1986	Candy Cane™	26.95	**173**	**280**
G.	1987	Mistletoe™	19.95	**100**	**155**
H.	1988	Poinsettia™	26.95	**99**	**155**
I.	1989	Memory™	34.95	**94**	**135**
J.	1990	Gingerbread™	32.95	**89**	**130**
		with Protector	37.90	**97**	**130**
		with Liner	45.90	**97**	**130**
		Combo (P/L)	50.85	**100**	**160**
K.	1991	Yuletide Traditions™	38.95	**93**	**140**
		with Protector	45.90	**104**	**145**
		with Liner	52.90	**104**	**145**
		Combo (P/L)	59.85	**122**	**185**
L.	1992	Season's Greetings™	44.95	**79**	**125**
		with Protector	49.90	**79**	**125**
		with Liner	57.90	**80**	**125**
		Combo (P/L)	53.95	**88**	**140**

* = Substitute R for Red or G for Green.

† = Product numbers are stated Red weave / Green weave

✎ = With Signatures.

A.   1981 Candle

9ᴸ x 5ᵂ x 5ᴴ

Form No: 1100-
No. Sold: 2,000

E.   1985 Cookie

7ᴿᴰ x 3ᴴ

Form No: 5400-A*
No. Sold:

First Christmas basket offered with an accessory. Liners were not offered again until 1990

I.   1989 Memory

8.75ᴸ x 4.75ᵂ x 6.5ᴴ

Form No: 5600-B*ST
No. Sold: 129,651

B. 1982 Grandad's Sleigh

.25L x 5.5W x 2FH x 5.5BH

Form No:	4900-Z
No. Sold:	3,200

Available with red tag only. Grandad with one 'd' was an intentional misspelling.

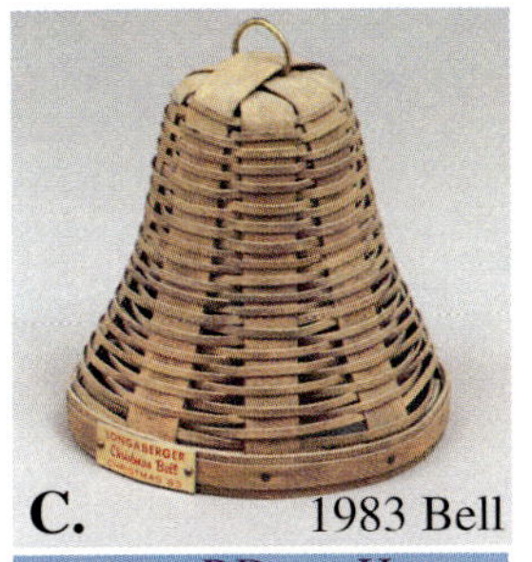

C. 1983 Bell

6.5RD x 7H

Form No:	4901-OO
No. Sold:	3,700

Available with red or green tag.

D. 1984 Holly

15L x 8W x 2.25H

Form No:	4600-AZ
No. Sold:	16,494

Only available in red.

F. 1986 Candy Cane

5L x 5W x 4.5H

Form No:	14000-A*T
No. Sold:	

G. 1987 Mistletoe

7L x 5W x 3.5H

Form No:	700-A*T
No. Sold:	

H. 1988 Poinsettia

7RD x 6.5H

Form No:	3900-B*ST
No. Sold:	

J. 1990 Gingerbread

10L x 6W x 4H

Form No:	3400-A*ST
No. Sold:	165,117

First year both liner and protector offered with basket.

K. 1991 Yuletide Traditions

13L x 7.5W x 3FH x 8BH

Form No:	5100-C*ST
No. Sold:	147,247

L. 1992 Season's Greetings

9.5L x 6W x 6H

Form No:	10316/10219†
No. Sold:	

Features:

This collection is usually promoted from September through the end of December.

MARKET VALUES

Photo		Description	Original	Avg.	High
M.	1993	Bayberry™	42.95	73	125
		with Protector	48.90	78	135
		with Liner	55.90	78	135
		Combo (P/L)	49.95	89	140
N.	1994	Jingle Bell™	47.95	90	125
		with Protector	54.90	90	130
		with Liner	62.90	90	130
		Combo (P/L)	59.95	98	136
		Full Set (Combo/Lid)	79.90	105	150
N.	1994	Jingle Bell Tie-On	6.95	14	28
O.	1995	Cranberry™	47.95	82	105
		with Protector	54.90	87	110
		with Liner	64.90	87	110
		Combo (P/L)	59.95	98	120
		Full Set (Combo/Lid)	79.90	98	130
O.	1995	Christmas Tie-On	6.95	13	20
O.	1995	Hanukkah Tie-On	6.95	9	10
P.	1996	Holiday Cheer™	47.95	64	100
		with Protector	53.90	64	100
		with Liner	64.90	64	100
		Combo (P/L)	59.95	76	129
		Full Set (Combo/Lid)	81.90	93	130
P.	1996	Christmas Tie-On	6.95	11	18
	1996	Hanukkah Tie-On[np]	6.95	—	—
Q.	1997	Snowflake™	49.95	70	90
		with Protector	58.90	73	95
		with Liner	71.90	73	100
		Combo (P/L)	69.95	86	135
		Full Set (Combo/Lid)	93.90	110	140
Q.	1997	Christmas Tie-On	6.95	12	18
Q.	1997	Hanukkah Tie-On	6.95	—	—
R.	1998	Glad Tidings™	49.00	64	75
		with Protector	57.00	64	80
		with Liner	70.00	83	100
		Combo (P/L)	69.00	90	115
		Full Set (Combo/Lid)	91.00	93	127
R.	1998	Christmas Tie-On	8.00	10	16
	1998	Hanukkah Tie-On	8.00	—	—
	1998-P	Kwanzaa Tie-On	8.00	—	—
S.	1999	Popcorn™	59.00	—	—
		with Protector	68.00	—	—
		with Liner	76.00	—	—
		Combo (P/L)	69.00	78	85
		Full Set (Combo/Lid)	101.00	113	125
S.	1999	Christmas Tie-On	8.00	—	—
S.	1999	Hanukkah Tie-On	8.00	—	—

M. 1993 Bayberry

9L x 9W x 4.5H

Form No: 11584/11592†
No. Sold:

Q. 1997 Snowflake

10L x 9.25W x 6.5H

Form No: 12645/12637†
Tie-On: 34738
No. Sold: 507,000

Tie-On and Lid not included in Combo.

  [np] = Not Pictured.

N. 1994 Jingle Bell

8RD x 6^H

Form No: 17906/17914†
Tie-On: 31437
No. Sold:

Tie-On and Lid not included in Combo.

O. 1995 Cranberry

8.5^L x 8.5^W x 7^H

Form No: 19500/19518†
Tie-On: 32441
No. Sold:

Tie-On and Lid not included in Combo.

P. 1996 Holiday Cheer

12^L x 8^W x 4.25^H

Form No: 18511/18520†
Tie-On: 31704
No. Sold: 403,248

Tie-On and Lid not included in Combo.

R. 1998 Glad Tidings

.75^L x 6^W x 9^{BH} x 7.5^{FH}

Form No: 12386/12394†
Tie-On: 33511
No. Sold:

Tie-On and Lid not included in Combo. Last year for Imperial Stripe fabric.

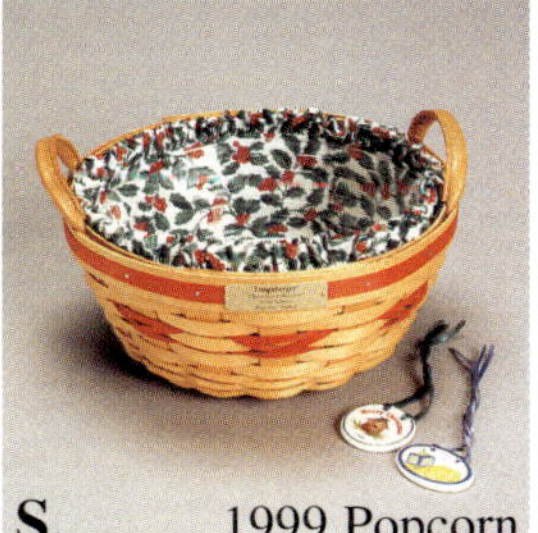

S. 1999 Popcorn

10.5RD x 5^H

Form No: 15156/15351†
Christmas Tie-On: 36935
Hanukkah Tie-On: 36943

Tie-Ons sold separately. Regular and divided protectors were offered.

Fun Fact

Longaberger has been working very hard to diversify its product line. In 1995, they introduced the very first Hanukkah Tie-On. Fabrics to celebrate both Hanukkah and Kwanzaa did not arrive until 1998. The popularity of these items can be seen in the customers' responses. Sales from these items alone exceeded more than $13 Million in 1998.

† = Product numbers are stated: Red weave / Green weave.

The Second Annual Basket Happening was again, a _great time!_

Collectors from all over the country came to Zanesville, Ohio to be a part of a weekend filled with selling, buying, trading, learning, sharing and FUN!

- Shop for **Retired Baskets & Products** throughout the hotel rooms.

- Wander through **a vendor area filled with basket accessories.**

- **Sit in on informal classrooms** designed by The Bentley Collection® and educate yourself. The topics covered at the 2000 Basket Happening included:

  - Dangers & Trends in the Market
  - Insuring Your Collection
  - Signatures – What to Know
  - Organizing and Inventorying your Collection
  - How to Identify and Value your Baskets

For more information about
The Basket Happening 2001
stay tuned to our website: www.bentleyguide.com

Come and enjoy yourself along with many other Collectors just like you!

Reservations can be made at 740-453-0771.
To receive more information, please call 614-855-8507.

Collectors Club™

Susan Grasso
Sellersville, Pennsylvania

This fantastic display is the work of a Consultant about to Branch. Susan started selling in 1992 and is <u>never</u> without a basket. Her favorite form is the Medium Market Basket, which means that the new Founder's Basket will soon be on her arm!

Features:

J.W.® Blue and Traditions™ Green Trim and Weave. Commemorative brass tag and collectors box.

MARKET VALUES

Photo	Description	Original	Avg.	High
	Membership Items:			
A.	1995-96 Charter Membership	75.00	**105**	**178**
	with **P**rotector	83.95	**120**	**180**
	with **L**iner	94.95	**127**	**180**
	Combo (**P/L**)	103.90	**127**	**265** ✍
A.	1997-P Membership	75.00	—	—
	with **P**rotector	83.95	—	—
	with **L**iner	94.95	—	—
	Combo (**P/L**)	103.90	—	—
	1996 Items:			
B.	1996 <u>Miniature</u>			
	J.W. Market®	125.00	**340**	**400**
	with **P**rotector	127.95	**375**	**410**
	with **L**iner	138.95	**375**	**410**
	Combo (**P/L**)	141.90	**388**	**675** ✍
C.	1996 Membership Tie-On	N/C	**41**	**75**
D.	1996 Small Serving Tray™	69.95	**150**	**200**
	with **P**rotector	79.90	**160**	**200**
	with **L**iner	92.90	**160**	**200**
	Combo (**P/L**)	102.85	**163**	**250**
E.	1996 Longaberger University Ornament™	29.95	**36**	**75**
	1997 Items:			
F.	1997 Renewal Basket™	39.95	**77**	**105**
	with **P**rotector	44.90	—	—
	with **L**iner	54.90	—	—
	Combo (**P/L**)	59.85	**98**	**149**
G.	1997 <u>Miniature</u>			
	J.W. Waste®	99.95	**171**	**225**
	with **P**rotector	102.90	—	—
	with **L**iner	113.90	—	—
	Combo (**P/L**)	116.85	**187**	**475** ✍
H.	1997 Handle Gripper	N/C	**19**	**25**
I.	1997 Welcome Home™	69.95	**133**	**145**
	with **P**rotector	79.90	**133**	**145**
	with **L**iner	92.90	**133**	**145**
	Combo (**P/L**)	102.85	**138**	**250** ✍
J.	1997 Caroling in Dresden Ornament™	29.95	**35**	**70**

✍ = With Signatures

A. 1996 Membership

9.5ᴸ x 5ᵂ x 9.5ᴴ

Form No: 62839
No. Sold: 105,304

Top half of basket woven with 1/2" weaving, while a 3/8" weave was used on the bottom half.

D. 1996 Serving Tray

11.5ᴸ x 15.5ᵂ x 3.75ᴴ

Form No: 12629
No. Given:

H. 1997 Membership Handle Gripper

N/A

Form No: unknown
No. Sold:

Sent FREE to all Members "CHARTER MEMBER" was embroidered for those who held that status.

B.   Miniature Market   1996

5.75^L x 4^W x 3^H

Form No:	150240
Signed:	15024
No. Sold:	

*Accessories sold separately.
Seal on the box designates
the basket was signed by a
family member.*

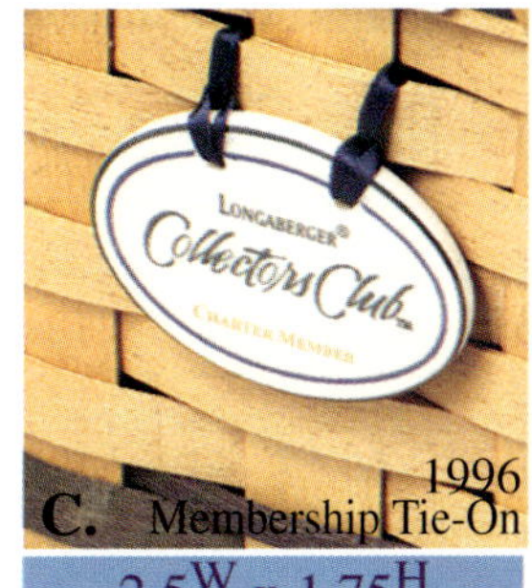

C.   Membership Tie-On   1996

2.5^W x 1.75^H

Form No:	83089
No. Given:	≈ 95,000

E.   1996 Ornament

3.5RD

Form No:	33758
No. Sold:	

*"Longaberger University
– Edition 1996"*

F.   1997 Renewal

9^L x 5^W x 5^H

Form No:	105702
No. Sold:	

G.   Miniature Waste   1997

3.75^L x 3.75^W x 4.75^H

Form No:	17797
No. Sold:	

About the Collectors Club™

The Longaberger Company® introduced The Collectors Club™ in December 95. With membership, each collector receives a Membership basket, a quarterly magazine, *Signatures*™, as well as a monthly issue designed to advertise baskets and products called *The Collectors Exchange*™.

I.   Welcome Home   1997

15^L x 9.5^W x 5.5^H

Form No:	10464
No. Sold:	

*Available to Members
between Aug. 1, 1997
through Sept. 30, 1997.*

J.   1997 Ornament

3.5RD

Form No:	34207
No. Sold:	

*"Caroling in Dresden –
Edition 1997"*

Features:
Most of the baskets feature two braided ears.

MARKET VALUES

Photo	Description	Original	Avg.	High
	1998 Items:			
K.	1998 Renewal Basket™	44.95	**68**	95
	with **P**rotector	50.90	**80**	95
	with **L**iner	62.90	**80**	95
	Combo (**P/L**)	68.85	**85**	101
L.	1998 <u>Miniature</u>			
	J.W. Apple®	139.95	**165**	200
	with **P**rotector	142.90	**170**	200
	with **L**iner	153.90	**170**	200
	Combo (**P/L**)	156.85	**177**	250
M.	1998 25th Anniversary™	115.00	**194**	250
	with **P**rotector	128.00	**200**	269
	with **L**iner	160.00	**200**	269
	Combo (**P/L**)	173.00	**217**	280
M.	1998 25th Anniversary Tie-On	N/C	**30**	55
N.	1998 Thyme™	N/C	**51**	71
	with **P**rotector	3.00	**55**	75
	with **L**iner	12.00	**55**	75
	Combo (**P/L**)	15.00	**70**	100
O.	1998 Harbor™	85.00	**107**	165
	with **P**rotector	95.00	**135**	170
	with **L**iner	110.00	**145**	170
	Combo (**P/L**)	120.00	**170**	225
	Full Set (**C/Lid**)	148.00	**195**	235
P.	1998 "25 Years in Pictures"	N/C	—	—
Q.	1998 Shopping in Dresden Ornament™	30.00	**35**	50
	1999 Items:			
R.	1999 Renewal Basket™	42.00	**50**	57
	with **P**rotector	46.00	—	—
	with **L**iner	58.00	—	—
	Combo (**P/L**)	62.00	**77**	89
S.	1999 <u>Miniature</u>			
	J.W. Two-Pie®	130.00	—	—
	with **P**rotector	133.00	—	—
	with **L**iner	144.00	—	—
	Combo (**P/L**)	147.00	**174**	210
T.	1999 Miniature Pie Plate 25th Anniversary	N/C	**51**	60
U.	1999 Mini Two-Pie Server	35.00	**49**	57
U.	1999 Miniature Pie Plate Set of 2, Blue design	45.00	**49**	62
V.	1999 Serving Tray™	99.00	—	—
	with **P**rotector	120.00	—	—
	with **L**iner	127.00	—	—
	Combo (**P/L**)	148.00	**183**	275

K.   1998 Renewal

8.5RD x 4^H

Form No: 13340
No. Sold:

O.   1998 Harbor

10^L x 8.25^W x 8.25^H

Form No: 10677
No. Sold:

S.   Miniature Two-Pie   1999

4.75^L x 5^W x 4^H

Form No: 19356
No. Sold:

Available to Members from Nov. 21, 1998 through Dec. 31, 1999.

L. 1998 Miniature Apple

5.25RD x 3.25^H

Form No: 13749
No.Sold:

M. 1998 25th Anniversary

16^L x 8^W x 11^H

Form No: 12297
Tie-On: 32492
No.Sold:

*Available to Members
from April 1 – 30, 1998*

N. 1998 Thyme

4.5RD x 3^H

Form No: 19224
No.Sold:

*Free to Members who
hosted a show in June 98
and received 2 bookings.*

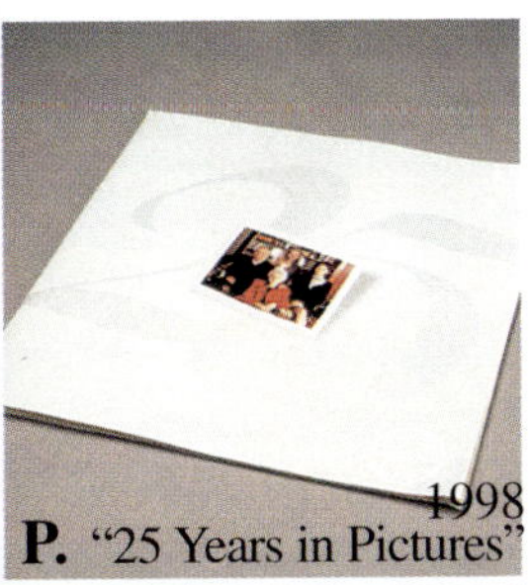

P. 1998 "25 Years in Pictures"

11^L x 11^W

Form No: 85804
No.Sold:

*Sent FREE to Club
Members.*

Q. 1998 Ornament

3.5RD

Form No: 32506
No.Sold:

*"Shopping in Dresden –
Edition 1998"*

R. 1999 Renewal

6.75^L x 5.75^W x 4.75^H

Form No: 12998
No.Sold:

*Available only within 90
days after membership
renewal.*

T. 1999 Miniature 25th Pie Plate

3.25RD

Form No: 33537
No. Sold:

*Offered FREE to Members
who purchased the Mini
Two-Pie™ Basket between
Nov. 21 – Dec. 31, 1998.*

U. 1999 Mini Server and Pie Plates

4RD x 6^H

Form No: 76902
Pie Plates: 35581

*First piece of Miniature
Wrought Iron offered.*

V. 1999 Serving Tray

20^L x 14^W X 3.75^H

Form No: 15849
No. Sold:

*Unlike other Club items,
this item **could** be purchased with Hostess
half-price benefits.* **43**

MARKET VALUES

Photo	Description	Original	Avg.	High
W.	1999 Riding Through the Snow Ornament™	30.00	—	—
X.	1999 Family Picnic™	225.00	**288**	**300**
	with **P**rotector	260.00	—	—
	with **L**iner	270.00	—	—
	Combo (**P/L**)	305.00	**315**	**330**
	Full Set (**C/Lid**)	364.00	**442**	**500**
X.	1999 Napkins - Set of 2	10.00	—	—
X.	1999 Place Mats - Set of 2	20.00	—	—
	1999 Handle Tie	7.00	—	—
Y.	1999 Tapestry Throw	60.00	**84**	**125**
Z.	1999 Homestead™			
	Combo (**P/L**)	79.00	—	—
	Full Set (**C/Lid**)	106.00	—	—
Z.	1999 Homestead Tie-On	8.00	—	—

2000 Items:

Photo	Description	Original	Avg.	High
A[1]	2000 Renewal Basket™	44.00	—	—
	with **P**rotector	48.00	—	—
	with **L**iner	61.00	—	—
	Combo (**P/L**)	65.00	—	—
B[1]	2000 <u>Miniature</u>			
	J.W. Bread & Milk®	130.00	—	—
	with **P**rotector	134.00	—	—
	with **L**iner	145.00	—	—
	Combo (**P/L**)	149.00	—	—
	2000 Miniature Milk Pitcher[np]	30.00	—	—
C[1]	2000 Century Celebration™	59.00	—	—
	with **P**rotector	66.00	—	—
	with **L**iner	78.00	—	—
	Combo (**P/L**)	85.00	—	—
	Full Set (**Combo/Lid**)	117.00	—	—
	2000 Spring Meadow™[np]	95.00	—	—
	with **P**rotector	104.00	—	—
	with **L**iner	121.00	—	—
	Combo (**P/L**)	130.00	—	—
	2000 Cottage Gate™ Tie-On	0.00	—	—

[np] = Not Pictured

W. 1999 Ornament

3.5RD

Form No: 35599
No. Sold:

This is the final ornament in the series of four.

A[1] 2000 Renewal

6.75L x 5.25W x 3.25

Form No: 18783
No. Sold:

New form. Renewing Members had to purchase within 30 days of renewal

X. 1999 Family Picnic

$20^L \times 14^W \times 9.5^H$

Form No:	13561
Napkins:	2363941
Place Mats:	2353141

Fabric items sold separatley.

Y. 1999 Tapestry Throw

$67^L \times 46^W$

Form No:	71587
No. Sold:	

Special feature offered from Aug. – Nov. 1999.

Z. 1999 Homestead

$10^{RD} \times 6.25^H$

Form No:	6609596
Tie-On:	37541
No. Sold:	

Sold only as a Combo. This version has a brass tag. Lid and Tie-On were not exclusive to Members.

B¹ 2000 Miniature Bread & Milk

$6.25^L \times 3.25^W \times 4.25^H$

Form No:	13391
No. Sold:	

Offered to Members from Jan. – Dec. 2000

C¹ 2000 Century Celebration

$10.5^L \times 6.25^W \times 4.75^H$

Form No:	15385
Tie-On:	36196

Special pewter tag. Lid and Tie-On were not exclusive to Members. Century Celebration logo on bottom.

Fun Fact

In just four years, The Longaberger Collectors Club has grown to be the *fifth largest club* in the nation. This is right behind the Hummels Club, which has been in existence for over 20 years!

Family Signatures

J.W. Longaberger was born in 1902. He left high school at age 17 to help his father make baskets full-time. He married Bonnie Jean Gist (Grandma Bonnie) in 1927. They had twelve children between 1928 and 1945. J.W. continued making baskets while he worked during the day at the Dresden Paper Mill. He sold each basket for about $1.50. Dave Longaberger joined his father making baskets in 1972. J.W. had since stopped making baskets for sale, but agreed to make a few for Dave to sell. J.W. passed away at age 71 before The Longaberger Company® was established.

Bonnie Jean
"Grandma Bonnie"
Born:
July 16, 1908

The Longaberger Children:

Genevieve #1
Born: Mar. 25, 1928
Spouse: Piercy Hard

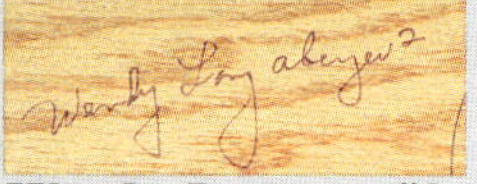

Wendy Jean #2
Born: Dec. 16, 1929
Spouse: Bob Little

Jerry Dean #3
Born: Nov. 23, 1931
Spouse: Donna

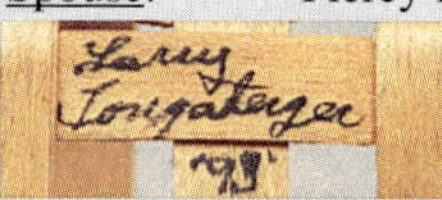

Dale "Larry" #4
Born: June 3, 1933

David Wendell #5
Born: Dec. 7, 1934
Died: Mar. 17, 1999

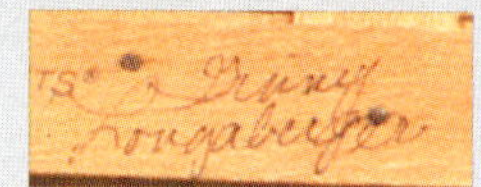

Richard Lee #6
Born: Dec. 18, 1936
Spouse: Joanne

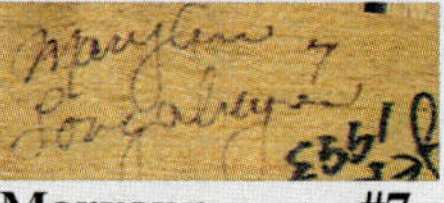

Maryann #7
Born: Nov. 29, 1937
Spouse:
Wendell McCafferty

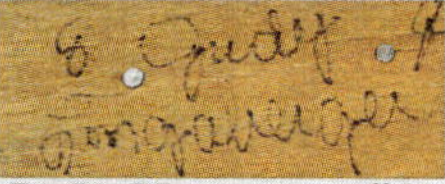

Judy Kay #8
Born: Sept. 19, 1939

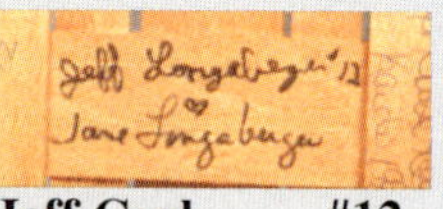

"Ginny" Lou #9
Born: Oct. 8, 1940
Spouse: Dick Wilcox

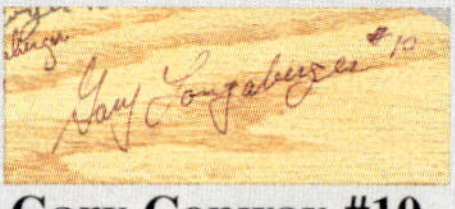

Gary Conway #10
Born: Jan. 6, 1943

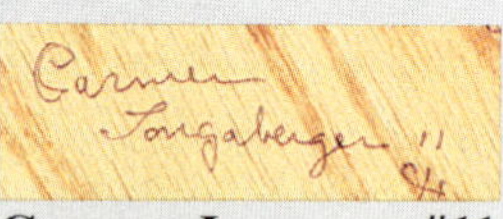

Carmen Lynn #11
Born: Nov. 23, 1943
Spouse: Ronald Fortney

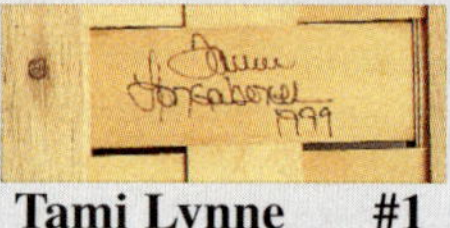

Jeff Carl #12
Born: Mar. 11, 1945
Spouse: Jane

Dave's Children:

Tami Lynne #1

Rachel Lynne #2

Cookie Molds

Janet Gardner
Gallipolis, Ohio

Janet has been collecting since 1993. Her first basket was the 1993 Inaugural basket, which she now has signed by President Clinton. After that first purchase, she got so hooked, that her husband convinced her to start selling in 1996. Her collection now exceeds over 500 baskets!

Features:

The stands being used to display the Cookie Molds and books throughout this section were not originally sold with the items. They are being used for photography purposes only.

MARKET VALUES

Photo	Description	Original	Avg.	High
	***Santa Series*™**			
A.	1990 Father Christmas™	18.95	**51**	**90**
B.	1990 1st Casting™	18.95	**92**	**115**
C.	1991 Kriss Kringle™	18.95	**30**	**50**
D.	1992 Santa Claus™	18.95	**30**	**50**
E.	1993 St.Nick™	18.95	**25**	**30**
	Santa Series Full Set of 4		**165**	**200**
	***Angel Series*™**			
F.	1993 Peace™	18.95	**25**	**40**
G.	1994 Hope™	19.95	**26**	**33**
H.	1995 Love™	19.95	**25**	**35**
I.	1996 Joy™	19.95	**25**	**33**
	***Easter Series*™**			
J.	1994 Mama & Baby Bunny™	18.95	**26**	**45**
K.	1994 Bunnies Book™	5.95	**13**	**30**
L.	1995 Grandpa Bunny & Herbie™	19.95	**21**	**40**

A. 1990 Father Christmas

8.5^H

Form No: 30066
No. Sold:

E. 1993 St. Nick

10.25^H

Form No: 31062
No. Sold:

Fun Fact

In June 1999, The Longaberger Company welcomed their 50,000th Consultant to the family.

Jackie Owens of Dumphries, VA received $100 in Homestead Gift Certificates, $100 in promotional literature and was recognized in *Your Success*, the Consultant monthly publication.

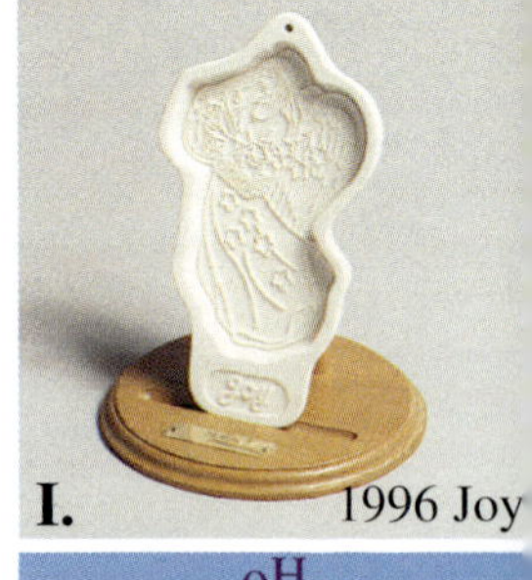

I. 1996 Joy

9^H

Form No: 31721
No. Sold:

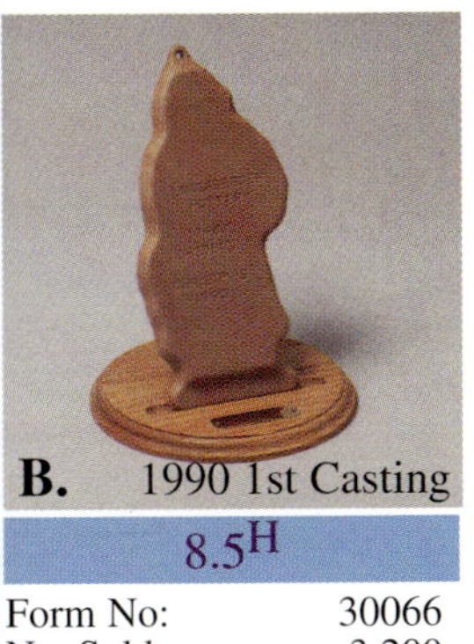

B. 1990 1st Casting

8.5^H

Form No:	30066
No. Sold:	3,200

*Inscription reads:
"Longaberger Pottery – First
Casting– Christmas 1990"*

C. 1991 Kriss Kringle

8.5^H

Form No:	30180
No. Sold:	

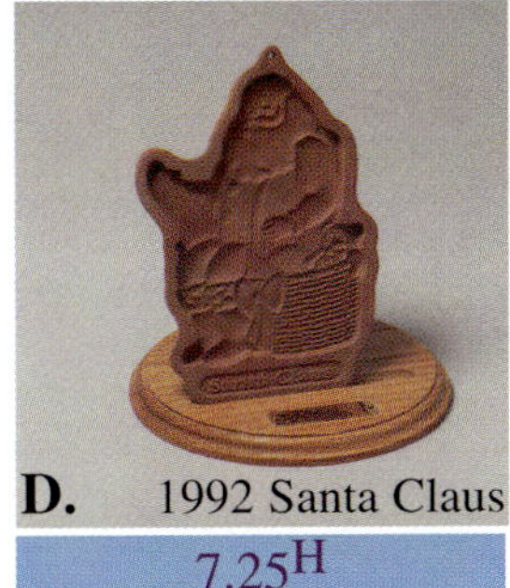

D. 1992 Santa Claus

7.25^H

Form No:	30457
No. Sold:	

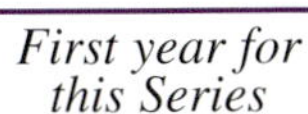

F. 1993 Peace

7.5^H

Form No:	31071
No. Sold:	

*First year for
this Series*

G. 1994 Hope

9^H

Form No:	31356
No. Sold:	

H. 1995 Love

7.5^H

Form No:	32468
No. Sold:	

J. 1994 Mama &
Baby Bunny

6.25^H

Form No:	31151
No. Sold:	

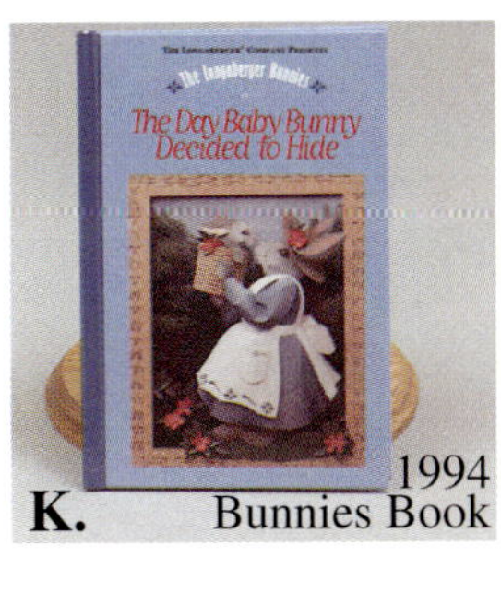

K. 1994 Bunnies Book

Form No:	72079
No. Sold:	

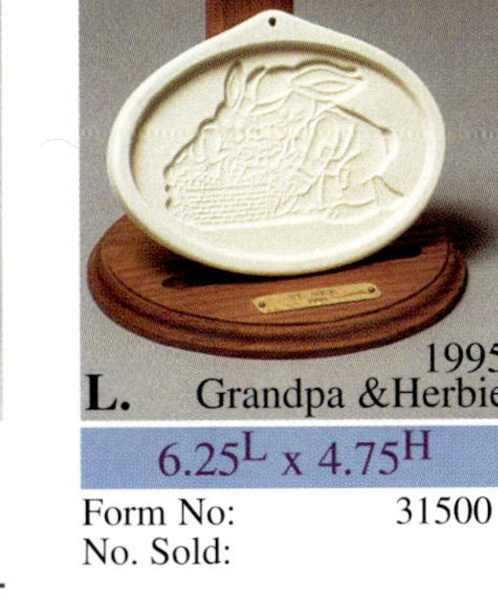

L. 1995 Grandpa & Herbie

6.25^L x 4.75^H

Form No:	31500
No. Sold:	

*The 1994 Book was available only with a purchase.
Only Hostesses were able to buy it for $5.95 and no
additional purchase necessary.*

MARKET VALUES

Photo	Description	Original	Avg.	High
	Easter Series™ (con't)			
M.	1995 Bunnies™ Book	14.95	**16**	**21**
N.	1996 Rosemary Bunny™	19.95	**20**	**30**
O.	1997 Grandma Bunny & Lavender™	19.95	**20**	**30**
	Gingerbread Series™			
P.	1995 Country Cottage™	29.95	**31**	**50**
Q.	1996 Country Cabin™	29.95	**30**	**36**
R.	1997 Holiday Home™	29.95	**32**	**35**
	Snow Friends Series™			
S.	1997 Chilly™	19.95	**29**	**40**
T.	1998 Sleigh Belle™	20.00	—	—
U.	1999 Set of 2 Flurry™ Snowball™	20.00	—	—

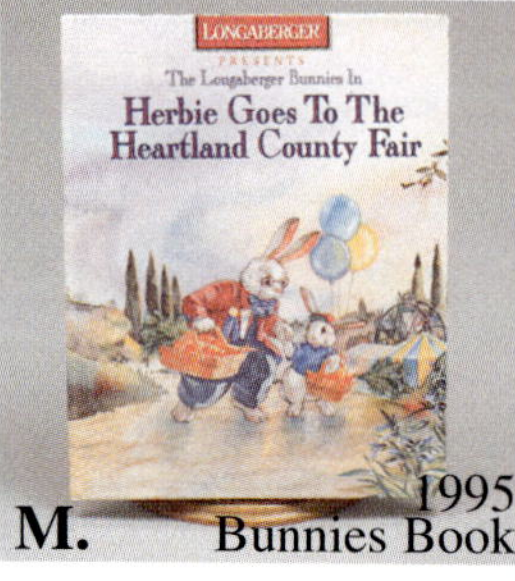

M. 1995 Bunnies Book

Form No: 72796
No. Sold:

Last year that a book was offered.

Q. 1996 Country Cabin

9ᴸ x 13.25ᵂ

Form No: 33090
No. Sold:

U. 1999 Flurry & Snowball

2.75ᴸ x 4.75ᵂ

Form No: 36994
No. Sold:

Sold only as a set.

N. Rosemary Bunny — 1996

6.5^L x 4.25^H

Form No: 32182
No. Sold:

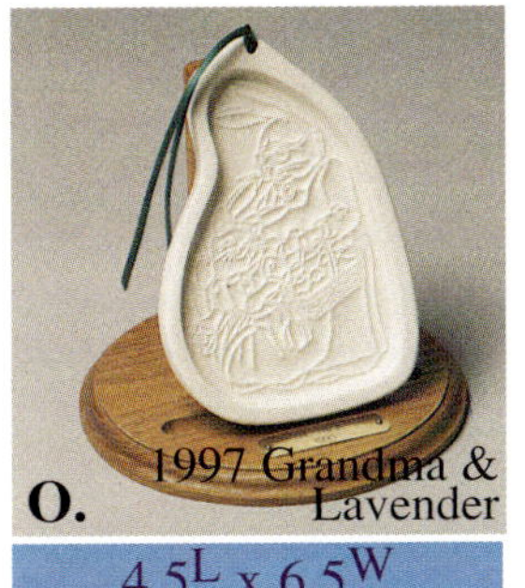

O. 1997 Grandma & Lavender

4.5^L x 6.5^W

Form No: 32191
No. Sold:

P. Country Cottage — 1995

9^L x 13.25^W

Form No: 32476
No. Sold:

First year for this Series.

R. Holiday Home — 1997

9^L x 13.25^H

Form No: 34720
No.Sold:

Last year for this series.

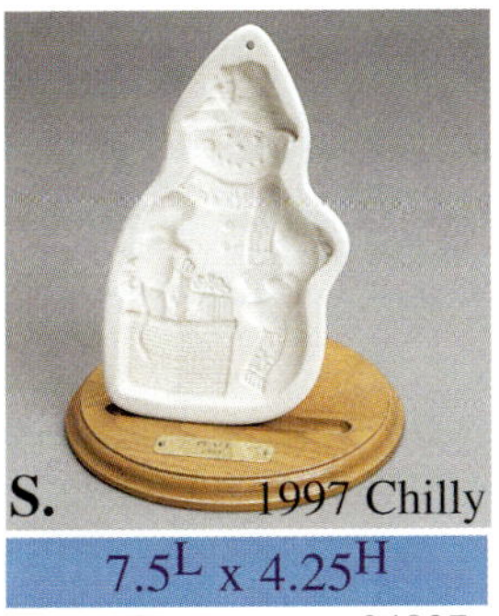

S. 1997 Chilly

7.5^L x 4.25^H

Form No: 34827
No.Sold:

First year for this Series.

T. 1998 Sleigh Belle

6^L x 7.5^H

Form No: 32484
No.Sold:

Fun Fact

65,000 Longaberger Sales Associates can be found through-out the country. Every state is represented. The top five states with the highest Consultant concentration are:

#5: Virginia

#4: Illinois

#3: Pennsylvania

#2: Indiana

#1: Ohio

Evaluating Condition

What should you look for when you are evaluating the quality or condition of a Longaberger Basket? It is first helpful to determine what is considered to be "normal" for these handmade baskets. In 1996, The Company started placing an informational card in with each basket, explaining what to accept as "normal and acceptable".

- It is normal for there to be some room between splints. This is a natural occurrence as the splints  dry and slightly shrink, therefore it is normal to be able to adjust the weaves up and down.

- If your basket has colored accent weaving, there will often be a small amount of dye on the upsplints where they touch. The dye is not completely color-fast, therefore this "bleeding" is very common.

- Small hairline cracks around the tacks are a natural occurrence as the wood dries. 

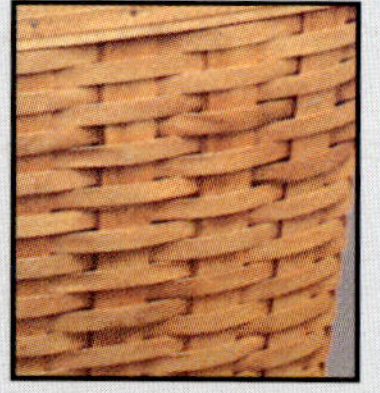

- Some wood has natural swirls or "beauty spots" in the grain that will absorb stain differently. This may cause the stain to appear darker in some areas.

- A trademark of Longaberger Baskets is the wrapping of the trim strip around the band for a cleaner finish. This "turn-under" may fray or crack as the wood dries. Because it is very difficult to bend wood at this angle, this fraying is very common.

Crisco® American™

Gretta Adams
Grayson, Kentucky

Gretta blames her daughter for her "basket addiction"! She is now, in turn, spreading her love for Longaberger to all of her friends. Her favorite basket is the Hostess Collection Wildflower™.

Features:

Red and Blue Weave and Trim.
Burned in Crisco® Logo.
Series completed in 1993.

MARKET VALUES

Photo	Description		Original	Avg.	High
A.	1991	Pie™	79.95	**355**	**500**
		with Protector	89.90	**376**	**510**
B.	1992	Cookie™	29.95	**128**	**175**
		with Protector	35.90	**128**	**175**
		with Liner	40.90	**130**	**175**
		Combo (P/L)	39.95	**132**	**192**
C.	1992	Crisco Apron	13.95	**31**	**65**
D.	1993	Baking™	39.95	**105**	**120**
		with Protector	44.90	**107**	**130**
		with Liner	48.90	**107**	**140**
		Combo (P/L)	45.95	**117**	**155**
	Full Crisco® Collection Set			**636**	**800**

Crisco® is a registered trademark of
The Procter & Gamble Company.

The Crisco® American Series started in 1991 when The Longaberger Company® was invited to create the official Pie Basket for the Crisco American Pie Celebration Bake-Off in New Orleans. Each of the 50 participants received the basket and then the company made it available to their customers to purchase. Although these baskets were sold during the All-American promotional season, they <u>are</u> <u>not</u> part of the All-American Series™. They were, however, designed to compliment that collection.

A. 1991 Pie

12^L x 12^W x 6^H

Form No:	100-DBRS
No. Sold:	

Sold with a divider.

B. 1992 Cookie

10RD x 4^H

Form No:	10081
No. Sold:	153,447

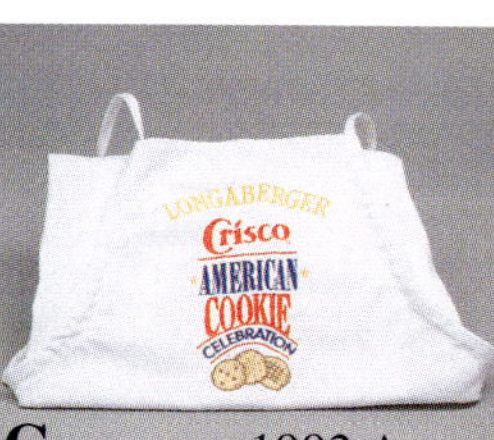

C. 1992 Apron

Form No:	20028
No. Sold:	

Not included in the Combo. Sold separately

D. 1993 Baking

14.5^L x 7.5^W x 3.75^H

Form No:	14745
No. Sold:	

Karen Weller
Seymour, Indiana

Starting her collection in 1996, was the Little Pumpkin™. Karen "just couldn't resist it!" Now, as a Consultant, her home is filled with baskets!

Features:
One stationary handle,
except 1987 Medium Chore.

MARKET VALUES

Photo	Description		Original	Avg.	High
	1987	Easter Signature Series			
A.		Medium Chore™	28.95	**246**	**326**
B.		Single Pie™	28.95	**233**	**375**
C.		Small Gathering™	28.95	**167**	**205**
D.		Spring™	25.95	**226**	**300**
E.	**1988**	Baby Easter™	18.95	**74**	**117**
F.		Small Easter™	22.95	**68**	**90**
G.		Medium Easter™	28.95	**84**	**105**
H.		Large Easter™	32.95	**87**	**110**
	1989	Stained Easter™[np]	29.95	**86**	**110**
I.		Blue Easter™	29.95	**76**	**105**
J.		Pink Easter™	29.95	**61**	**105**
K.	**1990**	Medium™	38.95	**55**	**100**
L.		Large™	43.95	**63**	**110**

[np] = Not Pictured

Each of the *Easter Signature Baskets* from 1987 were delivered with Dave Longaberger's signature on it. In addition, only 100 total baskets also have Grandma Bonnie's signature.

A. 1987 Medium Chore

13^L x 8^W x 5^H

Form No: 3500-CX
No. Sold:

Easter Signature Series: Blue, red and green weave. Signed by Dave.

E. 1988 Baby Easter

7^L x 5^W x 3.5^H

Form No: 700-AN
No. Sold:

Available in natural only; blue, green, lilac, or pink weave.

I. 1989 Blue Easter

10RD x 4^H

Form No: 5500-ABS
No. Sold:

Available stained only; pink or blue weave, or no color.

B. 1987 Single Pie

12^L x 12^W x 4^H

Form No: 2200-AX
No. Sold:

Easter Signature Series: Blue, red and green weave. Signed by Dave.

C. 1987 Small Gathering

14^L x 9^W x 4.5^H

Form No: 2300-AX
No. Sold:

Easter Signature Series: Blue, red and green weave. Signed by Dave.

D. 1987 Spring

11^L x 8^W x 5.5^H

Form No: 900-AX
No. Sold:

Easter Signature Series: Blue, red and green weave. Signed by Dave.

F. 1988 Small Easter

10^L x 6^W x 4^H

Form No: 3400-AN
No. Sold:

Available in natural only; blue, green, lilac, or pink weave.

G. 1988 Medium Easter

13^L x 8^W x 5^H

Form No: 3500-AN
No. Sold:

Available in natural only; blue, green, lilac, or pink weave.

H. 1988 Large Easter

14^L x 7.75^W x 5.25^H

Form No: 3600-AN
No. Sold:

Available in natural only; blue, green, lilac, or pink weave.

J. 1989 Pink Easter

10RD x 4^H

Form No: 5500-APS
No. Sold:

Available stained only; pink or blue weave, or no color.

K. 1990 Medium Easter

8RD x 4.5^H

Form No: 40000-APVBS
No. Sold:

Available stained only; Dresden blue, violet and pink weave.

L. 1990 Large Easter

9.5^{RD} x 5^H

Form No: 41000-APVBS
No. Sold:

Available stained only; Dresden blue, violet and pink weave.

Features:

This series is usually promoted during the months of January and February.

MARKET VALUES

Photo		Description	Original	Avg.	High
M.	1991	Customer™	26.95	**53**	**75**
N.		Hostess™	21.95	**39**	**60**
O.	1992	Easter™	27.95	**50**	**75**
		with **P**rotector	32.90	**60**	**75**
		with **L**iner	40.90	**60**	**75**
		Combo (**P/L**)	39.95	**62**	**80**
P.	1993	Small Easter™	24.95	**44**	**60**
		with **P**rotector	28.90	**58**	**60**
		with **L**iner	34.90	**58**	**60**
		Combo (**P/L**)	35.95	**60**	**75**
Q.	1993	Large Easter™	27.95	**60**	**80**
		with **P**rotector	32.90	**60**	**85**
		with **L**iner	38.90	**62**	**85**
		Combo (**P/L**)	38.95	**67**	**90**
R.	1994	Easter™	49.95	**51**	**75**
		with **P**rotector	55.90	**52**	**75**
		with **L**iner	65.90	**52**	**75**
		Combo (**P/L**)	59.95	**55**	**80**
S.	1995	Easter™	49.95	**65**	**90**
		with **P**rotector	55.90	**65**	**90**
		with **L**iner	65.90	**65**	**90**
		Combo (**P/L**)	59.95	**68**	**95**
S.	1995	Happy Easter Tie-On	6.95	**9**	**15**
T.	1996	Easter™	39.95	**60**	**83**
		with **P**rotector	44.90	**63**	**85**
		with **L**iner	54.90	**63**	**85**
		Combo (**P/L**)	49.95	**67**	**100**
	1996	Easter Egg Tie-On	6.95	**12**	**15**
U.	1997	Small Easter™			
		Combo (**P/L**)	29.95	**47**	**70**
U	1997	Large Easter™	42.95	**55**	**60**
		with **P**rotector	48.90	**55**	**60**
		with **L**iner	57.90	**60**	**80**
		Combo (**P/L**)	52.95	**65**	**90**
U.	1997	Easter Tie-On	6.95	**10**	**15**
V.	1998	Small Easter™	32.95	**45**	**55**
		with **P**rotector	36.90	**45**	**55**
		with **L**iner	43.90	**45**	**60**
		Combo (**P/L**)	29.95	**47**	**65**
V.	1998	Large Easter™	43.95	**—**	**—**
		with **P**rotector	48.90	**—**	**—**
		with **L**iner	58.90	**—**	**—**
		Combo (**P/L**)	52.95	**63**	**90**
V.	1998	Easter Tie-On	6.95	**9**	**10**

M. 1991 Customer

11^L x 8^W x 5.5^H

Form No: 900-ATM*
No. Sold:

Available stained or natural; teal and mauve 3/8" weave.

Q. 1993 Large Easter

10^L x 6^W x 4^H

Form No: 13439/13412†
No. Sold:

Available stained or natural; teal shoestring weave.

U. 1997 Easter

Sm: 8.5^L x 5^W x 3.5^H
Lg: 12^L x 7^W x 4.5^H

Small: 63541/63550†
Large: 13447/13455†
Tie-On: 30007

Available stained or natural. Small only available as Combo and with a $42.95 purchase.

N. 1991 Hostess

7^L x 5^W x 3.5^H

Form No: 700-ATM•
No. Sold:

Available stained or natural; teal and mauve 3/8" weave.

O. 1992 Easter

10.5^L x 7.5^W x 4.5^H

Form No:34000-APVCNK
No. Sold:

Available stained or natural; Dresden blue, violet and pink weave.

P. 1993 Small Easter

7^L x 5^W x 3.5^H

Form No: 10774/10766†
No. Sold:

Available stained or natural; teal shoestring weave.

R. 1994 Easter

13.5^L x 8.25^W x 5.25^H

Form No: 16926/16934
16900/16918†
No. Sold:

vailable stained, natural, tained with color or natural with color; Heartland® blue with pink accent weave.

S. 1995 Easter

10.75^L x 8.75^W x 5.25^H

Form No: 18708
Tie-On: 31518
No. Sold: 109,970

Available stained only; rose pink and purple weave. Tie-On sold separately.

T. 1996 Easter

7.5^L x 5^W x 6^H

Form No: 12912/12939†
Tie-On: 32271
No. Sold: 220,416

Available stained or natural; pink, green and purple double shoestring weave with purple and green.

1998 Easter

Sm: 6^L x 6^W x 3^H
Lg: 9^L x 9^W x 4.5^H

Small: 11959/11967†
Large: 11851/11860†
Tie-On: 34100

Both baskets available in stained or natural.

Market Report

In the past year, a growing interest in the market has surfaced for the Easter Signature Baskets.

Speculation is that the increased activity is due to the fact that each one was signed by Dave.

† = Product numbers are stated: Stained/ Natural weave.

Features:

Since 1991, Easter Baskets have been offered in both the stained and unstained finishes, with the exception of 1995.

1999 Easter

Sm: 5.75^L x 5.75^W x 3^H
Lg: 7.5^L x 7.5^W x 3.75^H

Small:	14052 / 14168†	
Large:	14061 / 14265†	
Tie-On:		35637

†Both baskets available in stained or unstained finishes.

MARKET VALUES

Photo	Description			Original	Avg.	High
W.	1999	Small Easter™		33.00	**50**	**60**
		with **P**rotector		37.00	**53**	**60**
		with **L**iner		45.00	**53**	**60**
		with **D**ivider		42.00	**53**	**60**
		Combo (**P/L/Div**)		49.00	**55**	**77**
W.	1999	Large Easter™		39.00	**50**	**55**
		with **P**rotector		44.00	**53**	**60**
		with **L**iner		54.00	**53**	**60**
		with **D**ivider		50.00	**53**	**60**
		Combo (**P/L/Div**)		59.00	**64**	**80**
W.	1999	Easter Tie-On		8.00	**14**	**16**
X.	2000	Jelly Bean™		34.00	—	—
		with **P**rotector		37.00	—	—
		with **L**iner		46.00	—	—
		Combo (**P/L**)		42.00	**52**	**59**
X.	2000	Jelly Bean Tie-On		8.00	**9**	**10**
X.	2000	Large Easter™		65.00	—	—
		with **P**rotector		72.00	—	—
		with **L**iner		86.00	—	—
		Combo (**P/L**)		79.00	**99**	**115**
		Full Set (**C/Riser**)		85.00	—	—
X.	2000	Happy Easter Tie-On		8.00	**9**	**10**

2000 Easter

Sm: 5.5RD x 3.75^H
Lg: 12.5RD x 6^H

Small:		19488
Large:	19186 / 19283†	
Jelly Bean TO:		38661
Easter TO:		38644

Small was offered whitewashed only, while the Large was available whitewashed or stained.

Margie Uhle – Canton, OH
Sitting pretty with her first basket.

Where's the Quiche Dish?

During the 2000 Easter campaign, The Company introduced a new Quiche Dish to the pottery line. At the time, it was promoted as "only available in February", however there is speculation that it will eventually be added to the Regular Line.

† = Product numbers are stated: Stained/ Natural weave.

Employee Baskets

Nancy McMahon
Covington, Indiana

Nancy believes in never going anywhere without a basket! The Cake™ is her favorite and was also her first. She was first invited to a party by her friends in 1983 and she's been a "Basket Lady" ever since!

Features:

Given to Employees for different occasions. No original costs are associated with these baskets.

MARKET VALUES

Photo	Description	Avg.	High
	Birthday – *Red shoestring weave and trim. Tags read "Longaberger Company Birthday Basket", Year of basket, and Employee's name (except 1990 did not have Employee's name).*		
A.	1988 5" Measuring™	77	105
B.	1989 Sweetheart™	76	95
C.	1990 Potpourri™	75	100
D.	1991 Ivy™	90	130
E.	1992 Tour™	62	85
	Recognition – *Given to Employees for years of service. Tag reads "Longaberger" or "Longaberger Company", the Year of award, and Achievement.*		
	(xx–97) Sophomore[np] (1 yr.)	67	75
F.	(xx–97) Junior (2 yrs.)	79	85
	(xx–97) Senior[np] (5 yrs.)	85	125
G.	(xx–97) Senior Employee	92	125
H.	(97–P) Senior Employee II	—	—
I.	(xx–97) Master (10 yrs.)	232	275
J.	(97–P) Master II (10 yrs.)	—	—
	Hartville Conversion Baskets		
K.	1992 Magazine	—	—
K.	1992 Cake	—	150

[continued next page]

[np] = Not Pictured

A. 1988 5" Measuring

5RD x 4.5^{H}

Form No: 3800-
No. Given:

E. 1992 Tour

8.75^{L} x 4.75^{W} x 6.5^{H}

Form No: 10022
No. Given:

Last year for a Birthday Basket.

I. 19xx-97 Master Employee

12.5^{RD} x 13.5^{H}

Form No: 1900
No. Given:

Given to Employees with 10 years of service with the company.

B.   1989 Sweetheart

5.75^L x 3.75^W x 3^H

Form No: 45000-
No. Given:

C.   1990 Potpourri

5^L x 5^W x 2.5^H

Form No: 13000-
No. Given:

*Tag did not include
Employee's name
in this year.*

D.   1991 Ivy

5.5^L x 5.5^W x 2.5^H

Form No: 13100-
No. Given:

F.   Junior Recognition

8.75^L x 4.75^W x 6.5^H

Form No: unknown
No. Given:

*Sophomore — same,
except no color weaving
Senior — same, except
with blue trim and weave.*

19xx-97
G.   Senior Employee

16^L x 9^W x 6^H

Form No: unknown
No. Given:

1997-P
H.   Senior Employee

6.5RD x 5^H

Form No: unknown
No. Given:

*Lilac weave and double
trim.*

1997-P
J.   Master Employee

8RD x 6.5^H

Form No: unknown
No. Given:

*Lilac weave and double
trim.*

1992 Conversion
K.   Baskets

Magazine: 16^L x 8^W x 11^H
Cake: 12^L x 12^W x 6^H

Form No: unknown
No. Given: ≈ 160 total

*Special brass tag. Dave's signature is on the
front of the basket, just below the tag. This
Magazine pictured still has the tag on it used to
return it to Hartville after it was stained.*

Conversion Baskets

In 1992, Longaberger con-
verted the weaving process
at their Hartville facility.
They moved to a piece rate
method of payment. To
compensate the weavers and
the runners for the change,
The Company allowed each
one to make their own
Magazine or Cake basket.
They were tagged and per-
sonally signed by Dave.

MARKET VALUES

Photo	Description	Avg.	High
	Perfect Attendance – *Given out once a year to Employees who have maintained Perfect Attendance. All have lilace trim and weave.*		
L.	1994 Small Fruit	**433**	**475**
M.	1995 Pansy	**425**	**475**
N.	1996 Candle	**400**	**425**
O.	1997 7" Measuring	—	—
P.	1998 Large Peg	—	—
Q.	1999 Spring	—	—
	Christmas – *Red and green alternating shoestring weave. No color on trim. Tags read "Merry Christmas" or "Happy Holidays", Year, and "Longaberger Company".*		
R.	1987 Medium Market™	**248**	**310**
S.	1988 Cake™	**143**	**180**
T.	1989 Candle™	**132**	**150**
U.	1990 Small Gathering™	**110**	**140**
V.	1991 Tall Key™	**108**	**140**
W.	1992 5" Measuring™	**94**	**120**

[continued next page]

199
L. Perfect Attendanc

6.5RD x 5H

Form No: unknow
No. Given: ≈ 20

*Lilac trim and shoestring w
around bottom. First Emple
Basket to include accessor*

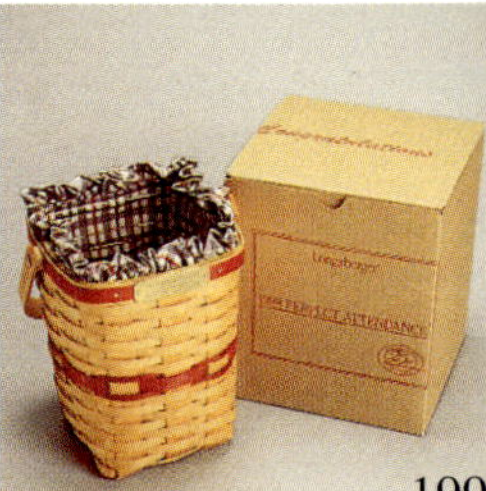

1998
P. Perfect Attendance

6.5L x 6.5W x 8H

Form No: unknowr
No. Given:

*First year award was
delivered to the employ
ee's home in a box.*

T.   1989 Candle

9L x 5W x 5H

Form No: 1100
No. Given:

M. Perfect Attendance 1995

7RD x 4.5^H

Form No: unknown
No. Given:

N. Perfect Attendance 1996

9^L x 5^W x 5^H

Form No: unknown
No. Given: ≈ 309

O. Perfect Attendance 1997

7RD x 6.5^H

Form No: unknown
No. Given:

Q. Perfect Attendance 1999

11^L x 8^W x 5.5^H

Form No: unknown
No. Given:

R. Medium Market 1987

15^L x 10^W x 7.5^H

Form No: 500-
No. Given:

S.   1988 Cake

12^L x 12^W x 6^H

Form No: 100-
No. Given:

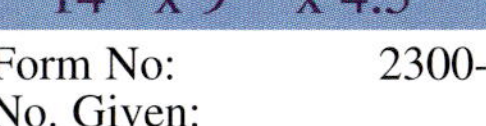

U. Small Gathering 1990

14^L x 9^W x 4.5^H

Form No: 2300-
No. Given:

V.   1991 Tall Key

9.5^L x 5^W x 9.5^H

Form No: 1000-
No. Given:

W.   1992 5" Measuring

5RD x 4.5^H

Form No: 3800-
No. Given:

Features:

All Christmas Employee Baskets have alternating red and green shoestring weave.

MARKET VALUES

Photo	Description		Avg.	High
X.	1993	Button™	95	125
Y.	1994	Tea™	95	125
Z.	1995	Ambrosia™	92	100
A¹	1996	Cracker™	80	100
B¹	1997	Chives™	115	130
C¹	1998	Small Berry™	71	115
D¹	1999	Tissue™	—	—

X. 1993 Button

7ᴿᴰ x 3ᴴ

Form No: 5400-
No. Given:

B¹ 1997 Chives

4ᴸ x 4ᵂ x 4ᴴ

Form No: unknown
No. Given:

First Weaver

K.R.B.

The first weaver, trained by Dave himself, was Ken Birkhimer. He and his wife live in Dresden, where he still works for The Longaberger Company. While he is no longer weaving, he does take care of the first shift maintenance. He says that he would eventually like to get back into weaving, just to keep his skills up.

Many collectors have started looking for his initials as a weaver (above). Or, you might be lucky enough to find his whole signature on a few baskets in the market.

Ken
1ˢᵗ Birkhimer

Y. 1994 Tea

7^L x 5^W x 3.5^H

Form No: 700-
No. Given:

Z. 1995 Ambrosia

5.5^L x 4^W x 4^H

Form No: 10120
No. Given:

First year for the tag to read "Happy Holidays".

A^1 1996 Cracker

11.5^L x 5^W x 3^H

Form No: 4500-
No. Given:

C^1 1998 Small Berry

6.5^L x 6.5^W x 3^H

Form No: unknown
No. Given:

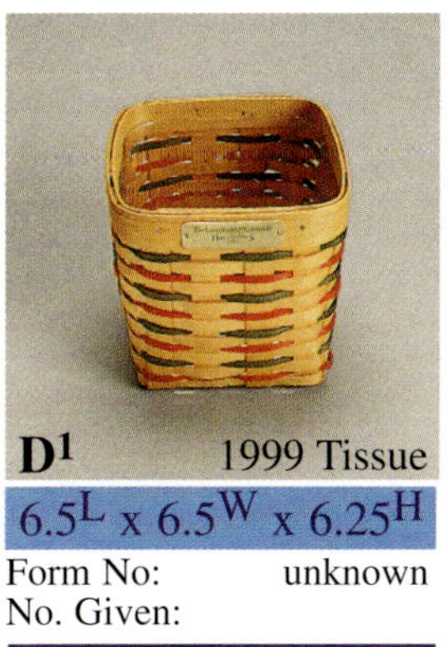

D^1 1999 Tissue

6.5^L x 6.5^W x 6.25^H

Form No: unknown
No. Given:

Did not come with the Tissue lid, but one could be purchased.

Fun Fact

Starting in 1999, all employees were allowed to weave their own Christmas baskets.

Hartville, Ohio

When Dave Longaberger first started The Longaberger Company®, he had to find a source for the maple splints to make the baskets. In Hartville, Ohio, he met Charles Kimberly of The Aspen Basket Company, who agreed to veneer for him on the weekends.

Two years later, Dave bought the plant on a "gentleman's agreement" and with the help of "owner financing". Shortly after, in February 1983, The Hartville Plant burnt to the ground. Even though official papers had not been signed, Dave stuck to his word and took the loss as his own. For a short time, the workers there were concerned that Dave would not rebuild 100 miles away from his other facilities. However, the plant was rebuilt with modern equipment and a promise to always have a plant in Hartville.

Maple trees from Ohio, West Virginia, Pennsylvania, Michigan and New York are brought into Hartville to be processed. Only 40% of what comes in is actually accepted to then be cut, debarked and veneered. The whole process takes place, right there at "Plant Number Two". Nothing is wasted, as the scraps are then used to fuel the furnace.

While it is not the size of Dresden, there is still much to see in Hartville. Along with the veneering process, you can also observe the dyeing process as well as watch the Hartville weavers at work. They have approximately 75 weavers per shift and run 3 shifts.

Unfortunately, tours are not open to the public. If you would like to tour the Hartville plant, you must do so with your Consultant.

Purdue Troy
Kokomo, Indiana

This creative photo is one of our favorites and is of
Purdue's favorite collection. His Mom first got him
interested in collecting back in 1995. Today he finds
uses for all of the baskets in his collection.

Features:

Dresden Blue and Burgundy
Trim and Weave.
Series completed in 1999.

Photo	Description			Original	Avg.	High
A.	1991	Spare Change™		21.95	**105**	**140**
		with **P**rotector		25.90	**105**	**140**
		with **L**iner		32.90	**105**	**140**
		with Combo (**P/L**)		32.95	**110**	**145**
B.	1992	Paper™		23.95	**105**	**130**
		with **P**rotector		27.90	**105**	**135**
		with **L**iner		33.90	**115**	**135**
		Combo (**P/L**)		33.95	**115**	**150**
C.	1992	Pencil™		20.95	**110**	**170**
		with **P**rotector		23.90	**110**	**180**
		with **L**iner		30.90	**110**	**180**
		Combo (**P/L**)		29.95	**127**	**200**
D.	1994	Tissue™		29.95	**84**	**100**
		with **P**rotector		35.90	**85**	**105**
		with **L**id		42.90	**85**	**110**
		Combo (**P/Lid**)		39.95	**90**	**115**
E.	1994	Business Card™		22.95	**88**	**150**
		Combo (**P**)		25.90	**93**	**155**
		with **L**iner (1995)		31.90	**93**	**155**
		Full Set (**Combo/L**)		34.85	**107**	**165**
F.	1995	Mini Waste™		46.95	**87**	**120**
		Combo (**P**)		49.95	**90**	**135**
		with **L**iner		63.95	**90**	**125**
		with **L**id		63.95	**90**	**140**
		Full Set (**P/L/Lid**)		83.85	**99**	**150**
G.	1996	Address™		29.95	**60**	**80**
		with **P**rotector		33.90	**63**	**85**
		Combo (**P/Card Holder**)		34.95	**63**	**85**
		with **L**iner		42.90	**65**	**90**
		Full Set (**Combo/L/Lid**)		61.85	**70**	**95**
H.	1997	Personal Organizer™		39.95	**66**	**80**
		with **P**rotector		46.90	**66**	**80**
		with **L**iner		57.90	**66**	**80**
		Combo (**P/L**)		54.95	**74**	**100**
		Full Set (**Combo/L/Lid**)		77.90	**93**	**110**
I.	1998	Finder's Keepers™		34.00	**48**	**65**
		Combo (**P**)		37.00	**60**	**80**
		with **L**iner		48.00	**60**	**80**
		Full Set (**Combo/L/Lid**)		67.00	**68**	**100**
J.	1999	Tee™		29.00	**38**	**45**
		with **P**rotector		33.00	**40**	**49**
		with **L**iner		40.00	**40**	**49**
		Combo (**P/L**)		39.00	**46**	**52**

A. 1991 Spare Change

6.5ᴸ x 6.5ᵂ x 3ᴴ

Form No: 1300-JCWS
No. Sold:

Liner also available in new design starting 1995.

E. 1994 Business Card

4.75ᴸ x 3.75ᵂ x 2.25ᴴ

Form No: 17477
No. Sold:

Hostess only. Liner was not originally offered – available for the first time in 1995, in new fabric design only.

I. 1998 Finder's Keepers

6ᴸ x 6ᵂ x 4.25ᶠᴴ x 5.25ᴮ

Form No: 12777
No. Sold:

B. 1992 Paper

.5^L x 5.5^W x 2^{FH} x 3.5^{BH}

Form No:	16000
No. Sold:	

Included note paper. Liner also available in new design starting 1995.

C. 1992 Pencil

4RD x 4.25^H

Form No:	15000
No. Sold:	

Liner also available in new design starting 1995.

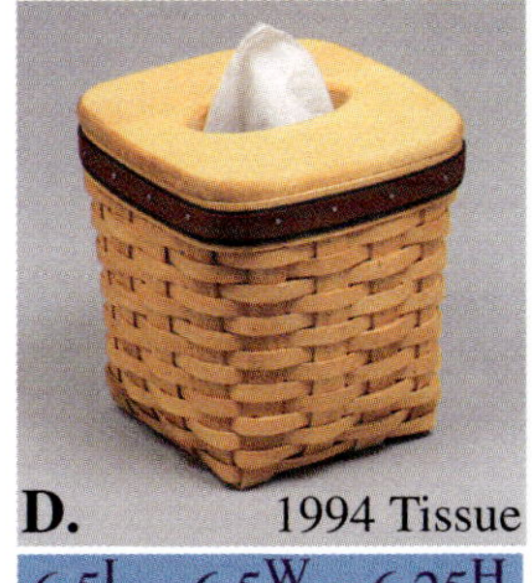

D. 1994 Tissue

6.5^L x 6.5^W x 6.25^H

Form No:	18490
No. Sold:	

No Liner available.

F. 1995 Mini Waste

7.5^L x 7.5^W x 10^H

Form No:	11266
No. Sold:	

Lid and Liner sold separately. First year for the newly designed fabric.

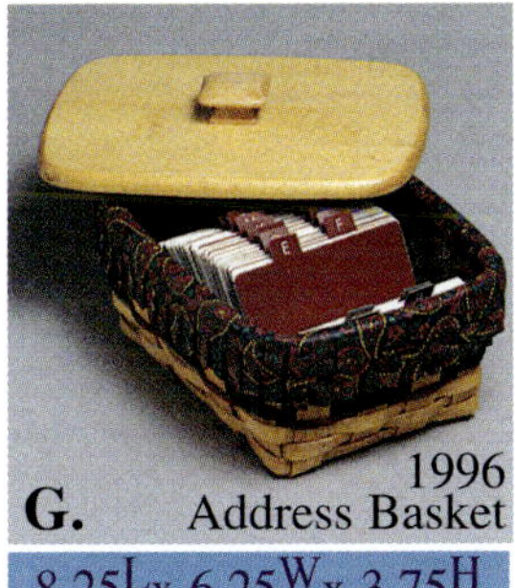

G. 1996 Address Basket

8.25^L x 6.25^W x 3.75^H

Form No:	12611
No. Sold:	173,381

Combo included Protector, Address Cards and Card Holder. Lid and Liner sold separately.

H. 1997 Personal Organizer

14^L x 6^W x 3^H

Form No:	13137
No. Sold:	

Combo came with divided protector. Regular protector was also available for $5.95.

J. 1999 Tee

5.25^L x 5^W x 3^H

Form No:	14940
No. Sold:	

Each Combo included a set of 50 Longaberger Golf Tees and an entry to win a Golf Outing at the new Longaberger Golf Course.

Fun Fact

New in April 2000, is the Golf Club Basket™. Only available at the Longaberger Golf Course or the Homestead, this special basket is the same form as the May Daisy™, but with green accent weave. It has a special burned-in logo on its board bottom and will be available through the end of 2000. Look for it to be featured in the *Tour Baskets* in next year's Bentley Guide. Yet another reason to "hit the links" at Longaberger's new tournament-caliber course.

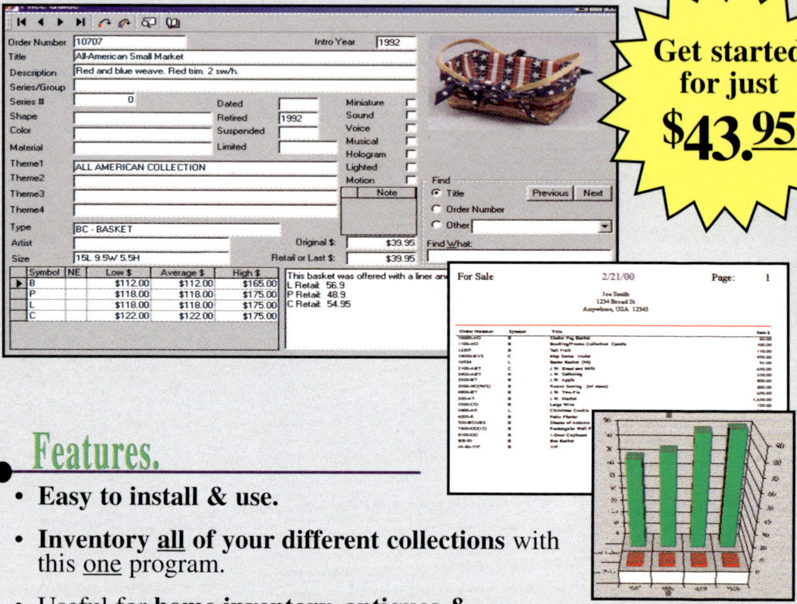

Feature Baskets

Donna Gilbert
Enola, Pennsylvania

Donna's collection started 16 years ago, but has grown tremendously since she became a Consultant in June 1998. The photo above shows some of her favorites around a dry-sink that her husband recently refinished, once belonging to his grandmother.

Features:

Baskets featured for a limited time.
This section is divided in two sections:
with and without color weaving.

MARKET VALUES

Photo	Description	Original	Avg.	High
	Baskets featured WITH Color Weaving:			
A.	1987 Resolution™	16.95	**90**	**135**
B.	1988 Memory™		**132**	**165**
& 89	with Longaberger Book	39.95	**162**	**200**
C.	1990 Basket O'Luck™		**110**	**150**
D.	1990 Shamrock™	19.95	**125**	**185**
E.	1993 All-Star Trio™	29.95	**57**	**95**
F.	1993 Thank-You Basket™	N/A	**126**	**150**
G.	1994 Boo™	34.95	**93**	**135**
	with **P**rotector	39.90	**93**	**150**
	with **L**iner	48.90	**93**	**150**
	Combo (**P/L**)	44.95	**94**	**175**
H.	1994 Three Key Baskets	98.85	**146**	**203**
	Small Key™	27.95	**40**	**55**
	Medium Key™	29.95	**37**	**55**
	Tall Key™	40.95	**55**	**80**
	1996-97 Six Baskets / Three Colors Promotion			
I.	1996-97 Medium Berry™	29.95	**41**	**50**
	with **P**rotector	33.90	**41**	**50**
	with **L**iner	42.90	**41**	**50**
	Combo (**P/L**)	36.43	**53**	**65**
J.	1996-97 Medium Spoon™	36.95	**53**	**60**
	with **P**rotector	42.90	**60**	**60**
	with **L**iner	52.90	**60**	**60**
	Combo (**P/L**)	44.93	**62**	**75**
K.	1996-97 Pantry™	46.95	**59**	**80**
	with **P**rotector	56.90	—	—
	with **L**iner	64.90	—	—
	Combo (**P/L**)	55.93	**86**	**90**
L.	1996-97 Large Vegetable™	61.95	**79**	**95**
	with **P**rotector	71.90	**84**	**95**
	with **L**iner	82.90	**84**	**95**
	Combo (**P/L**)	72.43	**85**	**95**

[continued next page]

A. 1987 Resolution

5RD x 4.5^{H}

Form No: 3800-ABS
No. Sold:

Offered in the month of December 1987

E. 1993 All-Star Trio

5.75^{L} x 3.75^{W} x 3^{H}

Form No: 64408
No. Sold:

Sold only as a three-piece combo. Form number for the basket can be found on the product card: 14494.

I. 1996-97 Med. Berry

7.5^{L} x 7.5^{W} x 3.5^{H}

Form No: 16241/25/33
No. Sold:

Liner was only available in stand-up.

B. 1988 & 89 Memory

8.75L x 4.75W x 6.5H

Form No: 5600-BBS
No. Sold:

Only sold as a combo of book and basket. Continued to be available through 1991.

C. 1990 Basket O'Luck

5.5RD x 3.75H

Form No: 17000-AGS
No. Sold:

Hostess only

D. 1990 Shamrock

5L x 5W x 2.5H

Form No: 13000-HGS
No. Sold:

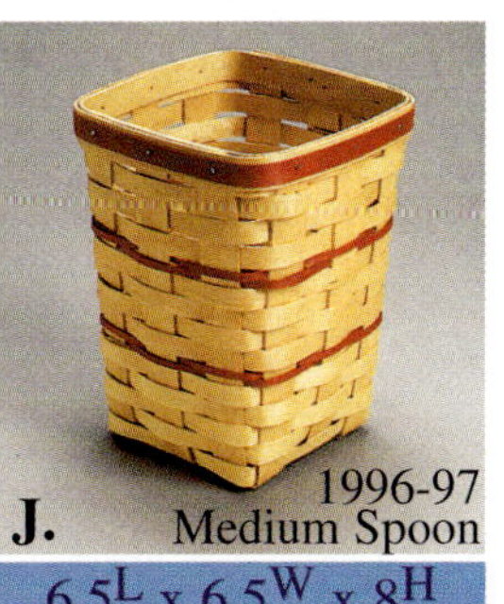

F. 1993 Thank-You

11L x 8W x 5.5H

Form No: 190xx
No. Sold: 7,478

This basket was sent as a Thank-You from Dave to the customers who had ordered the Red Pottery and waited for it through its production problems.

G. 1994 Boo

11L x 8W x 5.5H

Form No: 10987
No. Sold:

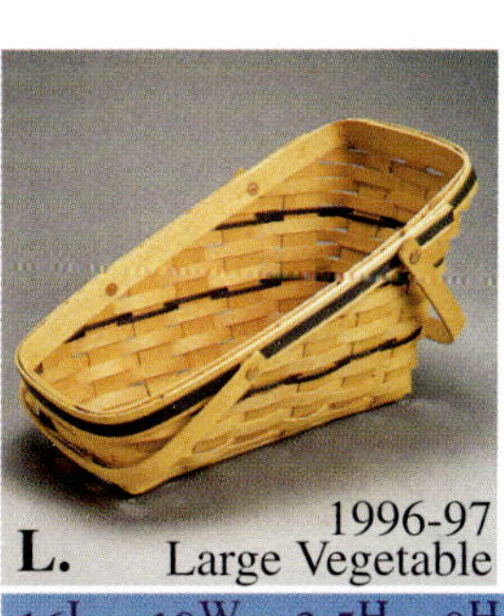

H. 1994 Key Basket Set

Form No:
Sm: **R**17078 /**B** -51 /**G** -60
Md: **R**15172 /**B** -99 /**G** -81
Tall: **R**14672 /**B** -99 /**G** -81

Available in Red, Blue, or Green weave.

J. 1996-97 Medium Spoon

6.5L x 6.5W x 8H

Form No: 16349/22/31
No. Sold:

K. 1996-97 Pantry

14L x 9W x 4.5H

Form No: 16446/20/38
No. Sold:

L. 1996-97 Large Vegetable

16L x 19W x 3.5H x 9H

Form No: 16543/27/35
No. Sold:

MARKET VALUES

Photo	Description	Original	Avg.	High
	1996 -97 Six Baskets / Three Colors (con't)			
M.	1996-97 Large Market™	77.95	**104**	**110**
	with **P**rotector	90.90	**105**	**110**
	with **L**iner	106.90	**112**	**115**
	Combo (**P/L**)	92.43	**130**	**140**
N.	1996-97 Remembrance™	99.95	**140**	**160**
	with **P**rotector	110.90	**140**	**180**
	with **L**iner	125.90	**140**	**180**
	Combo (**P/L**)	112.93	**142**	**190**
	1997-99 Sleigh Baskets			
O.	Large Holiday Sleigh™	47.95	**90**	**100**
	with **P**rotector	55.90	**92**	**105**
	with **L**iner	65.90	**92**	**105**
	Combo (**P/L**)	59.95	**95**	**125**
	Full Set (**C/Runners**)	85.85	**99**	**135**
O.	Med Dash Away Sleigh™	36.00	**50**	**75**
	with **P**rotector	41.00	**55**	**78**
	with **L**iner	50.00	**55**	**78**
	Combo (**Runners**)	50.00	**66**	**85**
	Full Set (**P/L/Runners**)	69.00	**70**	**90**
O.	Small Santa's Little Helper™	30.00	—	—
	with **P**rotector	33.00	—	—
	with **L**iner	40.00	—	—
	Combo (**P/L**)	42.00	—	—
	Full Set (**C/Runners**)	55.00	**69**	**71**
P.	1999 Little Joy™	38.00	**65**	**80**
	with **P**rotector	41.00	—	—
	with **L**iner	50.00	—	—
	Combo (**P/L**)	53.00	**70**	**85**
Q.	1999 Lots of Luck™	29.00	**90**	**130**
	with **P**rotector	32.00	**90**	**130**
	with **L**iner	41.00	**90**	**130**
	Combo (**P/L**)	39.00	**98**	**142**
	Full Set (**Combo/Lid/HT**)	58.00	**125**	**150**
Q.	1999 Shamrock Tie-On	6.00	**18**	**33**
R.	1999 Homestead™	59.00	—	—
	with **P**rotector	67.00	--	—
	with **L**iner	83.00	—	—
	Combo (**P/L**)	79.00	**99**	**120**
	Full Set (**C/Lid**)	113.00	**115**	**138**
R.	1999 Homestead Tie-On	8.00	**14**	**16**
S.	1999 Candy Corn™	29.00	**46**	**53**
	with **P**rotector	33.00	**50**	**55**
	with **L**iner	41.00	**51**	**55**
	Combo (**P/L**)	39.00	**53**	**65**
S.	1999 Candy Corn Tie-On	8.00	**13**	**18**

M. 1996-97 Lg. Market

16^L x 11^W x 9^H

Form No: 16641/24/32
No. Sold:

Liner was only available in over-the-edge.

Q. 1999 Lots of Luck

4.25^L x 4.25^W x 3^H

Form No: 18465
Tie-On: 36056
No. Sold:

Basket features a unique burned in shamrock logo and date on its bottom.

Retired Section

Baskets listed are in chronological order by the year they were featured.

N. Remembrance *1996-97*

10.5^L x 9^W x 8^H

Form No: 16748/21/30
No. Sold:

*Hostess Only.
Liner was only available in over-the-edge.*

O. Sleigh Basket *1997-99*

13^L x 7.5^W x 3^{FH} x 8^{BH}
7.75^Lx 4.5^Wx 2.25^{FH}x 4.5^{BH}
5.75^Lx 3.75^Wx 1.5^{FH}x 3.5^{BH}

This unofficial collection was started in 1997 and added to each year until 1999.

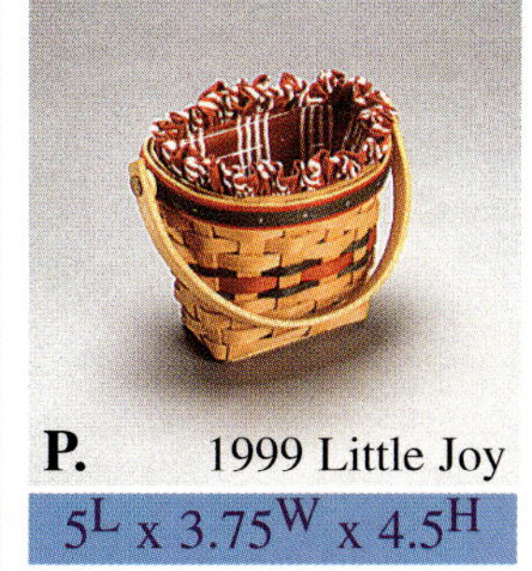

P. 1999 Little Joy

5^L x 3.75^W x 4.5^H

Form No: 19445
No. Sold:

Hostess Appreciation Basket. Available FREE to Hostesses sponsoring a $250 show in both Oct.98 and Jan.99.

R. 1999 Homestead

10RD x 6.25^H

Form No: 13871
Tie-On: 37541
No. Sold:

There are 2 versions of this basket: this one for all customers, and another for Collectors Club Members.

S. 1999 Candy Corn

7.75^L x 4^W x 3.75^H

Form No: 14354
Tie-On: 36676
No. Sold:

Unique form is shaped like a candy corn.

Fun Fact

Throughout the year 2000, Longaberger is celebrating the new millennium with a special burned-in logo.

Every feature basket made in 2000, with the exception of the Founders Basket, will have this special logo to commemorate the new century. Collectors Club baskets have their own special burned-in logo, incorporating both the Century Celebration Logo and the Collectors Club logo.

Features:

Many of these basket are first tested as a Feature, but then return in the Regular Line.

MARKET VALUES

Photo		Description		Original	Avg.	High
T.	2000	Hostess Appreciation				
		Century Celebration	44.00	—	—
		with **Protector**	48.00	—	—
		with **Liner**	59.00	—	—
		Combo (**P/L**)	63.00	—	—
		Full Set (**C/Lid**)	80.00	—	—
T.	2000	Century Star Tie-On	8.00	—	—
T.	2000	Cheers™	39.00	**61**	70
		with **Protector**	43.00	—	—
		with **Liner**	54.00	—	—
		Combo (**P/L**)	49.00	—	—
		Full Set (**C/Lid**)	72.00	—	—

T. 2000 Celebration Baskets

7.5^L x 4.5^W x 3.5^H

Hostess:	13498
Cheers:	18945
Tie-On:	36196

*Hostess Appreciation is th[e]
natural with color version[s]*

Baskets featured
WITHOUT Color Weaving

MARKET VALUES

Photo		Description		Original	Avg.	High
A.	1981	Grandma Bonnie's Bread & Milk™		**675**	800
B.	1982	Old Oak Lid Picnic™		**536**	600
	1983-84	Cake (2 sw/h)[WL]	20.95	—	—
C.	1984	Patio Planter™	21.95	**90**	135
D.	1984	Shaker Peg Basket™	14.95	**45**	60
	1985	Single Pie™[WL]	19.95	—	50
E.	1985	Pantry™	21.95	**62**	70
F.	1985 & 87	Two-Quart™	28.95	**74**	85
G.	1985 & 87	Round Sewing™ (no stand)	37.95	**207**	218
		1985 & 88 Berry Baskets™ (1 st/h)			
H.		Small	16.95	**38**	45
I.		Medium	17.95	**35**	45
J.		Large	18.95	**44**	60

[continued next page]

D. 1984 Shaker Peg

5.5^L x 5.5^W x 6^H

Form No:	10000-AO
No. Sold:	

About the Value

If you have reported [a]
value to us and do not [see]
it reflected, it could b[e]
because it was out of t[he]
range of other transacti[ons]
reported for that item. [We]
do not report transacti[ons]
that are either much hig[h]
or much lower than th[e]
range of values we ar[e]
reviewing. If you hav[e]
questions, do not hesit[ate]
to call our Research De[pt.]

[WL] =Wish List™. It is similar to what is available today. Pictures can be found in a current Wish List™. See the Quick Find for dimensions and form numbers.

A. 1981 Bread & Milk

16^L x 8^W x 11^H

Form No: 2100-
No. Sold:

First Tagged Basket

B. 1982 Oak Lid Picnic

12^L x 12^W x 6^H

Form No: unknown
No. Sold: < 2,500

2,500 were to be made, but far less were actually produced.

C. 1984 Patio Planter

10RD x 5.5^H

Form No: 6000-R
No. Sold:

E. 1985 Pantry

14^L x 9^W x 4.5^H

Form No: 2300-JO
No. Sold:

F. 1985,1987 Two-Quart

9.5^L x 5^W x 9.5^H

Form No: 1000-CO
No. Sold:

G. 1985, 1987 Round Sewing

13RD x 8.5^H

Form No: 3200-EO
No. Sold:

H. 1985, 1988 Small Berry

6.5^L x 6.5^W x 3^H

Form No: 1300-AO
No. Sold:

I. 1985, 1988 Medium Berry

7.5^L x 7.5^W x 3.5^H

Form No: 1400-AO
No. Sold:

J. 1985, 1988 Large Berry

8.5^L x 8.5^W x 5^H

Form No: 1500-AO
No. Sold:

These 1985 and 1988 features were the only times that the Berry Baskets™ were offered with 1 stationary handle.

Features:

Horizon of Hope™ Baskets were moved to their own in collection in 1999. See page 104.

MARKET VALUES

Photo	Description	Original	Avg.	High
	1986 Chore Baskets™ (2 sw/h)			
	Small [np]	17.95	**55**	**60**
K.	Medium	18.95	**53**	**55**
	Large[np]	23.95	**51**	**60**
	1986 Daisy™, Natural[np]	27.95	**63**	**70**
L.	1986 Daisy™, Stained & 87	25.95	**68**	**95**
M.	1986 Large Hamper™	79.95	**223**	**295**
N.	1986 Herb™		**72**	**100**
O.	Garden™		**83**	**110**
	Sold <u>only</u> as a Set	32.90	—	—
P.	1987 Bakery™	19.95	**48**	**50**
Q.	1987 Lg.Inverted Waste™	59.95	**124**	**150**
R.	1987 Med.Market™	41.95	—	—
S.	1987 Med.Gathering™	41.95	**70**	**85**
T.	1987 Weekender™ & 88	54.95	**125**	**175**
	1988 Planters (with legs)			
U.	Small Fern™	35.95	**125**	**140**
V.	Large Fern™	42.95	**140**	**140**

[continued next page]

[WL] =Wish List™. It is similar to what is available today. Pictures can be found in a current Wish List™. See the Quick Find for dimensions and form numbers.

[np] = Not Pictured

K. 1986 Medium Cho...

13^L x 8^W x 5^H

Form No: 3500-C...
No. Sold:

Small: 10^L x 6^W x 4^H
Large: 14^L x 7.75^W x 5.2...

O. 1986 Garde...

15^L x 8^W x 2.25^H

Form No: 4600-A...
No. Sold:

S. 1987 Medium Gathering...

18^L x 11^W x 4.5^H

Form No: 2400-C...
No. Sold:

Hostess Only. Offered only in Natural or Natural with color: re... blue, green or brown.

L. 1986, 87 Daisy, Stained

10RD x 4^H

Form No: 5500-AO
No. Sold:

M. 1986 Large Hamper

16.5^L x 16.5^W x 21.5^H

Form No: 1600-OO
No. Sold:

N. 1986 Herb

11.5^L x 5^W x 3^H

Form No: 4500-AO
No. Sold:

In '86, this basket was available in both Natural and Stained. In '87, it was only offered Stained.

This was a May feature where only Hostesses could purchase it half priced. No lid. First time for hand slots.

P. 1987 Bakery

14.5^L x 7.5^W x 3.75^H

Form No: 4700-JO
No. Sold:

Q. 1987 Large Inverted Waste

14RD x 16^H

Form No: 2000-BO
No. Sold:

R. 1987 Medium Market

15^L x 10^W x 7.5^H

Form No: 500-
No. Sold:

Hostess Only. Offered only in Natural or Natural with color: red, blue, green or brown.

T. 1987, 88 Weekender

10.5^L x 9^W x 8^H

Form No: 200-YO
No. Sold:

U. 1988 Small Planter

8.5RD x 7.5^H

Form No: 2900-RO
No. Sold:

V. 1988 Large Planter

13RD x 8.5^H

Form No: 3200-RO
No. Sold:

MARKET VALUES

Photo	Description			Original	Avg.	High
W.	1989	Bed™		18.95	**85**	**105**
		with **Liner**		29.95	**89**	**110**
X.	1989	Breakfast™		24.95	**85**	**110**
		with **Liner**		37.95	**96**	**125**
		Bed / Breakfast Set		43.90	**140**	**150**
		with **Liner**		67.90	**152**	**160**
Y.	1989	Friendship™		21.95	**55**	**80**
Z.	1991	Doll Cradle™		69.95	—	—
		with **Protector**		80.90	—	—
		with **Liner**		86.90	—	—
		Combo (**P/L**)		97.85	—	—

Shades of Autumn Hostesses

Photo	Description			Original	Avg.	High
A¹	1991	Small Hamper™		99.95	**153**	**165**
		with **Protector**		113.90	—	—
A¹	1991	Large Hamper™		149.95	**227**	**295**
		with **Protector**		169.90	—	—
	1993	Large Hamper™[WL]		179.95	**235**	**275**
	&94	Combo (**P**)		185.95	**244**	**280**
B¹	1994	Hostess Appreciation		N/C	**62**	**125**
C¹	1996	Hostess Appreciation		N/C	**50**	**70**
D¹	1998	Hostess Appreciation		N/C	**56**	**85**

1998 January Sale – Naturals

Photo	Description			Original	Avg.	High
E¹	1998	Cake™ (Natrl)		43.95	—	—
		with **Protector**		54.90	—	—
		with **Liner**		67.90	—	—
		Combo (**P/L**)		78.85	—	—
		Full Set (**C/Lid**)		121.80	—	—
F¹	1998–00	Gathering™ (Natrl)		39.95	—	—
		with **Protector**		49.90	—	—
		with **Liner**		61.95	—	—
		Combo (**P/L**)		71.85	—	—
	1998	Market, Med™ (Natrl)		53.95	—	—
		with **Protector**		64.90	—	—
		with **Liner**		80.90	—	—
		Combo (**P/L**)		91.85	—	—
G¹	1998	Purse, Kiddie™ (Natrl)		27.95	—	—
		with **Protector**		33.90	—	—
		with **Liner**		45.90	—	—
		Combo (**P/L**)		51.85	—	—
H¹	1998,00	Spoon, Sm.™ (Natrl)		19.95	—	—
		with **Protector**		24.90	—	—
		with **Liner**		34.90	—	—
		Combo (**P/L**)		39.85	—	—
		Full Set (**C/Lid**)		59.80	—	—

W. 1989 Bed

11.5^L x 5^W x 3^H

Form No: 4500-AO
No. Sold:

A¹ 1991 Shades of Autumn

12^L x 12.25^W x 16.25^H

Sm. Hamper: 1700-DS
Lg. Hamper: 1600-DS

Large: 16.5^L x 16.5^W x 21.5
Only available to Hostesses during the Shades of Autumn campaign in 1991. Both hampers have detached lids, knob in center of lid and two hand slots.

E¹ 1998 Natural Cake

12^L x 12^W x 6^H

Form No: 10481
No. Sold:

[WL] =Wish List™. It is similar to what is available today. Pictures can be found in a current Wish List™. See the Quick Find for dimensions and form numbers.

X. 1989 Breakfast

14.5^L x 7.5^W x 3.75^H

Form No: 4700-AO
No. Sold:

Y. 1989 Friendship

5.5^L x 5.5^W x 2.5^H

Form No: 13100-JO
No. Sold:

Made using 1/2" weave.

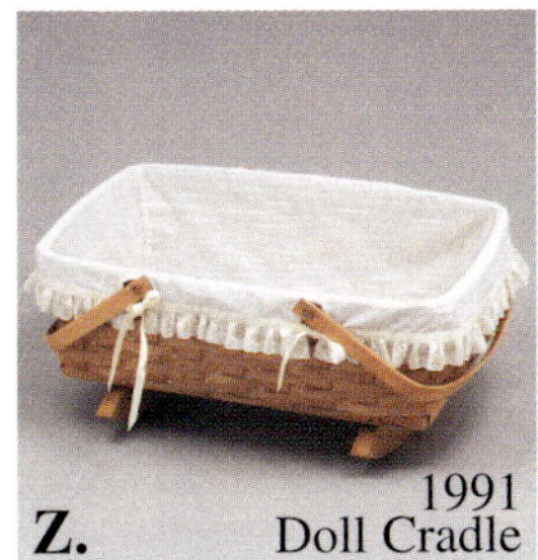

Z. 1991 Doll Cradle

19^L x 12^W x 6^H

Form No: 2500-LO
No. Sold:

Featured for a short time during the 1991 Christmas season. Muslin liner and protector sold separately.

B¹ 1994 Hostess Appreciation

8^L x 4^W x 2^H

Form No: unknown
No. Sold:

Given to Hostesses with shows in both Oct. 93 and Jan. 94.

C¹ 1996 Hostess Appreciation

5.5^L x 5.5^W x 2.5^H

Form No: unknown
No. Sold: 181,337

Given to Hostesses with shows in both Oct. 95 and Jan. 96. Liner was sold separately.

D¹ 1998 Hostess Appreciation

5.75^L x 3.75^W x 3^H

Form No: unknown
No. Sold:

Given to Hostesses with shows in both Oct. 97 and Jan. 98. Liner was sold separately.

F¹ 1998-99 Natural Small Gathering

14^L x 9^W x 4.5^H

Form No: 12572
No. Sold:

Offered in Jan. 98, Feb. 99 and then again in the Jan. 2000 sales.

G¹ 1998 Natural Kiddie Purse

7^L x 5^W x 3.5^H

Form No: 10898
No. Sold:

H¹ 1998 Natural Small Spoon

5.5^L x 5.5^W x 6^H

Form No: 10871
No. Sold:

Offered in Jan. 98 and then again in Jan. 2000

Features:
During the January Sales campaign,
Regular Line baskets are also offered
at a discounted price.

MARKET VALUES

Photo	Description		Original	Avg.	High
I[1]	1998	Spring (Natrl)	29.95	**37**	50
		with **P**rotector	34.90	—	—
		with **L**iner	46.90	—	—
		Combo (**P/L**)	51.85	—	—
J[1]	1998	Tea (Natrl)	19.95	**27**	33
		with **P**rotector	25.90	—	—
		with **L**iner	31.90	—	—
		Combo (**P/L**)	37.85	—	—
	1998	Waste, Med. (Natrl)	71.95	—	—
		with **P**rotector	87.90	—	—
		with **L**iner	95.90	—	—
		Combo (**P/L**)	111.85	—	—
		Full Set (**C/Lid**)	156.80	—	—
K[1]	1998	Grandma Bonnie's Two-Pie™	95.00	**130**	150
		with **P**rotector	110.00	**145**	200
		with **L**iner	131.00	**145**	210
		Combo (**P/L**)	124.00	**176**	225
		Full Set (**C/Lid**)	182.00	**208**	250

1999 January Sale – Naturals

Photo	Description		Original	Avg.	High
L[1]	1999	Berry, Large (Natrl)	28.00	—	—
		with **P**rotector	33.00	—	—
		with **L**iner	43.00	—	—
		Combo (**P/L**)	48.00	—	—
M[1]	1999	Darning (Natrl)	31.00	—	—
		with **P**rotector	40.00	—	—
		with **L**iner	48.00	—	—
		Combo (**P/L**)	57.00	—	—
N[1]	1999	Picnic, Large (Natrl)	89.00	—	—
		with **P**rotector	104.00	—	—
		with **L**iner	125.00	—	—
		Combo (**P/L**)	140.00	—	—
O[1]	1999	Pie (Natrl)	39.00	**41**	60
		with **P**rotector	48.00	—	—
		with **L**iner	59.00	—	—
		Combo (**P/L**)	68.00	—	—
P[1]	1999	Spoon, Med. (Natrl)	28.00	—	—
		with **P**rotector	35.00	—	—
		with **L**iner	44.00	—	—
		Combo (**P/L**)	51.00	—	—
Q[1]	1999	Vegetable, Lg. (Natrl)	48.00	—	—
		with **P**rotector	58.00	—	—
		with **L**iner	69.00	—	—
		Combo (**P/L**)	79.00	—	—

continued next page

I[1] 1998 Natural Spring

11L x 8W x 5.5H

Form No: 10880
No. Sold:

First offered in Jan. 98, but then brought back during the Feb. 99 sale.

M[1] 1999 Natural Darning

10RD x 4H

Form No: 19640
No. Sold:

Both a regular and divided protector were offered.

Q[1] 1999 Natural Large Vegetable

16L x 9W x 3.5FH x 9BH

Form No: 19551
No. Sold:

Only available during January 1999.

J[1] 1998 Natural Tea

7^L x 5^W x 3.5^H

Form No: 10847
No. Sold:

K[1] 1998 Grandma Bonnie's Two-Pie

12^L x 12^W x 10^H

Form No: 19241
No. Sold:

Basket features Grandma Bonnie's signature burned in on one handle. Created in celebration of her 90th Birthday.

L[1] 1999 Large Berry

8.5^L x 8.5^W x 5^H

Form No: 19844
No. Sold:

N[1] 1999 Natural Large Picnic

17^L x 14^W x 11^H

Form No: 19755
No. Sold:

Only available during January 1999.

O[1] 1999 Natural Pie

12^L x 12^W x 4^H

Form No: 19441
No. Sold:

Availability extended through Feb.28, 1999.

P[1] 1999 Natural Medium Spoon

6.5^L x 6.5^W x 8^H

Form No: 19658
No. Sold:

Only available during January 1999.

January Sale

The Longaberger Company has offered a January Sale since 1998. During this campaign, Regular Line baskets are placed on sale along with a Natural version. After the sale, the Natural baskets are no longer available.

Features:

Natural Baskets are different from the new Whitewash finish. Natural means that the basket is in its "natural form", with no stain applied.

R¹ 2000 Natural Baskets

see Quick Find

Form No.
Small Fruit: 17671
Small Berry: 17841
Small Picnic: 18040

S¹ 2000 Founder's Basket

15ᴸ x 10ᵂ x 7.5ᴴ

Form No: 18791
No. Sold:

Basket made in memory of Dave Longaberger.

MARKET VALUES

Photo	Description	Original	Avg.	High
	2000 January Sale – Naturals			
R¹	2000 Berry, Small (Natrl)	22.00	—	—
	with **P**rotector	26.00	—	—
	with **L**iner	34.00	—	—
	Combo (**P/L**)	38.00	—	—
	2000 Bread,			
	W. Traditions (Natrl)	33.00	—	—
	with **P**rotector	38.00	—	—
	with **L**iner	49.00	—	—
	Combo (**P/L**)	54.00	—	—
	Full Set (**C/Lid**)	79.00	—	—
R¹	2000 Fruit, Small (Natrl)	25.00	—	—
	with **P**rotector	29.00	—	—
	with **L**iner	41.00	—	—
	Combo (**P/L**)	45.00	—	—
	Full Set (**C/Lid**)	63.00	—	—
R¹	2000 Picnic, Small (Natrl)	59.00	—	—
	with **P**rotector	70.00	—	—
	with **L**iner	88.00	—	—
	Combo (**P/L**)	99.00	—	—
	2000 Vegetable, Med (Natrl)	37.00	—	—
	with **P**rotector	45.00	—	—
	with **L**iner	55.00	—	—
	Combo (**P/L**)	63.00	—	—
S¹	2000 Dave Longaberger			
	Founder's Baske™	189.00	—	—
	with **P**rotector	200.00	—	—
	with **L**id	248.00	—	—
	Combo (**P/Lid**)	249.00	—	—

The Dave Longaberger Founder's Basket

In some way, every feature of this basket is connected to Dave. He helped to develop the unique stairstep weaving, which is created by alternating each weave over two upsplints and then under two upsplints. It is, by far, the hardest basket The Company has made, taking 2-3 times longer to weave than any other basket.

Foundry Collection®

Connie Boring
Columbus, Ohio

Connie's license plate reads "BSKTNUT", but actually she is a "Wrought Iron Nut"! She owns at least one of every foundry piece the company has made. She uses them in her shows and in her home!

Features:

Most pieces have a small maple leaf with the
signature four-petal mark of authenticity.

MARKET VALUES

Photo	Description	Original	Avg.	High
	Basket Tree			
A.	(95-97) Ten Level Tree	119.95	**142**	157
	(95-97) Hanging Tree [np]	69.95	**75**	105
B.	(95-97) Table Top Tree	64.95	—	—
C.	(96-97) Hook Finial	10.95	—	—
C.	(95-97) Leaf Finial	12.95	—	—
	Herb Markers			
D.	(96-97) Gift Sets:			
	Basil & Chives	19.95	**15**	25
	Parsley & Thyme	19.95	**15**	25
	Dill & Cilantro	19.95	**15**	25
	Sage & Oregano	19.95	**15**	25
	Spice Rack			
E.	(97-98) Spice Rack	74.95	—	—
E.	with Mug Rack	104.90	—	—
	with Shelf [np]	139.90	—	—
	Full Set	169.85	—	—
	Wall Hangings			
F.	(96-98) Plant Hanger	39.95	**45**	45
G.	(96-98) Wall Arch	29.98	**35**	40
	Miscellaneous Items			
H.	(95-98) Two-Pie Server	59.95	**60**	77
I.	(99) Snowman Stand	99.00	**121**	140

[np] = Not Pictured

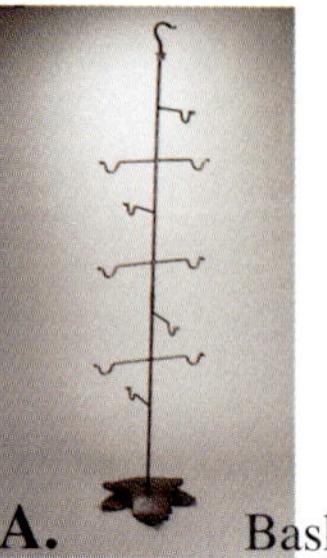

A. 95-97 Basket Tree

4'7" H

Form No:	74012
Hanging	70084

*The Tree is made up of
the Hanging Tree [top
part] and the Table Top
Tree [lower section].*

E. 97-98 Spice Rack

17^L x 3.5^W x 8.5^H

Form No:	71307

*The additional shelf is
not pictured. Mug Rack
included 4 "S" hooks
for the mugs.*

Foundry Note

Each piece of Longaberg
Foundry features signature s
work and maple leaf mot

The natural iron finish make
furniture suitable to both in
and outdoor use.

The Longaberger Compar
suggests occasionally using
wax to protect the natural i
finish from rusting.

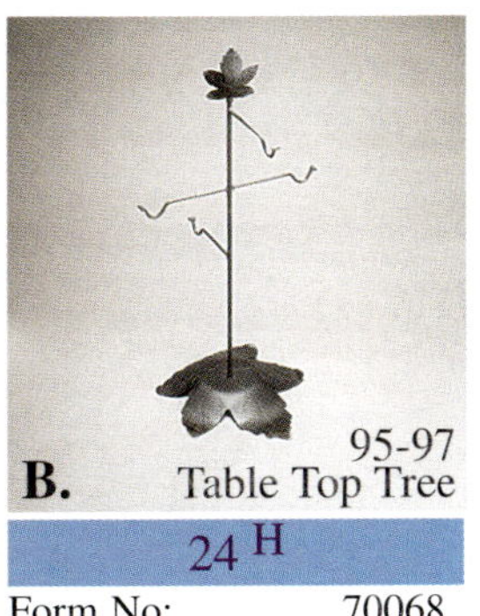

B. 95-97 Table Top Tree

24 H

Form No: 70068

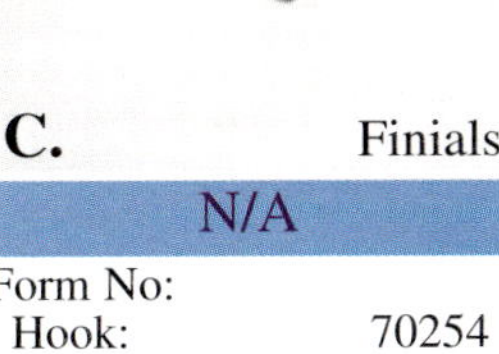

C.   Finials

N/A

Form No:
Hook: 70254
Leaf: 74039

D.   Herb Markers   96-97

Form No:
Basil & Chives   32905
Parsley & Thyme   32808
Dill & Cilantro   33006
Sage & Oregano   33014

Basket is for display only.

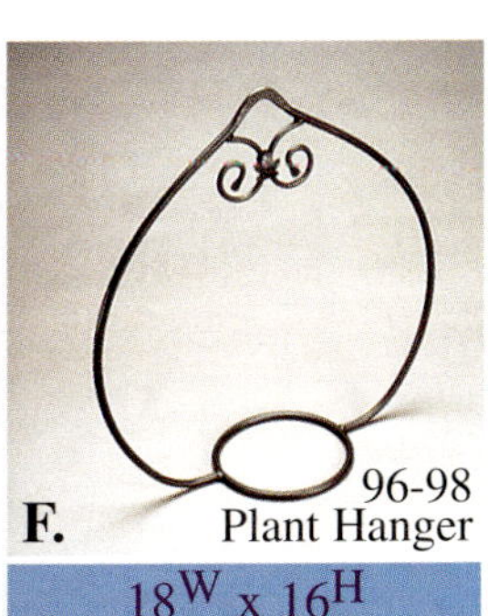

F. 96-98 Plant Hanger

18 W x 16 H

Form No: 70271

*Discontinued after
8/31/98.*

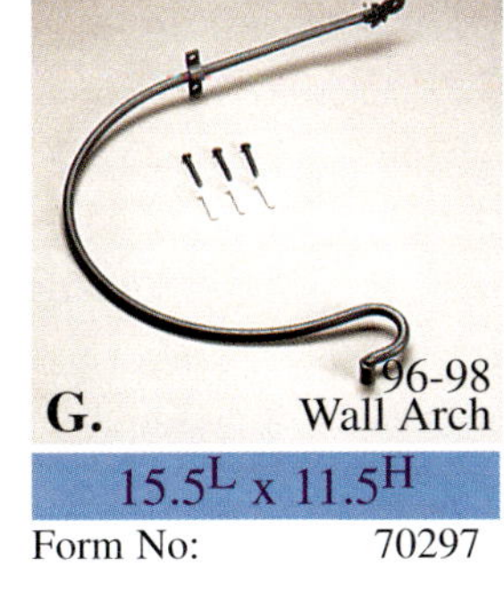

G. 96-98 Wall Arch

15.5 L x 11.5 H

Form No: 70297

*Discontinued after
8/31/98.*

H. 95-98 Two-Pie Server

10.5 RD x 14 H

Form No: 74004

*There is still a Two-Pie
Server in the Regular
Line. It was made to be
more decorative in 1998.*

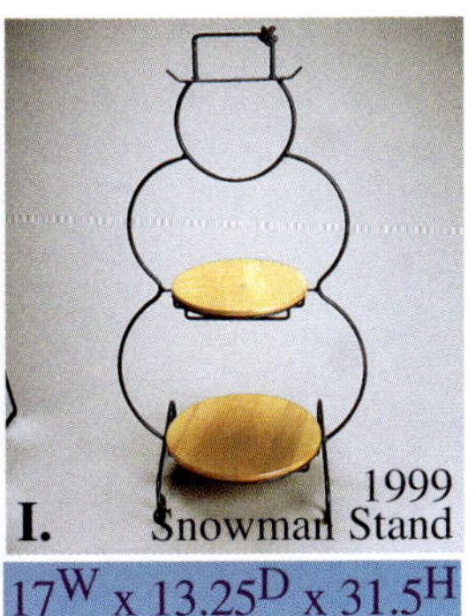

I. 1999 Snowman Stand

17 W x 13.25 D x 31.5 H

Form No: 75795

Shelves sold separately.

Basket Fun Fact

Repairing your Heirlooms

What should you do if one of your beloved baskets, heaven forbid, gets damaged? Many Collectors approach us with this question. The next question is usually, "How will it affect its value?"

Because these baskets are handmade, they often receive repairs before they even leave the plant. As long as the repair does not negatively affect its beauty or function, it should not negatively affect its value. For this reason, The Bentley Collection recommends that all repairs be sent to The Longaberger Company. Your Consultant should be able to provide you with a Basket Repair Form, or you can contact The Company directly at 740-322-5000.

It is important to be able to identify the part that needs repaired. Here is a brief anatomy of a basket to help you in your repairs, as well as in the market as a whole:

Leather loops, or "ears"

Leather Shoestring

"Trim Strip"

"Band" (beneath the Trim Strip)

"Wood Wheel" (between handle and basket)

Dowel   Lid   Leather Hinge

1/2" Weaving

Copper "Rivet"

Filler Splints

Tack   Swinging Handle

Reinforcement Splints

Upsplint

90

Good Ol' Summertime™

Kim Malkiewicz

Valrico, Florida

Kim doesn't have a favorite basket, she "falls in love with them all!" She fell under the spell at an open house when she won the door prize: a Medium Market woven "right in front of my eyes!"

Features:

Series first introduced in 1998. Promoted during the month of July.

A. 1998 Picnic Pal

9.5^L x 9.5^W x 2.75^H

Form No:	18643
No. Sold:	

Red and blue trim strip.

MARKET VALUES

	Description	Original	Avg.	High
A.	1998 Picnic Pal™	37.00	**50**	**60**
	with **P**rotector	44.00	**51**	**64**
	with **L**iner	53.00	**51**	**64**
	Combo (**P/L**)	51.00	**53**	**70**
B.	1999 Seashell™	39.00	**60**	**85**
	with **P**rotector	46.00	**60**	**85**
	with **L**iner	55.00	**60**	**85**
	Combo (**P/L**)	49.00	**68**	**120**
	Full Set (**C/Lid**)	69.00	**80**	**135**
C.	1999 Seashell Tie-On	8.00	**13**	**17**
C.	1999 Beachcomber™	67.00	—	—
	with **P**rotector	83.00	—	—
	with **L**iner	91.00	—	—
	Combo (**P/L**)	97.00	**100**	**110**
	Full Set (**C/Lid**)	127.00	**129**	**190**
	2000 Shaker Taker™[np]	39.00	—	—
	with **P**rotector	43.00	—	—
	with **L**iner	54.00	—	—
	Combo (**P/L**)	49.00	—	—
	2000 Salt/Pepper Tie-On[np]	8.00		
D.	2000 Barbeque Buddy™	49.00	—	—
	with **P**rotector	54.00	—	—
	with **L**iner	67.00	—	—
	Combo (**P/L**)	59.00	—	—
	2000 BBQ Buddy Tie-On[np]	10.00	—	—

[np] = Not Pictured

B. 1999 Seashell

7.75^L x 5.75^W x 5^H

Form No:	15296
Tie-On:	36561
No. Sold:	

Both baskets in 1999 were offered to everyone No Hostess Only.

C. 1999 Beachcomber

10.5^L x 9^W x 8^H

Form No:	15342
No. Sold:	

D. 2000 Barbeque Buddy

12^L x 5.25^W x 3^H

Form No:	16284
No. Sold:	

Heartland Collection®

Suzanne Tobin
Williamsport, Ohio

This past Christmas, Suzanne's husband helped her to complete her Heartland Collection® by giving her the 1990 Getaway™. She also owns every Booking Basket ever offered. Her only wish is that she "would have started collecting EARLIER!"

Features:

Dresden Blue® shoestring weave. Series created in 1988. Special burnt in logo on bottom.

MARKET VALUES

Photo	Description		Original	Avg.	High
A.	(88-97)	Chore, Medium™	36.95	**50**	90
B.	(89-97)	Chore, Mini™	19.95	**40**	75
C.	(89-97)	Chore, Small™	22.95	**43**	55
D.	(1990)	Getaway™	65.95	**140**	200
E.	(88-97)	Key, Medium™	26.95	**44**	60
F.	(94-97)	Key, Small™	21.95	**37**	50
G.	(88-97)	Key, Tall™	34.95	**54**	75
H.	(89-97)	Market, Medium™	43.95	**74**	90
I.	(89-97)	Peg, Large™	28.95	**52**	70
J.	(88-98)	Purse, Small™	36.95	**52**	80
K.	(88-99)	Spoon, Small™	23.95	**37**	45
L.	(90-97)	Spring™	34.95	**48**	60

[continued next page]

A. 1988-97 Medium Chore

13^L x 8^W x 5^H

Form No:	13528
No.Sold:	

One of the first in the series.

E. 1988-97 Medium Key

9^L x 5^W x 5^H

Form No:	11118
No.Sold:	

One of the first in the series.

Heartland® Logo

All Heartland Baskets have this burned-in logo on the bottom, authenticating the collection.

I. 1989-97 Large Peg

6.5^L x 6.5^W x 8^H

Form No:	11177
No.Sold:	

B. 1989-97
Mini Chore

7^L x 5^W 3.5^H

Form No: 10758
No.Sold:

C. 1989-97
Small Chore

10^L x 6^W x 4^H

Form No: 13404
No.Sold:

D. 1990
Heartland Getaway

17^L x 14^W x 11^H

Form No: 300-CCS
No. Sold:

Hostess only.
Featured in 1990.

F. 1994-97
Small Key

7^L x 5^W x 3.5^H

Form No: 10782
No.Sold:

One of the first in the series.

G. 1988-97
Tall Key

9.5^L x 5^W x 9.5^H

Form No: 11061
No.Sold:

One of the first in the series.

H. 1989-97
Medium Market

15^L x 10^W x 7.5^H

Form No: 10545
No.Sold:

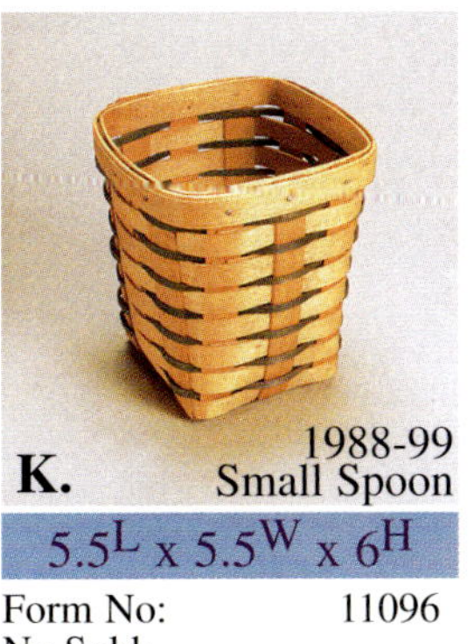

J. 1988-98
Small Purse

9.5^L x 6^W x 6^H

Form No: 10839
No.Sold:

K. 1988-99
Small Spoon

5.5^L x 5.5^W x 6^H

Form No: 11096
No.Sold:

L. 1990-97 Spring

11^L x 8^W x 5.5^H

Form No: 10936
No.Sold:

1997-9
M. Medium Vegetabl

13^L x 7.5^W x 3^{FH} x 8^B

Form No: 16713
No.Sold:

Features:

There are still Heartland baskets being offered in the Regular Line. Items listed here are those that have been retired.

MARKET VALUES

Photo	Description	Original	Avg.	High
M.	(97-99) Vegetable, Med.™	50.95	**54**	75

Fun Fact

Top Regular Line Sellers
1998-1999

#4: Tissue Basket™   127,000

#3: Candle Basket™   130,000
Tea Basket™   130,000

#2: Darning Basket™ 155,000

#1: Recipe Basket™   175,000

LeAnn Starner
Dover, Pennsylvania

Doesn't this room scream "BASKET CRAZY"!

LeAnn has been an Advisor for a year now and has over 300+ baskets throughout her home. She decorates each room in a different theme.

Features:
Red and Green Weave.
Red or Green Trim.

MARKET VALUES

Photo	Description		Original	Avg.	High
A.	1987	Tray™	32.95	**109**	200
B.	1988	Tall Key™	30.95	**92**	125
C.	1988	Weekender™	65.95	**183**	225
D.	1988	Large Market™	49.95	**114**	161
E.	1988	Small Laundry™	67.95	**240**	342
F.	1989	Medium Gathering™	40.95	**104**	135
G.	1989	Large Fruit™	49.95	**121**	172
H.	1989	Magazine™	53.95	**122**	160
I.	1990	13" Measuring™	69.95	**123**	155
J.	1990	Large Gathering™	65.95	**127**	165
K.	1991	Tree Trimming™	79.95	**150**	200
		Combo (**P**)	92.90	**160**	225
L.	1992	Gift Giving™	124.95	**158**	220
		with **P**rotector	137.90	**175**	225
		with **L**iner	146.90	**175**	225
		Combo (**P/L**)	169.85	**178**	250

A. 1987 Tray
14^L x 9^W x 4.5^H
Form No: 2300-JGRS
No. Sold:

E. 1988 Small Laundry
24^L x 17^W x 10^H
Form No: 2600-ORGS
No. Sold:

Holiday Hostess Values

Holiday Hostess baskets are only available to hostesses during the Holiday selling season. This season usually begins Sept. 1 and goes through the end of the year. It is very common for the original collector to have purchased these baskets at half price, using their hostess benefits. This explains why some of the values in the market look as if they are below original retail.

I. 1990 13" Measuring
13RD x 12.5^H
Form No: 4200-CGRS
No. Sold:

B. 1988 Tall Key

9.5^L x 5^W x 9.5^H

Form No: 1000-IRGS
No. Sold:

C. 1988 Weekender

10.5^L x 9^W x 8^H

Form No: 200-YRGS
No. Sold:

D. 1988 Large Market

16^L x 11^W x 9^H

Form No: 600-ARGS
No. Sold:

F. Medium Gathering — 1989

18^L x 11^W x 4.5^H

Form No: 2400-AGRS
No. Sold:

G. Large Fruit — 1989

13RD x 8.5^H

Form No: 3200-BGRS
No. Sold:

H. 1989 Magazine

16^L x 8^W x 11^H

Form No: 2100-CGRS
No. Sold:

J. Large Gathering — 1990

19^L x 12^W x 6^H

Form No: 2500-CGRS
No. Sold:

K. Tree Trimming — 1991

12.5^RD x 13.5^H

Form No:
1900-BRGS/BGRS
No. Sold:

L. 1992 Gift Giving

20.5^L x 15^W x 10.5^H

Form No: 12700/12718[†]
No. Sold:

† = Product numbers are stated: Red weave / Green weave

Features:

Available only to Hostesses during September through December.

MARKET VALUES

	Description	Original	Avg.	High
M.	**1993 Homecoming™**	109.95	**140**	**200**
	with **Protector**	120.90	**140**	**210**
	with **Liner**	131.90	**140**	**210**
	with **Lid**	145.90	**150**	**210**
	Combo (**P/L/Lid**)	149.95	**154**	**220**
N.	**1994 Sleigh Bell™**	139.95	**182**	**250**
	with **Protector**	154.90	**185**	**250**
	with **Liner**	167.90	**185**	**250**
	with **Lid**	175.90	**185**	**250**
	Combo (**P/L/Lid**)	199.95	**199**	**250**
O.	**1995 Evergreen™**	139.95	**180**	**225**
	with **Protector**	154.90	**180**	**225**
	with **Liner**	167.90	**180**	**225**
	with **Lid**	179.90	**189**	**225**
	Combo (**P/L/Lid**)	199.95	**189**	**250**
	with **Divider**	146.90	—	—
P.	**1996 Yuletide Treasures™**	129.95	**149**	**200**
	with **Protector**	144.90	**149**	**200**
	with **Liner**	159.90	**149**	**200**
	with **Lid**	179.90	**149**	**200**
	Combo (**P/L/Lid**)	199.95	**169**	**225**
Q.	**1997 Snowflake™**	129.95	**140**	**185**
	with **Protector**	156.90	**160**	**185**
	with **Liner**	156.90	**160**	**190**
	Combo (**P/L**)	159.95	**170**	**215**
	Full Set (**C/Lid**)	204.90	**180**	**250**
R.	**1998 Winter Wishes™**	95.00	**100**	**130**
	with **Protector**	110.00	**100**	**130**
	with **Liner**	122.00	**100**	**130**
	Combo (**P/L**)	115.00	**119**	**165**
	Full Set (**C/Lid**)	149.00	**130**	**185**
S.	**1999 Pinecone™**	99.00	—	—
	with **Protector**	119.00	—	—
	with **Liner**	123.00	—	—
	Combo (**P/L**)	129.00	**123**	**150**
	Full Set (**C/Lid**)	174.00	**151**	**178**

M. 1993 Homecoming

15^L x 15^W x 7.5^H

Form No: 12084/12092†
No. Sold:

Q. 1997 Snowflake

14^L x 12.75^W x 11.5^H

Form No: 12661/12653†
No. Sold:

Three-level protector and wooden lid (with or without a knob) sold separately. Also features an open-weave bottom.

N. 1994 Sleigh Bell

16.5RD x 11.5^H

Form No: 14427/14435†
No. Sold:

Lid available with red or green knob.

O. 1995 Evergreen

15.5^L x 15.5^W x 12.25^H

Form No: 19607/19615†
No. Sold:

Lid available with red or green knob. Divider shelf sold separately.

P. 1996 Yuletide Treasures

20.25^L x 13.75^W x 7.5^H

Form No: 18619/18627†
No. Sold:

The lid that was introduced for this basket is still available in the regular line.

R. 1998 Winter Wishes

.5^L x 8.25^W x 10.5^{FH} x 12^{BH}

Form No: 12483/12491†
No. Sold:

Lid available with red or green knob.

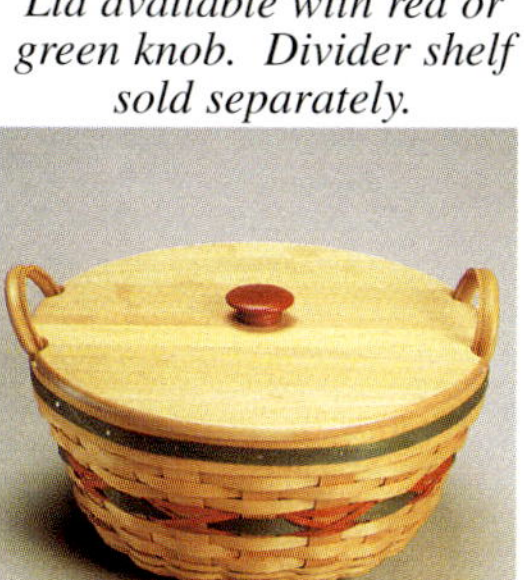

S. 1999 Pinecone

13RD x 6.25^H

Form No: 15253 / 15164†
No. Sold:

Lid available with red or green knob. Divider shelf sold separately.

Fun Fact

The Longaberger Sales force continues to break records! The top Sales Person for the company in the 1998 - 1999 sales year sold almost $290,000. In the same year, Sales Consultants set a new record with 88,000 shows during the Lots of Luck™ campaign, while the Basketmakers were busy with their own benchmark of 57,000 baskets in one day.

† = Product numbers are stated: Red weave / Green weave

Ever wonder where the values in the Bentley Guide come from?

☆ Ever look at a value and disagree with it?

☆ The Bentley Guide is based on *actual selling prices*.

☆ Most of the research we gather comes from Collectors like you!

☆ **We need you to accurately represent your area.**

☆ Whenever you buy, sell or trade, **SEND US YOUR RESULTS!**

☆ The more results we have, the more accurate your Guide will be.

HERE'S HOW

☆ **Call Us**
1-800-837-4394
Monday through Friday
9am - 5pm (EST)

☆ **Fax Us**
1-888-275-8484
24 hours a day, 7 days a week

☆ **E-mail Us**
research@bentleyguide.com
24 hours a day, 7 days a week

☆ **Mail Us**
Bentley Guide Research
P.O. Box 2245
Westerville, Ohio 43086

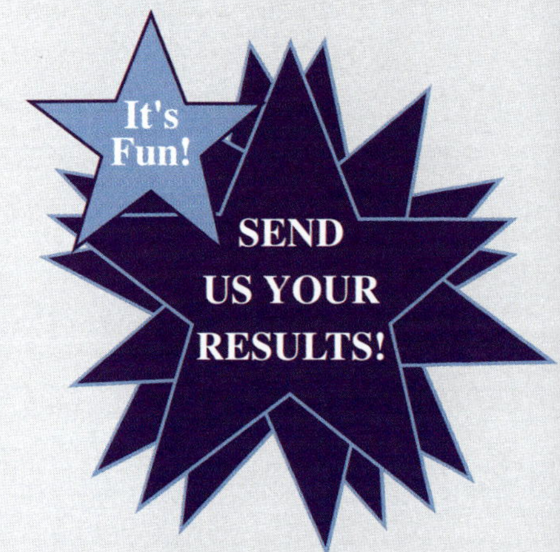

HERE'S THE INFO WE NEED

? Name of Basket and its Collection
? Year
? Did you buy, sell or trade it?
? Selling Price (not including shipping)
? Condition
? Accessories (liner, protector, tie-on, lid, divider, etc...)
? Signatures (who and how many)
? Which forum was used to make the transaction (internet, auction, etc...)
? In which state was the transaction made (selling state and buying state)

Angela Lundgren
Los Angeles, California

Angela first started collecting in 1987 and began selling in 1988. The Horizon of Hope® Collection is her favorite because of the important role that it plays in Breast Cancer Awareness. She also has the complete May Series™ and all of the Bee Baskets™, back to 1991.

Features:

No color weave or trim. Each basket has the American Cancer Society logo burned into the bottom.

MARKET VALUES

Photo	Description		Original	Avg.	High
A.	1995	Horizon of Hope™	28.95	75	95
		with **Protector**	31.90	78	100
		with **Liner**	38.90	87	120
		Combo **(P/L)**	41.85	103	131
B.	1996	Horizon of Hope™	28.95	63	80
		with **Protector**	31.90	63	85
		with **Liner**	38.90	70	85
		Combo **(P/L)**	41.85	75	95
C.	1997	Horizon of Hope™	28.95	50	60
		with **Protector**	31.90	62	63
		with **Liner**	38.90	62	65
		Combo **(P/L)**	41.85	64	85
D.	1998	Horizon of Hope™	31.00	50	75
		with **Protector**	34.00	53	78
		with **Liner**	41.00	53	78
		Combo **(P/L)**	44.00	67	95
D.	1998	Oval Tie-On	8.00	12	15
E.	1999	Horizon of Hope™	31.00	60	75
		with **Protector**	34.00	—	—
		with **Liner**	44.00	—	—
		Combo **(P/L)**	47.00	65	80
		Full Set **(C/Lid)**	46.00	—	—
E.	1999	Heart Tie-On	8.00	12	16

These baskets are made in cooperation with The American Cancer Society® to help with the fight against breast cancer. With every basket sold, The Longaberger Company® donates $2.00 towards breast cancer research and education projects. To date, a total of $4.3 Million has been raised.

A. Horizon of Hope 1995

5.75^L x 3.75^W x 3^H

Form No:	17124
No. Sold:	180,579

All Regular line fabrics were made available for this Liner.

E. Horizon of Hope 1999

6.25^L x 5.25^W x 3^H

Form No:	14150
Tie-On:	36625
No. Sold:	368,000

All Regular line fabrics were made available for this Liner. $1.3 Million was raised in 1999.

6.75L x 4.75W x 2.25H	
Form No:	15911
No. Sold:	248,886

Each basket came with a set of 12 recipes chosen by The American Cancer Society®. Liner offered in all regular line fabrics.

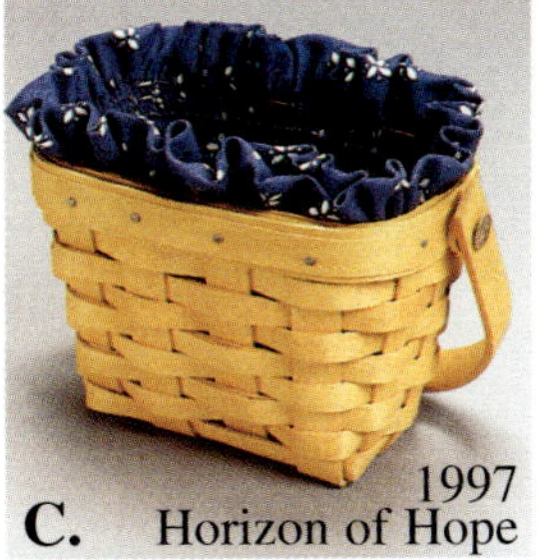

5.75L x 4W x 4H	
Form No:	18724
No. Sold:	290,000

Liner available only as stand-up, but in all the regular line fabrics.

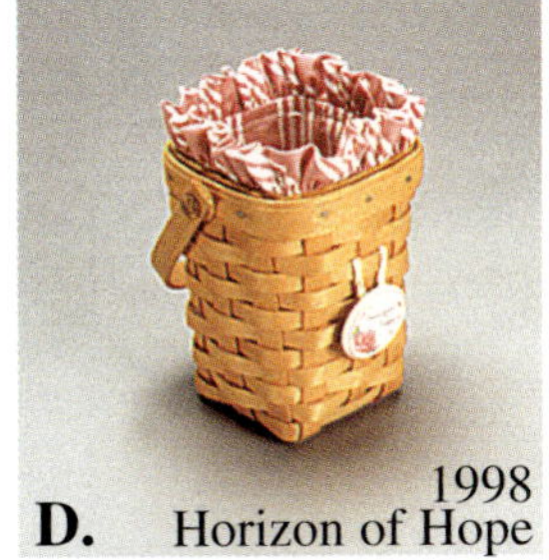

4L x 4W x 5.5H	
Form No:	10472
Tie-On:	33677
No. Sold:	

Each basket included a sheet of 12 breast self-exam reminder stickers. Liner offered in all regular line fabrics.

Big Basket of Hope™

A special, one-of-a-kind, large version of the 1999 Horizon of Hope Basket™ was given away through a random drawing on December 18, 1999. Vicki Lee of Peoria, Illinois was the lucky winner.

Consultants at the 1999 Bee were first able to purchase tickets for the drawing for $2. After August 9, the Big Basket of Hope was moved to the Longaberger Homestead, where visitors could also purchase tickets until December 15. *All of the proceeds* went to Breast Cancer Research, totaling nearly $56,000.

The Big Basket of Hope has its own special liner and a brass tag that reads "Longaberger – Big Basket of Hope – 1999 – Horizon of Hope – One-of-a-kind Edition". Tami, Rachel, Grandma Bonnie and all of the siblings completed the special edition with their signatures.

Basket Fun Fact

Large Hamper Basket History . . .

The Large Hamper™ is a form that has shown up in the Longaberger product line in many different variations.   Following is a brief history time line describing the different looks of the Large Hamper.

Prior to 1979 – July, 1986
- Available through the Regular Line.
- Attached Woven Lid with knob <u>at front</u> of Lid.
- No hand slots.
- Darker "old" stain, Natural or Natural with color.

August, 1986 – 1990
- Available through the Hostess Collection.
- Attached Woven Lid with knob <u>at front</u> of Lid.
- No hand slots.
- Darker "old" stain, Natural or Natural with color.
- After 1987: Lighter "new' stain <u>only.</u>

May 1986
- Available as a Feature Basket.
- No Lid.
- First time for two hand slots.
- Darker "old" stain <u>only</u>.

1991
- Featured for Shades of Autumn Hostesses only for one month.
- 3/8" Hostess Weaving.
- Detached Woven Lid with knob in <u>middle</u> of Lid.
- Two hand slots.
- Lighter 'new' stain <u>only</u>.

1993 – 1994
- Available through the Regular Line.
- Detached Woven Lid with knob in middle of Lid.
- Two hand slots.
- Lighter "new' stain <u>only</u>.

1995 – present (See Wish List™)
- Available through the Hostess Collection.
- 3/8" Hostess Weaving.
- Detached Woven Lid with knob in middle of Lid.
- Two hand slots.
- Lighter 'new' stain <u>only</u>.

Prior to 1979 – 1990
Large Hamper

1986 Feature Hamper

1991 Shades of Autumn
Hostess Hamper

1993 – 1994 Hamper looks like this with, $\frac{1}{2}$" weave. Returned to $\frac{3}{8}$" weave in 1995 Hostess Collection.

Hostess Collection™

Rita Scaggs
Raceland, Kentucky

While this "Spring Cleaning" photo shows the extent of Rita's collection, her favorite baskets are from the All-American Collection®. This past April, she had the opportunity to attend her first Collectors Club Gathering and was lucky enough to win a basket signed by Rich!

Features:

Available only to Hostesses. Baskets from 1990 to present have 3/8" weave.

MARKET VALUES

Photo	Description	Original	Avg.	High
	1986 – 1990:			
A.	Large Hamper™	109.95	**241**	**305**
	Medium Hamper™[np]	69.95	**131**	**175**
B.	Doll Cradle™	44.95	**183**	**240**
C.	Large (Infant) Cradle™	109.95	**357**	**400**
D.	Large Laundry™	96.95	**242**	**300**
	1990 – 1992:			
E.	Heirloom™	87.95	**110**	**150**
F.	Hearthside ™	59.95	**87**	**130**
	with Protector	68.90	**105**	**140**
G.	Remembrance™	79.95	**150**	**200**
	with Protector	88.90	**169**	**240**
H.	Harvest™	54.95	**96**	**122**
	with Protector	66.90	**118**	**125**
	1992 – 1995:			
I.	Gourmet Picnic™	99.95	**130**	**170**
	with **Protector**	110.90	**130**	**170**
	with **Liner**	121.90	**130**	**170**
	Combo (**P/L**)	132.85	**140**	**175**
	1992 – 1996:			
J.	Mail™	79.95	**118**	**140**
	with **Protector**	89.90	**127**	**155**
	with **Liner**	96.90	**127**	**155**
	Combo (**P/L**)	106.85	**138**	**160**
	1992 – 1998:			
K.	Wildflower™	64.95	**101**	**125**
	with **Protector**	75.90	**104**	**125**
	with **Liner**	84.90	**104**	**125**
	Combo (**P/L**)	95.85	**122**	**175**
	1995 – 1998:			
L.	Tea Pot	59.95	**96**	**140**

[continued next page]

[np] = Not Pictured

A. 1986 - 1990
Large Hamper

16.5^L x 16.5^W x 21.5^H

Form No: 1600-DO
No. Sold:

<u>Med:</u> 12^L x 12.25^W x 16.25^H
Attached lid, knob towards front of lid, no handles.

E. 1990 – 1992
Heirloom

15^L x 10^W x 7.5^H

Form No: 500-HOS
No. Sold:

I. 1992 – 1995
Gourmet Picnic

13.25^L x 11.25^W x 9^H

Form No: 10413
No. Sold:

B. 1986 – 1990
Doll Cradle

19^L x 12^W x 6^H

Form No: 2500-LO
No. Sold:

Liner sold separately.

C. 1986 – 1990
Large Cradle

30^L x 20^W x 10.5^H

Form No: 2800-M
No. Sold:

Available Stained, Natural, or Natural with color. Available stained from 1990 – 1984, and then again from 8/89 - 1/90.

D. 1986 – 1990
Large Laundry

30^L x 20^W x 10.5^H

Form No: 2800-O
No. Sold:

Available Stained, Natural, or Natural with color. Available stained from 1990 – 1984, and then again from 8/89 - 1/90.

F. 1990 – 1992
Hearthside

11.75RD x 6.5^H

Form No: 42000-AOS
No. Sold:

G. 1990 – 1992
Remembrance

10.5^L x 9^W x 8^H

Form No: 200-YOS
No. Sold:

H. 1990 – 1992
Harvest

16^L x 9^W x 6^H

Form No: 3700-AOS
No. Sold:

J. 1992 – 1996 Mail

12^L x 8^W x 11.5^H

Form No: 10600
No. Sold:

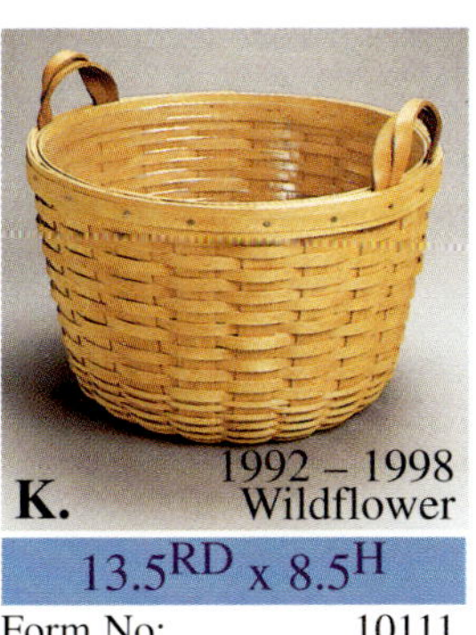

K. 1992 – 1998
Wildflower

13.5RD x 8.5^H

Form No: 10111
No. Sold:

Available at the $250 show level.

L. 1995 – 1998 Teapot

40 oz.

Form No: 32069/42/51
Ivory   33782

Available in red, blue, green or ivory at the $250 show level.

Features:

Hostesses were able to earn some of these baskets at half-price once their show totaled at least $250.

MARKET VALUES

Photo	Description	Original	Avg.	High
	1995 – 1999:			
M.	Corn™	139.95	**142**	**250**
	with **Protector**	158.90	**147**	**265**
	with **Liner**	169.90	**147**	**265**
	Combo **(P/L)**	193.85	**234**	**295**
	1995 – 2000:			
N.	Sewing™	89.95	--	—
	with **Protector**	105.90	—	—
	with **Liner**	113.90	—	—
	Combo **(P/L)**	129.85	—	—
	1996 – 1999:			
O.	Large Gathering™	89.95	**103**	**120**
	with **Protector**	102.90	—	—
	with **Liner**	118.90	—	—
	Combo **(P/L)**	131.85	**153**	**190**

M. 1995 – 1999 Corn

17RD x 11.5^{H}

Form No: 14443
No. Sold:

Available at the $500 show level. Lid sold separately.

N. 1995 – 2000 Sewing

13RD x 8.5^{H}

Form No: 13234
No. Sold:

Available at the $500 show level. Accessories sold separately.

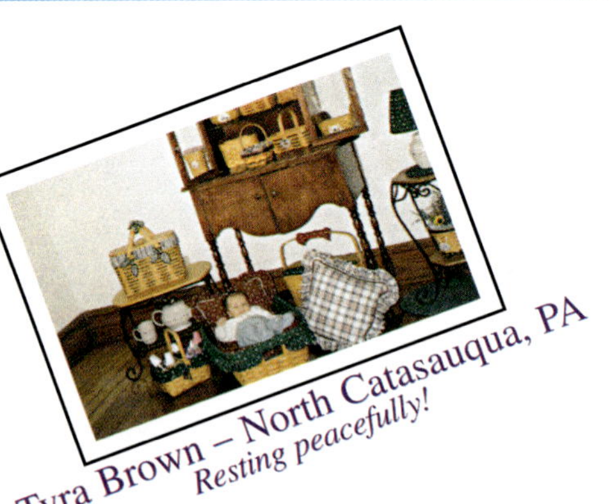

Tyra Brown – North Catasauqua, PA
Resting peacefully!

O. 1996 – 1999 Large Gathering

19^{L} x 12^{W} x 6^{H}

Form No: 12564
No. Sold:

Available at the $250 show level.

Incentive/Award Baskets

Elizabeth Sanders
Crown Point, Indiana

This beautiful display was created to celebrate Elizabeth's new Branch. *The Heartfelt Traditions Branch* was established in December 1999 after much hard work. The 1995 Family Traditions basket pictured here was Elizabeth's very first feature purchase. Five years later, she is motivating her very own Branch!

Features:

Available only to Consultants, Advisors, & Sales Directors. Most have commemorative tags. No original prices.

MARKET VALUES

Photo	Description	Avg.	High
	Recruit / Sponsor Baskets:		
	1988 "Recruiting – Building Branches"		
	Sm.Fruit [WL] –1 recruit	—	**140**
	Md. Fruit [WL] –2 recruits	—	**165**
	Lg. Fruit [WL] –3+ recruits	—	—
	1988 "Share the Tradition"		
A.	& 89 Recruit	**170**	**220**
B.	Sponsor	**207**	**325**
	Set:	—	**425**
	1990 "Together – We're Growing"		
C.	Recruit	**169**	**180**
D.	Sponsor	**175**	**200**
	1990 "Longaberger Rising Star"		
E.	& 91 Recruit	**175**	**175**
	Sponsor [np]	**185**	**230**
	*Superstar Sponsor [np]	**155**	**200**
	1992 "Flying High with Longaberger"		
F.	Recruit	**119**	**125**
G.	Sponsor (Large)	**125**	**175**
	*Sponsor (Small) [np]	**118**	**175**
	1993 "All-Star Recruiting"		
H.	Recruit	**138**	**200**
I.	Sponsor (Large)	**130**	**175**
	*Sponsor (Small) [np]	**113**	**160**
	1996 "Opportunity Reigns"		
J.	Recruit / Sponsor Umbrella	**63**	**75**
	1996 "Pegged for Your Success"		
K.	Recruit	**102**	**135**
	with **Protector**	—	—
	with **Liner**	—	—
	Combo (**P/L**)	--	—
K.	Sponsor	**193**	**225**
	with **Protector**	—	—
	with **Liner**	—	—
	Combo (**P/L**)	—	—
	1997 "Watch Your Business Bloom"		
L.	Recruit / Sponsor	**92**	**99**

* Given to Sponsors with more than one recruit.
[np] = Not Pictured

A. 1988-89 Recruit

5^L x 5^W x 2.5^H

Form No: 13000-BBRS
No. Given:

"Share the Tradition"
No tag on basket.

E. 1990-91 Recruit

12^L x 12.25^W x 16.25^H

Form No: 1700-DST
No. Given:

Superstar Sponsor:
Same as above, except
tag is different.
Sponsor (Lg.Hamper)
16.5L x 16.5W x 21.5H

I. 1993 Sponsor (Large)

8.5^L x 5^W x 3.5^H

Form No: 13323
No. Given:

"All-Star"

B. 1988-89 Sponsor

8.5^L x 8.5^W x 5^H

Form No: 1500-BBRS
No. Given:

"Share the Tradition"
No tag on basket.

C. 1990 Recruit

5.75^L x 3.75^W x 3^H

Form No: 45000-ABRST
No. Given:

Tag reads: "Together –
1990 Recruit"

D. 1990 Sponsor

9^L x 5^W x 5^H

Form No: 1100-ABRST
No. Given:

Tag reads: "Together –
1990 Sponsor"

F. 1992 Recruit

5RD x 4.5^H

Form No: 10154
No. Given:

G. 1992 Sponsor (Large)

7RD x 6.5^H

Form No: 10162
No. Given:

"Flying High with Longaberger"

1992 Sponsor (Small)
Looks the same as the 1992 Recruit, except tag is different

H. 1993 Recruit

8^L x 4^W x 2^H

Form No: 16101
No. Given:

"All-Star"

1993 Sponsor (Small)
Looks the same, except
tag is different.

J. 1996 Recruit/Sponsor

34^H

Form No: N/A
No. Given:

"Opportunity Reigns"
Given to both the quali-
fied Recruit and Sponsor
between 1/27 – 3/29/96.

K. 1996 Recruit & Sponsor

<u>Sm</u>: 5^L x 5^W x 4.5^H
<u>Lg</u>: 6.5^L x 6.5^W x 8^H

"Pegged for Success"
Accessories could be earned
with additional recruits.
Available to both Recruit and
Sponsor from 4/22 – 5/31/96.

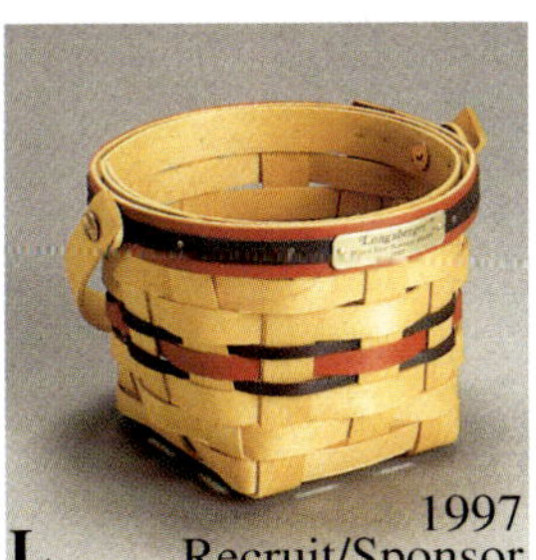

L. 1997 Recruit/Sponsor

5RD x 4.5^H

Form No: unknown
No. Given:

"Watch Your Business Bloom"
Given to both the qualified
Recruit and Sponsor from
3/22 – 6/27/97. **113**

Features:

All V.I.P. Baskets are the same size with 2 sw/h. No other basket shares this form.

Photo	Description	Original	Avg.	High
	Recruit / Sponsor (con't):			
M.	1997 Christmas Sponsoring Snowflake™		127	150
N.	1998 Flag Sponsoring		200	250
	1998 Flag Recruit		192	200
O.	1999 Recruit		146	200
	1999 Recruit Tie-On[np]		—	—
	National Sponsoring Awards:			
P.	1992 Blue-Green Trim & Weave		—	—
Q.	1993 Red Trim & Weave			
	Sm. Gathering (5-9 recruits)		—	250
	Md. Gathering (10-14 recruits)		—	—
	Lg. Gathering (15-19 recruits)		—	—
	Lg. Gathering (20+ recruits)		—	—
R.	1994 Pink/Purple Trim & Weave			
	Sm. Gathering (5-9 recruits)		200	220
	Md. Gathering (10-14 recruits)		—	—
	Lg. Gathering (15-19 recruits)		—	—
	Lg. Gathering (20+ recruits)		—	—
S.	1995 Purple/Green Trim & Weave			
	Sm. Gathering (5-9 recruits)		150	180
	Md. Gathering (10-14 recruits)		—	—
	Lg. Gathering (15-19 recruits)		—	—
	Lg. Gathering (20+ recruits)		—	—
T.	1996 Blue/Gold/Red Trim & Weave			
	Sm. Gathering (5-9 recruits)		108	120
	Md. Gathering (10-14 recruits)		—	—
	Lg. Gathering (15-19 recruits)		—	—
U.	XLg. Gathering (20+ recruits)		—	—
V.	1997 Red/Blue/Green Trim & Weave			
	Sm. Gathering (5-9 recruits)		—	—
	Md. Gathering (10-14 recruits)		—	—
	Lg. Gathering (15-19 recruits)		—	—
	XLg. Gathering (20+ recruits)		—	—
W.	1998 Green/Yellow/Blue/Red Trim & Weave			
	Sm. Gathering (5-9 recruits)		—	—
	Md. Gathering (10-14 recruits)		—	—
	Lg. Gathering (15-19 recruits)		—	117
	XLg. Gathering (20+ recruits)		—	—
X.	1999 Rose, Green, Blue, Purple Trim & Weave			
	Small (5-9 recruits)		—	—
	Medium (10-14 recruits)		—	—
	Large (15-19 recruits)		—	—
	XLarge (20+ recruits)		—	—

[np] = Not Pictured

M. 1997 Sponsor

10^L x 9.25^W x 6.5^H

Form No: unknown
No Given:

Available to anyone sponsoring a recruit between 6/28 – 8/29/97. Accessories were not given with this award.

Q. Natl. Sponsoring 1993

14^L x 9^W x 4.5^H

Form No: unknown
No Given:

*Woven by Larry Longaberger. Unique open-weave bottom and **personalized** brass tag. Engraved lid included.*

U. XLg. Gathering 1996

23^L x 15^W x 8^H

Form No: unknown
No. Given:

The lid at this level is also engraved with recipient's name. First year for XLarge Size at the 20+ level.

N.   1998 Recruit

7^L x 3.5^W x 4.75^H

Form No: unknown
No. Given:

The Recruit and Sponsor baskets are identical, except for the tag.

O.   1999 Recruit

5.5RD x 4.5^H

Form No: unknown
No. Given:

Woven by Larry Longaberger. The open-weave bottom is a unique and rare characteristic.

1992
P.   Natl. Sponsoring

19.75^L x 12^W x 3.5^H

Form No: unknown
No. Given:

Woven by Larry Longaberger. The open-weave bottom is a unique and rare characteristic.

1994
R.   Natl. Sponsoring

14^L x 9^W x 4.5^H

Form No: unknown
No Given:

Engraved lid included.

1995
S.   Natl. Sponsoring

19^L x 12^W x 6^H

Form No: unknown
No Given:

Engraved lid included.

1996
T.   Natl. Sponsoring

14^L x 9^W x 4.5^H

Form No: unknown
No. Given:

Engraved lid included.

1997
V.   Natl. Sponsoring

14^L x 9^W x 4.5^H

Form No: unknown
No. Given:

Engraved lid included.

1998
W.   Natl. Sponsoring

14^L x 9^W x 4.5^H

Form No: unknown
No. Given:

Engraved lid included.

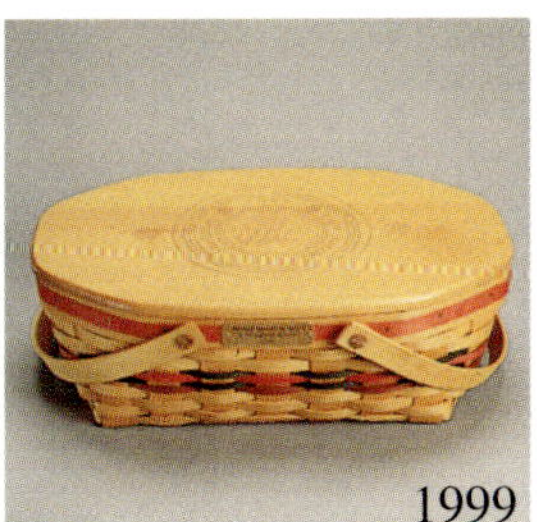

1999
X.   Natl. Sponsoring

14^L x 9^W x 4.25^H

Form No: unknown
No. Given:

First year for this new form. Engraved lid included.

Features:

The V.I.P. Honorable Mention has been the only Tie-On given as an award.

MARKET VALUES

Photo	Description	Avg.	High
	VIP – Honorable Mention:		
	1995 VIP Honorable Mention[np]	—	—
Y.	1996 VIP Honorable Mention	—	—
Z.	1997 VIP Honorable Mention	—	33
A[1]	1998 VIP Honorable Mention	—	—
B[1]	1999 VIP Honorable Mention	—	—
	VIP – $30,000+ sales for the year:		
C[1]	1986 Blue weave & trim	375	400
D[1]	1987 Green or Red weave & trim	363	400
E[1]	1988 Blue weave & trim	310	400
F[1]	1989 Red/Blue weave; Red trim	313	370✍
G[1]	1990 Pink/Blue weave; Pink trim	367	450✍
H[1]	1991 Blue weave & trim	310	425
I[1]	1992 Green weave & trim	270	340
J[1]	1993 Teal/Pink weave; Teal trim	285	350

continued next page

✍ = With Signatures
[np] = Not Pictured

Fun Fact

When a new Consultant signs up to sell, they must purchase what is known as a "Business Kit". In the Classic Kit, they receive a variety of pottery and fabric items and the following baskets to help them get started in their Home Shows:

Classic Cake™
Classic Magazine™
Classic Medium Market™
Classic Recipe™
Classic Small Spoon™
Classic Tea™
Heartland Darning™
Woven Traditions Bread™
Hostess Serving Tray™
Booking Oregano™

Y. Honorable Mention — 1996

3RD x 2.5^{H}

Form No: N/A
No. Given:

Given to Consultants who attain $20,000 - $34,999 in sales.

C[1] 1986 VIP

12^{L} x 7^{W} x 10^{H}

Form No: N/A
No. Given: 69

*Selling Period:
Jan 1985 – Dec 1985*

G[1] 1990 VIP

12^{L} x 7^{W} x 10^{H}

Form No: N/A
No. Given: 359

*Selling Period:
July 1989 – June 1990*

1997
Z. Honorable Mention

3RD x 2.5^H

Form No: N/A
No. Given:

Given to Consultants who attain $20,000 - $34,999 in sales.

1998
A¹ Honorable Mention

3RD x 2.5^H

Form No: N/A
No. Given: ≈ 2,800

Given to Consultants who attain $20,000 - $34,999 in sales.

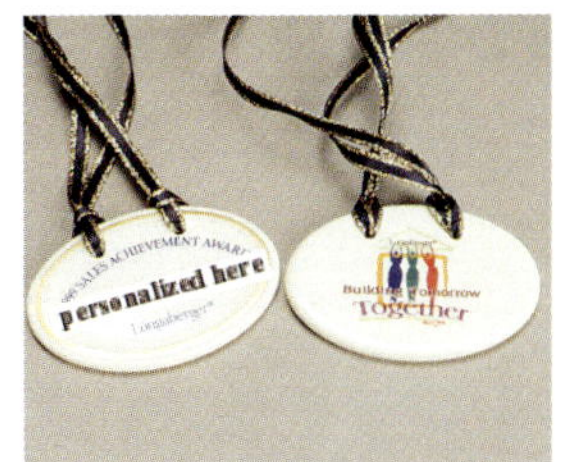

1999
B¹ Honorable Mention

3RD x 2.5^H

Form No: N/A
No. Given:

First time for this award to be personalized and printed on both sides.

D¹ 1987 VIP

12^L x 7^W x 10^H

Form No: N/A
No. Given:

Selling Period:
Green: 1/86 – 6/86
Red: 7/86 – 6/87

E¹ 1988 VIP

12^L x 7^W x 10^H

Form No: N/A
No. Given:

Selling Period:
July 1987 – June 1988

F¹ 1989 VIP

12^L x 7^W x 10^H

Form No: N/A
No. Given: 163

Selling Period:
July 1988 – June 1989

H¹ 1991 VIP

12^L x 7^W x 10^H

Form No: N/A
No. Given:

Selling Period:
July 1990 – June 1991

I¹ 1992 VIP

12^L x 7^W x 10^H

Form No: N/A
No. Given:

Selling Period:
July 1991 – June 1992

J¹ 1993 VIP

12^L x 7^W x 10^H

Form No: N/A
No. Given:

Selling Period:
July 1992 – June 1993

Features:
Commemorative Plates, Pottery, Jewelry and
Trips are examples of other awards given.

MARKET VALUES

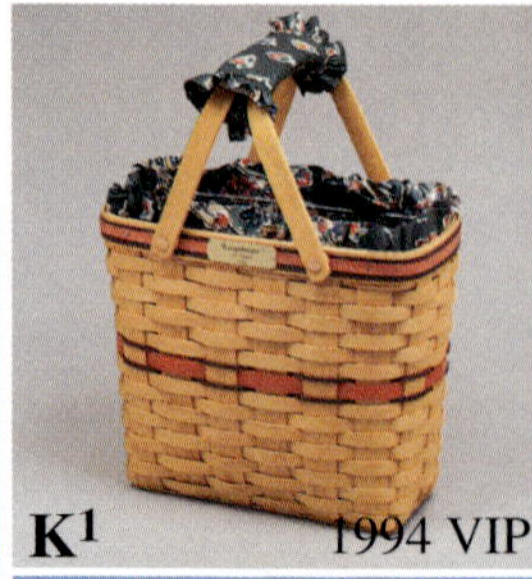

K[1]   1994 VIP

$12^L \times 7^W \times 10^H$

Form No:	N/A
No. Given:	

Selling Period:
July 1993 – June 1994

Photo	Description			Avg.	High
	VIP – $35,000+ sales for the year:				
K[1]	1994	Rose/Purple		**210**	**220**
L[1]	1995	Purple/Green		**245**	**300**
M[1]	1996	Red/Blue/Gold		—	—
N[1]	1997	Red/Blue/Green		—	—
O[1]	1998	Green/Yellow/Blue/Red		**213**	**270**
P[1]	1999	Green/Rose/Blue/Purple		—	—
	National Sales Awards:				
Q[1]	1983	Tin Punched Plaque		—	—
R[1]	1984	Sketched Print		—	—
S[1]	1988	Coverlet Basket™		—	—
T[1]	1989	Flag Basket™		—	—
	1993	Red Accents			
		Sm.Fruit [np]	(Level 1)	—	**190**
U[1]		Md. Fruit	(Level 2)	—	**135**
		Lg. Fruit [np]	(Level 3)	—	—
	1994	Pink/Purple Accents			
		5" Measuring [np]	(Level 1)	—	**235**
V[1]		7" Measuring	(Level 2)	**168**	**185**
		9" Measuring [np]	(Level 3)	—	—
		11" Measuring [np]	(Level 4)	—	**400**

continued next page

[np] = Not Pictured

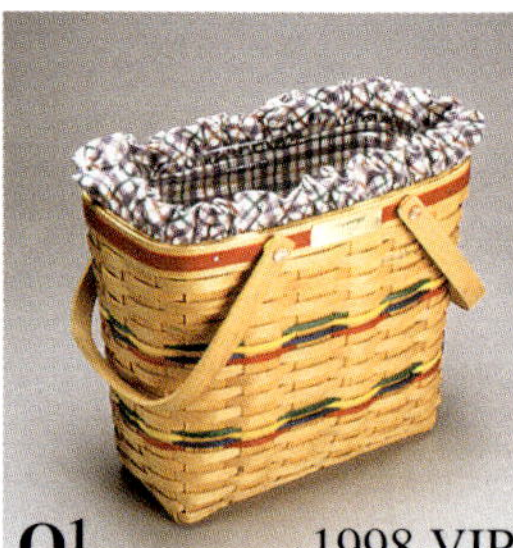

O[1]   1998 VIP

$12^L \times 7^W \times 10^H$

Form No:	N/A
No. Given:	≈ 1,800

Selling Period:
July 1997 – June 1998

S[1]   1988 Coverlet

$16^L \times 16^W \times 8^H$

Form No:	unknown
No. Given:	

Top selling consultants
in 1988.

L¹　　　　　1995 VIP

12^L x 7^W x 10^H

Form No:　　　　　N/A
No. Given:

Selling Period:
July 1994 – June 1995

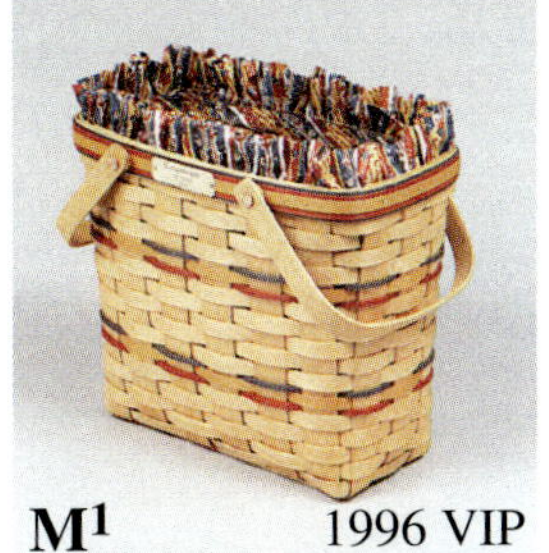

M¹　　　　　1996 VIP

12^L x 7^W x 10^H

Form No:　　　　　N/A
No. Given:　　　　1356

Selling Period:
July 1995 – June 1996

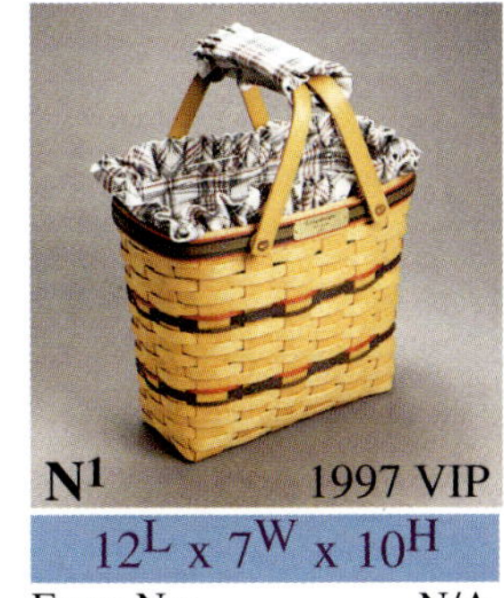

N¹　　　　　1997 VIP

12^L x 7^W x 10^H

Form No:　　　　　N/A
No. Given:

Selling Period:
July 1996 – June 1997

P¹　　　　　1999 VIP

12^L x 7^W x 10^H

Form No:　　　　　N/A
No. Given:

Selling Period:
July 1998 – June 2000

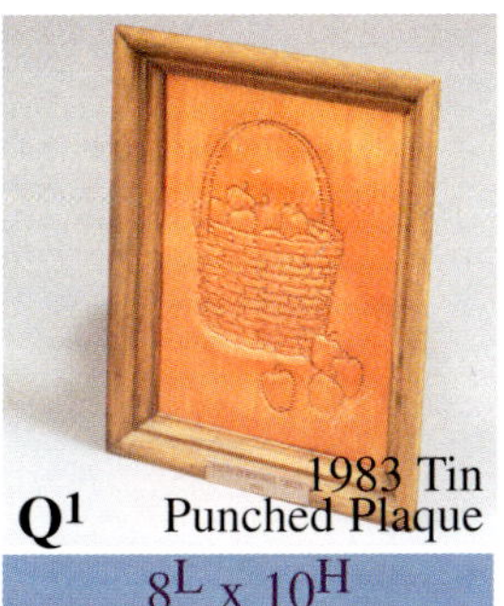

Q¹　　1983 Tin
Punched Plaque

8^L x 10^H

Form No:　　　　　N/A
No. Given:　　　　35

Top selling consultants
in 1983.

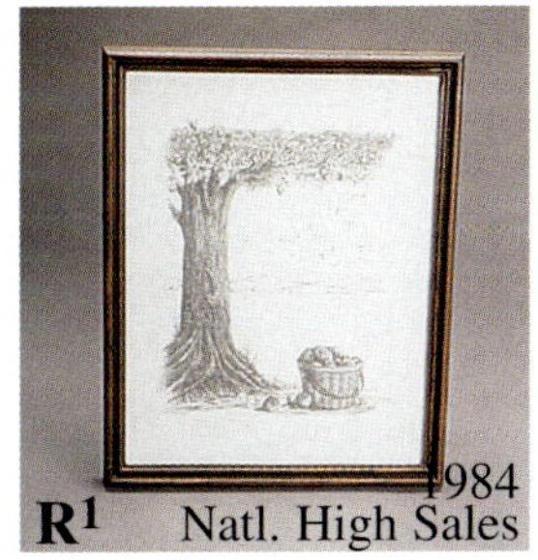

R¹　　1984
Natl. High Sales

Form No:　　　　unknown
No. Given:

Given as a Top Sales
award.

T¹　　　　　1989 Flag

10.75^L x 5.75^W x 7.5^H

Form No:　　　　unknown
No. Given:　　　　20

Given to the Top selling
Consultants during the
"Weave Your American
Dream" Bee in 1989.

U¹　　1993
Natl. High Sales

8RD x 6.5^H

Form No:　　　　unknown
No. Given:

$60,000 – 74,999 Sales
in 1993.

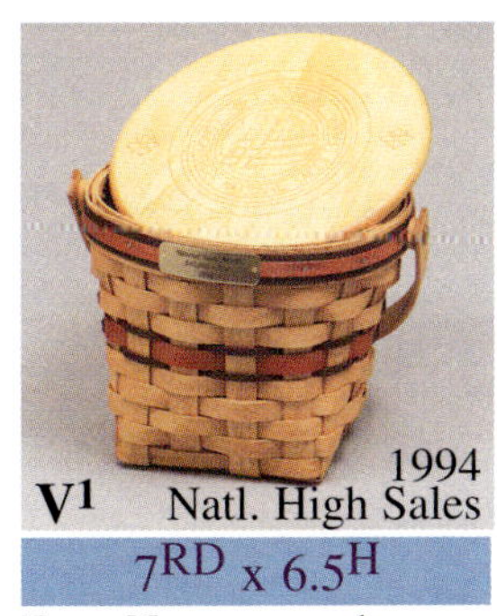

V¹　　1994
Natl. High Sales

7RD x 6.5^H

Form No:　　　　unknown
No. Given:

$60,000 – 74,999
Sales in 1994.

MARKET VALUES

Photo	Description	Avg.	High
	National Sales Awards (con't):		
	1995 Purple/Green Accents		
W[1]	5" Measuring [np] (Level 1)	—	—
	7" Measuring (Level 2)	—	—
	9" Measuring [np] (Level 3)	—	**280**
	11" Measuring [np] (Level 4)	—	—
	1996 Blue/Gold/Red Accents		
X[1]	5" Measuring (Level 1)	**188**	**250**
	7" Measuring [np] (Level 2)	—	—
	9" Measuring [np] (Level 3)	—	—
	11" Measuring [np] (Level 4)	—	**400**
	1997 Green/Red/Blue Accents		
Y[1]	5" Measuring (Level 1)	—	—
	7" Measuring [np] (Level 2)	—	—
	9" Measuring [np] (Level 3)	—	—
	11" Measuring [np] (Level 4)	—	—
	1998 Green/Yellow/Blue/Red Accents		
Z[1]	5" Measuring [np] (Level 1)	—	—
	7" Measuring (Level 2)	—	—
	9" Measuring [np] (Level 3)	—	—
	11" Measuring [np] (Level 4)	—	—
	13" Measuring [np] (Level 4)	—	—
	1999 Green/Rose/Blue/Purple		
A[2]	Small (Level 1)	—	—
	Medium [np] (Level 2)	—	—
	Large [np] (Level 3)	—	—
	XLarge [np] (Level 4)	—	—
	Miscellaneous Award and Incentives:		
B[2]	1985 Meadow Blossoms Pottery™		
B[2]	Dinner Plates	—	**6**
B[2]	Mugs	—	—
B[2]	Napkin Rings	—	—
	Salad Plates [np]	**7**	**11**
	Sugar/Creamer Set [np]	—	—
B[2]	Pitcher	—	—
	Honey Pot [np]	—	**20**
	Soup Tureen [np]	—	**33**
	Soup Bowls [np]	—	—
	Buffet Trays [np]	—	—
	Oval Bowl [np]	—	—
	Piepan w/ Lattice Cover [np]	—	—
C[2]	Hurricane Lamp	—	—
D[2]	1986 December Special Recognition		
	Bread Basket	**145**	**175**
E[2]	1986 Advisor Recognition Basket	**87**	**95**
	1987 10th Anniversary Recruiting Award "We're Building New Traditions"		
F[2]	Medium Market™	**262**	**320**
G[2]	Plate	**154**	**200**
	Candelabra [np]	—	—

[np] = Not Pictured

W[1] 1995 Natl. High Sales

7RD x 6.5H

Form No: unknown
No. Given:

$60,000 – 74,999 Sales in 1995.

A[2] 1999 Natl. High Sales

5RD x 4.5H

Form No: unknown
No. Given:

First year for this new, exclusive form.

D[2] 1986 December Recognition

14.5L x 7.5W x 3.75H

Form No: 4700-AO
No. Given:

Sales of $500 or more for month of December. Some are signed by Dave.

X[1] 1996 Natl. High Sales

5RD x 4.5H

Form No: unknown
No. Given:

$45,000 – 59,999 Sales in 1996.

Y[1] 1997 Natl. High Sales

5RD x 4.5H

Form No: unknown
No. Given:

$45,000 – 59,999 Sales in 1997.

Z[1] 1998 Natl. High Sales

7RD x 6.5H

Form No: unknown
No. Given:

$45,000 – 59,999 Sales in 1998.

B[2] Meadow Blossoms 1985

Form No: N/A
No. Given:

Different groupings were available for each Recruit earned from 4/1/85 – 7/29/85

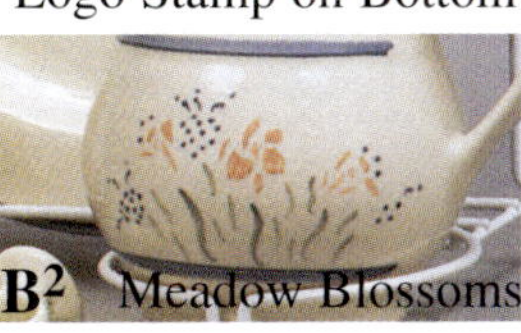

B[2] Meadow Blossoms

The design uses red, blue and green. Stamp on the bottom says "Longaberger Pottery – by Heartstone"

C[2] Hurricane Lamp

Form No: unknown
No. Given:

This candle holder should also have a hurricane glass.

E[2] 1986 Advisor Recognition

14L x 9W x 4.5H

Form No: 2300-
No. Given:

Given to all Advisors during a 1986 Meeting.

F[2] 1987 Tenth Anniversary

15L x 10W x 7.5H

Form No: 500-A
No. Given:

Blue shoestring weave. Given for each new Recruit earned from 8/15 – 9/25/87.

G[2] 1987 Plate

Form No: N/A
No. Given: 660

Three $1000 months from Sept. – Nov.

Features:

Award baskets given during the Bee will have the same colors as that year's Bee Basket.

MARKET VALUES

Photo	Description	Avg.	High
H^2	**1987** <u>May Basket</u> Herb™ (5 shows + \$1000 sales)	**80**	**80**
H^2	**1988** <u>May Incentive</u> Herb™ (\$500 + 1 recruit) Garden™ [np] (\$1000 + 1 recruit) Set:	**80** **80** **142**	**80** **80** **175**
I^2	**1991** Basket Planter Sleeve	**445**	**500**
J^2 J^2 J^2	**1992-98** <u>"Success Start"</u> Pencil Basket™ Paper Basket™ **Set:** Gold Pen	74 65 **123** —	90 75 **138** —
K^2	**1993** "Holiday Basket of Thanks"	72	115
L^2	**1996-97** Growing Strong Together	—	—
M^2	**19xx-P** Growing Strong Together	—	—
N^2	**1997** \$500 Million Celebration	**194**	**275**
O^2	**1997** Christmas Votive	—	—
P^2	**1998** 25th Anniversary Basket Sleeve	—	—
Q^2	**1999** "Thanks a Million" Basket	—	—
R^2 R^2 R^2 R^2 R^2	**1999** <u>"Success Start"</u> Pencil Basket™ Note Paper Basket™ Business Card Basket™ Mini Waste Basket™ Tapered Paper Tray™ Pen [np]	— — — — — —	— — 75 — — —
S^2	**2000** January Advisors Meeting	—	—
	2000 Associate Homestead Tour[np]	—	—

[np] = Not Pictured

H^2 1987 & 88 Herb

11.5^L x 5^W x 3^H

Form No: 4500-
No. Given:

<u>Garden:</u> 15^L x 8^W x 2.25^H

L^2 1996-97 Growing Strong Together

9.5^L x 5^W x 9.5^H

Form No: unknown
No. Given: ≈ 50

Given to Regional Advisors & Directors for facilitating Branch Advisor Trainings.

P^2 1998 25th Anniversary Sleeve

31.5^{RD} x 18^H

Form No: unknown
No. Given: 26

Given as a surprise thank you to all Directors at the 1998 Bee.

I² 1991 Planter Sleeve

31.5^RD x 18^H

Form No:	N/A
No. Given:	190

"High Road to Success"

J² 1992 – 98 Success Start

Pencil:	15000-
Paper:	16000-
Pen:	N/A

Consultants receive pen if reach $1000 in sales in first 90 days. Add Paper if achieve goal within 60 days, all three if within 30 days.

K² 1993 Holiday Basket of Thanks

7^L x 5^W x 3.5^H

Form No:	unknown
No. Given:	

Red and green trim. Given for December Sales.

M² 19xx Growing Strong Together

9.5^L x 5^W x 9.5^H

Form No:	unknown
No. Given:	

Given to Regional Advisors & Directors for facilitating Branch Advisor Trainings.

N² 1997 $500 Million

10^L x 6^W x 4^H

Form No:	unknown
No. Given:	≈ 1,225

Given to all advisors at Jan 97 Advisor meeting to celebrate achieving $500 Million in Sales in Nov 96.

O² 1997 Christmas Votive

3RD x 2.5^H

Form No:	34932
No. Given:	

Given to all consultants who hosted a Christmas Open House by September 12, 1997

Q² 1999 Thanks-A-Million

5.5^L x 4^W x 4^H

Form No:	14940
No. Given:	

Given to all Advisors who attended JAM 1999. This is 1997 Horizon of Hope basket that has been retagged.

R² 1999 Success Start

Pencil:	15000
Note Paper:	16000
Business Card:	17361
Mini Waste:	11258
Tapered Tray:	19062

These baskets can be earned exclusively by Consultants during their first 90 days. Each basket has a brass tag that reads "Longaberger – Success Start".

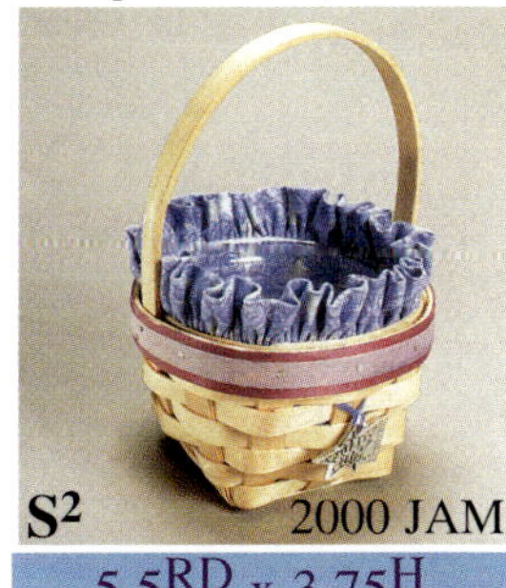

S² 2000 JAM

5.5^RD x 3.75^H

Form No:	unknown
No. Given:	

This basket, including accessories & tie-on, were given to all Advisors who attended JAM 2000.

Features:

Bee Speaker baskets are given to those who volunteer their time at the Bee to speak to other consultants about various topics.

MARKET VALUES

Photo	Description		Avg.	High
	Bee Speaker Baskets:			
T^2	1988	Medium Market™	—	—
U^2	1990	Harvest™	**120**	**130**
V^2	1991	Spring™	—	—
W^2	1992	Spring™	**145**	**189**
X^2	1993	Spring™	**235**	**260**
Y^2	1994	Spring™	**230**	**250**
Z^2	1995	Spring™	—	—
A^3	1996	Spring™	—	**200**
B^3	1997	Spring™	—	—
	1998	Spring™ [np]	—	—
C^3	1999	Spring™	—	—
	1988–P Cnsultant Advancement Baskets:			
D^3	MBA Basket™		**198**	**220**
E^3	Branch Basket™		**300**	**312**
F^3	Regional Basket™		**250**	**250**

continued next page

[np] = Not Pictured

T^2   1988 Bee Speaker

15^L x 10^W x 7.5^H

Form No: 500-
No. Given: 15

Blue shoestring weave.

X^2   1993 Bee Speaker

11^L x 8^W x 5.5^H

Form No: 900-
No. Given:

Teal and pink weave and trim.

B^3   1997 Bee Speaker

11^L x 8^W x 5.5^H

Form No: 900-
No. Given:

Green, red and blue weave and trim.

C^3   1999 Bee Speaker

11^L x 8^W x 5.5^H

Form No: 900-
No. Given:

Rose trim. Green, rose, blue and purple accents. Accessories sold separate

U² 1990 Bee Speaker

16^L x 9^W x 6^H

Form No: 3700-
No. Given:

No color. Brass tag.

W² 1992 Bee Speaker

11^L x 8^W x 5.5^H

Form No: unknown
No. Given:

Green trim and weave.

V² 1991 Bee Speaker

11^L x 8^W x 5.5^H

Form No: 900-
No. Given:

Blue trim and weave.

Y² 1994 Bee Speaker

11^L x 8^W x 5.5^H

Form No: 900-
No. Given:

Pink and purple trim and weave.

Z² 1995 Bee Speaker

11^L x 8^W x 5.5^H

Form No: 900-
No. Given:

Purple and green trim and weave.

A³ 1996 Bee Speaker

11^L x 8^W x 5.5^H

Form No: 900-
No. Given:

Blue, gold and red trim and weave.

D³ MBA

9.5^L x 5^W x 9.5^H

Form No: 1000-FO
No. Given:

No tag.

E³ Branch Advisor

15.75^L x 6.5^W x 11^H

Form No: unknown
No. Given:

Red trim and weave. No tag.

F³ Regional Advisor

15.75^L x 6.5^W x 11^H

Form No: unknown
No. Given:

Blue rim and weave. No tag.

MARKET VALUES

Photo	Description	Avg.	High
	Consultant Advancement Baskets (con't):		
G[3]	Director Basket™	—	—
	Branch Sponsored Awards:		
H[3]	1997 Branch Bouquet	**138**	**140**
I[3]	1998 Branch Excellence	**92**	**110**
I[3]	1998 Branch Sponsoring Excellence	—	—
J[3]	1999 Branch Excellence	**83**	**90**
J[3]	1999 Branch Sponsoring Excellence	**70**	**85**
K[3]	2000 Branch Excellence	—	—
K[3]	2000 Branch Sponsoring Excellence	—	—
	Regional Sponsored Awards:		
L[3]	1991 Small Chore	**188**	**225**
M[3]	1992 Small Oval	**195**	**275**
N[3]	1993 Potpourri with Lid	**187**	**275**
O[3]	1994 Small Purse, no Lid	**226**	**250**
P[3]	1995 Medium Berry	**234**	**300**
Q[3]	1996 Darning	**190**	**210**
R[3]	1997 Rose Garden	**108**	**127**
S[3]	1998 Regional Excellence	**150**	**170**
S[3]	1998 Reg. Sponsoring Excellence	—	**127**

[continued next page]

G[3] Director Advisor

15.75^L x 6.5^W x 11^H

Form No: unknown
No. Given:

*Green trim and weave.
No tag.*

K[3] 2000 Branch Awards

Lg: 7.75^L x 3.75^W x 4.5^H
Sm: 5.75^L x 3.75^W x 3^H

*Red trim. Green, red,
blue weave.
Sponsoring (Lg):
2+ recruits.
Excellence (Sm):
$12,000 sales.*

O[3] 1994 Regional Sponsored

9.5^L x 6^W x 6^H

Form No: 800-
No. Given:

*Blue trim and shoe-
string weave. Two
braided ears.*

P[3] 1995 Regional Sponsored

7.5^L x 7.5^W x 3.5^H

Form No: 1400-
No. Given:

*Blue trim and
shoestring weave.*

H³ 1997 Branch Bouquet

10.5ᴸ x 6ᵂ x 4ᴴ

Form No: unknown
No. Given:

First year for a Branch Advisor to sponsor an award.

I³ 1998 Branch Awards

6.5ᴸ x 6.5ᵂ x 3ᴴ

Form No: unknown
No. Given:

Excellence:
Basket given with 50+ shows
Sponsoring Excellence:
Charm given to all with at least one qualified recruit.

J³ 1999 Branch Awards

Lg: 9.5ᴸ x 6ᵂ x 6ᴴ
Sm: 7ᴸ x 5ᵂ x 3.5ᴴ

Red trim with green, red, blue weave.
Sponsoring (Lg):
2+ recruits.
Excellence (Sm): 50+ shows, or $12,000 sales.

L³ 1991 Regional Sponsored

10ᴸ x 6ᵂ x 4ᴴ

Form No: 3400-
No. Given:

Blue weave and trim. Given for High Sales in the Region.

M³ 1992 Regional Sponsored

8ᴸ x 5ᵂ x 3ᴴ

Form No: 33000-
No. Given:

Green, blue and red shoestring weave.

N³ 1993 Regional Sponsored

5ᴸ x 5ᵂ x 2.5ᴴ

Form No: 11321
No. Given:

Blue weave and trim.

Q³ 1996 Regional Sponsored

10ᴿᴰ x 4ᴴ

Form No: 500-
No. Given:

Red trim and shoe-string weave at bottom.

R³ 1997 Regional Sponsored

12ᴸ x 7ᵂ x 4.5ᴴ

Form No: unknown
No. Given:

Green trim and shoe-string accent weave.

S³ 1998 Regional Sponsored

Lg: 8.5ᴸ x 8.5ᵂ x 5ᴴ
Sm: 4.25ᴸ x 4.25ᵂ x 3ᴴ

Blue trim with green, red, and blue weave.
Excellence (Lg): Top Regional performers.
Sponsoring (Sm):
4+ recruits.

Features:

The Regional Sponsored Awards are funded and given out by each Regional Advisor. The number of awards given out is determined by the size of their Region.

MARKET VALUES

Photo	Description	Avg.	High
	Regional Sponsored Awards (con't):		
T³	1999 Regional Sales Excellence	—	150
T³	1999 Reg. Sponsoring Excellence	—	—
U³	2000 Regional Sponsored	—	—
	Director Sponsored Awards:		
V³	1988 Top Performer	—	—
W³	1989 Top Performer	—	—
X³	1990 Top Performer	—	—
Y³	1991 Top Performer	—	—
Z³	1991 Pom Pom Peggy™	128	130
A⁴	1992 Treasure Chest™	200	280
B⁴	1992 Top Performer	198	200
C⁴	1993 Paint the Town™	100	150
D⁴	1993 Top Performer	144	200
E⁴	1994 "Over the Rainbow"		
	Gold Nugget (Small)	178	235
	Pot of Gold (Medium)	91	160 ✍
	Gold Rush (Large)	178	270
F⁴	Top Performer	267	380

continued next page

✍ = With Signatures

T³   1999 Regional Sponsored

15ᴸ x 9.5ᵂ x 5.5ᴴ

Form No: unknown
No. Given:

Blue trim with green, blue, and red weave.
Stained:
Top Sales in Region.
Unstained:
Top Sponsors in Region

X³   1990 Top Performer

10.5ᴸ x 9ᵂ x 8ᴴ

Form No: unknown
No. Given:

Red weave and trim. Available both stained and natural.

B⁴   1992 Top Performer

10.5ᴸ x 9ᵂ x 8ᴴ

Form No: unknown
No. Given:

Green, blue, and red weave. Top 10 Consultants in the Directorship.

C⁴   1993 Paint the Town

5.75ᴸ x 3.75ᵂ x 3ᴴ

Form No: 45000-
No. Given:

Green, blue, and red weave. 50+ shows.

U³ 2000 Regional Sponsored

9.25^L x 5^W x 6.5^H

Form No: unknown
No. Given:

Natural or stained. Blue trim with green, blue, and red weave.

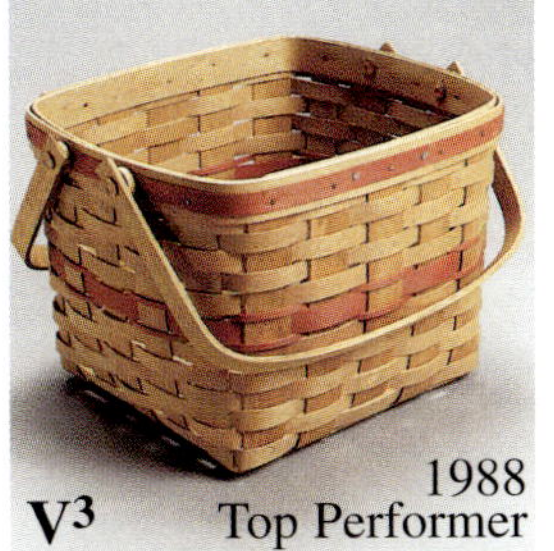

V³ 1988 Top Performer

10.5^L x 9^W x 8^H

Form No: unknown
No. Given:

Red weave and trim. Available both stained and natural.

W³ 1989 Top Performer

10.5^L x 9^W x 8^H

Form No: unknown
No. Given:

Blue weave and trim. Available both stained and natural.

Y³ 1991 Top Performer

10.5^L x 9^W x 8^H

Form No: unknown
No. Given:

Purple weave and trim. Available both stained and natural.

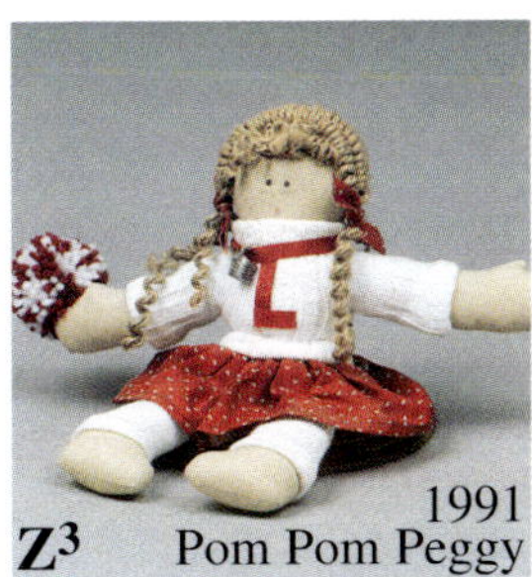

Z³ 1991 Pom Pom Peggy

12^H

Received doll for 50+ shows . The basket charm attached at her neck could be earned with 1 recruit.

A⁴ 1992 Treasure Chest

5.75^L x 3.75^W x 3^H

Form No: 45000-
No. Given:

Given to consultants with 50+ shows.

D⁴ 1993 Top Performer

10.5^L x 9^W x 8^H

Form No: unknown
No. Given:

Green, blue, and red weave. Top 10 consultants in the Directorship.

E⁴ 1994 Over the Rainbow

Form No: unknown

Small: 4.5RD x 3H
4+ recruits
Medium: 5.5RD x 3.75H
50+ shows
Large: 6.5RD x 4.75H
$40,000+ sales

F⁴ 1994 Top Performer

10.5^L x 9^W x 8^H

Form No: unknown
No. Given:

Teal Weave; Top 10 consultants in the Directorship.

Features:

The Director Sponsored award, Top Performer, is the same as the High Achiever. When the shape of the basket was changed in 1991, it was renamed as well.

MARKET VALUES

Photo	Description	Avg.	High
	Director Sponsored Awards (con't):		
	1995 "Reach for the Stars"		
G[4]	Star Bound (Small)	**215**	**300**
H[4]	Shining Star (Medium)	**185**	**300**
I[4]	Star Team (Large)	**219**	**300**
J[4]	High Achiever	**202**	**275**
	1996 "Our Business is Show Business"		
K[4]	Associate Producer (Small)	**128**	**130**
L[4]	Show Star (Medium)	**118**	**160**
M[4]	Best Supporting Role (Large)	**105**	**150**
N[4]	High Achiever	**177**	**210**
	1997 "Everything's Coming Up Roses"		
O[4]	Rose Bud (Small)	**155**	**200**
P[4]	Rose Petal (Medium)	**121**	**130**
Q[4]	Rose Bud Flower Pots	—	—
R[4]	American Beauty	—	**140**

continued next page

G[4]
1995
Star Bound

4.75[L] x 3.75[W] x 2.25[H]

Form No: unknown
No. Given:

4+ recruits

K[4]
1996 Associate
Producer

5.5[RD] x 2.5[H]

Form No: unknown
No. Given:

4+ Recruits

O[4]
1997
Rose Bud

8[L] x 4[W] x 2[H]

Form No: unknown
No. Given:

50+ shows

H⁴ 1995 Shining Star

5.75^L x 3.75^W x 3^H

Form No: unknown
No. Given:

50+ shows

I⁴ 1995 Star Team

7^L x 5^W x 3.5^H

Form No: unknown
No. Given:

Available only to Branch Advisors when 30% of their Branch achieves the Shining Star.

J⁴ 1995 High Achiever

12RD x 5.75^H

Form No: unknown
No. Given:

Top 10 consultants

L⁴ 1996 Show Star

7RD x 3^H

Form No: unknown
No. Given:

50+ shows

M⁴ 1996 Best Supporting Role

8.5RD x 4^H

Form No: unknown
No. Given:

Awarded to Branch Advisors when 30% of their Branch achieves the Show Star.

N⁴ 1996 High Achiever

12RD x 5.75^H

Form No: unknown
No. Given:

Top 10 Consultants in the Directorship.

P⁴ 1997 Rose Petal

8.5^L x 5^W x 3.5^H

Form No: unknown
No. Given:

50+ shows

Q⁴ 1997 Rose Bud Pots

2.5RD x 2.5^H

Form No: 33693
No. Given:

Available only to Branch Advisors when 30% of their Branch achieves the 50+ shows.

R⁴ 1997 American Beauty

13.5^L x 8.25^W x 5.25^H

Form No: unknown
No. Given:

Top 10 Consultants in the Directorship.

Features:

The "theme" for the Director Sponsored Awards are developed by actual Consultants well over a year before they are actually awarded.

S⁴ 1998 Director Sponsored

12^L x 12^W x 4^H

Form No: unknown
No. Given:

Green trim with green, red and blue weave. <u>Stained</u> given to Top Sales Performers. <u>Unstained</u> given to Top Sponsors.

MARKET VALUES

Photo	Description	Avg.	High
	Director Sponsored Awards (con't):		
S⁴	1998 Sales Excellence	—	**125**
S⁴	1998 Sponsoring Excellence	—	—
T⁴	1998 Team Excellence	**111**	**119**
U⁴	1999 Sales Excellence	—	—
U⁴	1999 Sponsoring Excellence	—	—
V⁴	1999 Team Excellence	—	—
W⁴	2000 Director Sponsored	—	—
X⁴	2000 Team Excellence	—	—

W⁴ 2000 Director Sponsored

14.5^L x 5.5^W x 9.5^H

Form No: unknown
No. Given:

Natural or stained. Green trim with green, red and blue weave.

T⁴ 1998 Team Excellence

8.25ᴸ x 8.25ᵂ x 3.5ᴴ

Form No: unknown
No. Given:

Green trim with green, red and blue weave. Available both stained and unstained.

U⁴ 1999 Director Sponsored

16ᴸ x 11ᵂ x 9ᴴ

Form No: unknown
No. Given:

Green trim with blue, green, and red weave. Stained given to Top Sales Performers. Unstained given to Top Sponsors.

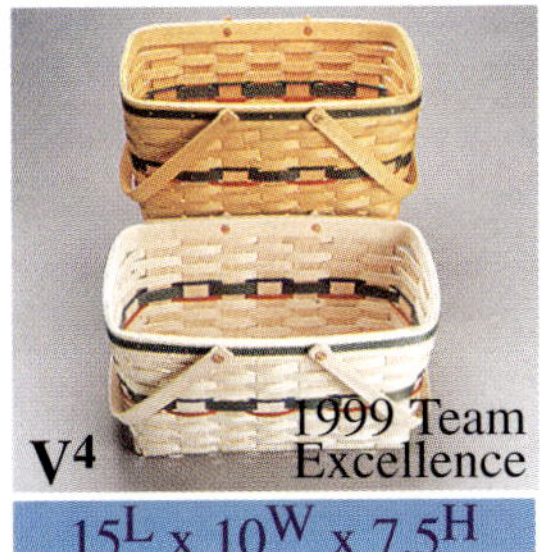

V⁴ 1999 Team Excellence

15ᴸ x 10ᵂ x 7.5ᴴ

Form No: unknown
No. Given:

Green trim with blue, green and red weave. Available both stained and unstained.

X⁴ 2000 Team Excellence

9.5ᴸ x 4.5ᵂ x 5ᴴ

Form No: unknown
No. Given:

Natural or stained. Green trim with green, red and blue weave.

New Success Start

Starting in 2000, The Company modified their *Success Start* incentive program for new Consultants. Specific goals are set for the new Consultant to obtain in a specific time frame. At each level, a special tagged basket is waiting.

<u>1st 30 days</u>:   **Goal:** $1000 in sales
Business Card Basket

<u>2nd 30 days</u>:   **Goal:** $1000 in sales
NEW Diskette Basket
   (Finder's Keepers form)

<u>3rd 30 days</u>:   **Goal:** $1000 in sales
Address Basket

<u>1st 180 days</u>:   **Goal:** One Recruit
NEW Catalog Caddy Basket
   (new form)

J.W. Collection®

J. Dianne Ricker

Chester Gap, Virginia

Dianne has only been collecting since 1985, but that has not stopped her from finding earlier baskets. Her collection includes at least one basket from every year, back to 1978. Her favorite basket is a Bread Basket™ that she wove herself at a Bee and then had signed by Dave.

Features:

Blue Accent Weave and Trim.
Commemorative Brass Tag.
Series Retired in 1994.

MARKET VALUES

Photo	Description		Original	Avg.	High	
A.	1983	Market™	32.95	**1346**	**1800**	✍
		with **L**iner (1993)	52.90	—	—	
B.	1984	Waste™	34.95	**1555**	**2100**	✍
C.	1985	Apple™	45.95	**631**	**850**	
D.	1986	Two-Pie™	34.95	**480**	**650**	
E.	1987	Bread and Milk™	43.95	**393**	**600**	
		with **P**rotector		**413**	**600**	
		with **L**iner (1993)		**413**	**600**	
		Combo **(P/L)**		**439**	**650**	
F.	1988	Gathering™	36.95	**300**	**550**	
		with **L**iner (1993)	57.90	**310**	**550**	
G.	1989	Banker's Waste™	59.95	**308**	**575**	
H.	1990	Large Berry™	48.95	**214**	**290**	
		Combo **(P)**	53.90	**222**	**290**	
		with **L**iner (1993)	66.90	**222**	**290**	
		Full Set **(P/L)**	71.85	—	—	
I.	1991	Corn™	89.95	**334**	**470**	
		Combo **(P)**	103.90	**341**	**490**	
J.	1992	Cake™	55.95	**167**	**290**	
		with **P**rotector	65.90	**175**	**290**	
		with **L**iner	67.90	**175**	**290**	
		Combo **(P/L)**	69.95	**197**	**375**	
K.	1993	Original Easter™	65.95	**165**	**225**	
		with **P**rotector	71.90	**169**	**225**	
		with **L**iner	83.90	**169**	**225**	
		Combo **(P/L)**	82.95	**172**	**270**	
L.	1994	Umbrella™	74.95	**177**	**250**	
		Combo **(P)**	79.95	**189**	**270**	
L.	1994	JW Commemorative Book	24.95	**28**	**51**	
Full Set JW Collection:				**4417**	**6000**	

In May & June of 1993, Hostesses only were given the opportunity to purchase liners for four previous J.W. Baskets: Medium Market, Medium Gathering, Large Berry and Bread & Milk. A set of 4 Place Mats and 4 Napkins were also offered in the Classic Plaid™ fabric.

✍ = With Signatures

A. 1983 Market

15^L x 10^W x 7.5^H

Form No: 500-AT
No. Sold: 6,300

A liner was made available in 1993.

E. 1987 Bread and Milk

16^L x 8^W x 11^H

Form No: 2100-ABT
No. Sold: 17,818

Did not originally sell with accessories. Liner first offered in 1993. Magazine protector used from the regular line.

I. 1991 Corn

17RD x 11.5^H

Form No: 4400-JBST
No. Sold: 48,332

B. 1984 Waste

| 9.5^L x 9.5^W x 12^H |

Form No: 1800-OT
No. Sold: 3,544

C. 1985 Apple

| 13RD x 8.5^H |

Form No: 3200-BT
No. Sold: 10,467

*Also referred to as a
Large Fruit.*

D. 1986 Two-Pie

| 12^L x 12^W x 10^H |

Form No: 4800-BT
No. Sold: 44,363

F. 1988 Gathering

| 18^L x 11^W x 4.5^H |

Form No: 2400-ABT
No. Sold: 49,495

*A liner was made avail-
able in 1993. See page
'24 for more information.*

G. 1989 Banker's Waste

| 12.5RD x 13.5^H |

Form No: 1900-BBST
No. Sold: 53,328

H. 1990 Large Berry

| 8.5^L x 8.5^W x 5^H |

Form No: 1500-BBST
No. Sold: 37,009

*A liner was made avail-
able in 1993. See page
124 for more information.*

J. 1992 Cake

| 12^L x 12^W x 6^H |

Form No: 100-CBST
No. Sold: 98,557

*Basket sold with
divider.*

K. 1993 Original Easter

| 16^L x 9^W x 6^H |

Form No: 13722
No. Sold: ≈ 77,000

L. 1994 Umbrella

| 10RD x 17.5^H |

Form No: 11215
Book: 72214
No. Sold: ≈ 95,000

Book sold separately.

Market Activity Report

Throughout the year, The Bentley Collection has collected and reviewed over 14,000 actual selling transactions from the secondary market. Below is a summary of the market activity reported to us during the 1999 – 2000 season.

Top 10 Collections
showing the highest market activity

Collections with the greatest activity	% of Activity
#10 Easter Series™	4.3%
#9 All-American Collection®	4.4%
#8 Sweetheart Collection™	4.4%
#7 Booking / Promo Baskets	4.5%
#6 Regular Line (items with discontinued features)	4.8%
#5 Retired Items	4.9%
#4 Collectors Club™	6.1%
#3 May Series™	6.5%
#2 Christmas Collection™	7.1%
#1 Feature Baskets	8.9%

J.W. Originals

Susan Ryan
Pickerington, Ohio

Featured among this beautiful collection of baskets, is Susan's prize possession: an authentic, handwoven J.W. Original Medium Market, which can be seen sitting on top of the crate. Members of the Longaberger family have authenticated and confirmed that it was woven somewhere in the 1950-1960 circa. On the bottom is the original stamp "Ohio Ware Basket Company – Dresden, Ohio" and the original price of $1.79 can still be seen on the handle! It is very rare to find these baskets with such great color and in such great condition. They all are beautiful!

Features:

These baskets were woven by John Wendell Longaberger (J.W.), himself and are very rare in the secondary market.

Photo

Description

Identifying features:

A. Braided trim

Color weaving (red, green or blue)

B. Continuous weaving

Double weaving

Handles: very smooth, hand-carved

C. Open-weave or splinted bottom

Signatures: many have family signatures, to confirm its authenticity.

D. Stamp: "Made in Dresden, Ohio" on *inside*

E. Trim strip: Used metal tacks or staples

F. Upside down 'V' pattern at stationary handles

Weave: very tight basket with square corners

Common forms:

Apple

Berry Baskets

Bread & Milk

G. Cake

H. Corn

Gathering Baskets

Hamper

Key Baskets

I. Laundry

J. Market, Medium

Picnic, Large

K. Pool Basket

Pottery Ware Basket

Purse

Two-Pie

Waste, Banker's

Waste, Square

Umbrella

PLEASE NOTE

Reporting values based on actual selling transactions is difficult for this collection due to the fact that each one is so unique and there are not many being bought and sold in the market. The majority of J.W. Original transactions reported to us are findings at garage sales, in basements, attics, or at auctions for well below value. Therefore, we cannot report values until we are able to obtain more detailed information.

G. Cake Baskets

12^L x 12^W x 6^H

These "blonde" baskets were most likely never stained, but would be considered "natural".

J. Medium Market

16.5^L x 11^W x 8.75^H

This darker look is more common among J.W. Originals. This basket is 1940 circa.

A.   Braided Trim

This is a smaller version of the braid used for trim. A wider, heavier material was also used.

B.   Continuous Weave

This technique is evident by a "split upsplint", seen here on the front left corner.

C. Open-weave bottom

While this technique was common among J.W.'s baskets, he also closed the bottoms with filler splints.

D.   Stamp

"Made in Dresden, Ohio" We are not clear when or for how long J.W. used this stamp on his baskets.

E.   Tacks vs. Staples

J.W. started out using tacks for his trims. He received a staple gun for Christmas one year and used it on "everything". Later in his basketmaking, he returned to using tacks.

F.   Upside down 'V'

Almost all of J.W.'s baskets with stationary handles have this trademark for added strength to the handle.

H.   Corn

19RD x 14^{H}

This Corn basket is much larger than what was once offered in the regular line. He also made Corn baskets with leather handles.

Bottom of Corn

These metal reinforcements were common on Corn, Laundry and Pottery Ware Baskets. The nail in the center is another J.W. trademark.

I.   Laundry

28^{L} x 16.5^{W} x 10.75^{H}

This Laundry Basket also has the cutout handles and metal reinforcements, common for this big of a basket.

J.   Medium Market

16.5^{L} x 11^{W} x 8.75^{H}

If you look closely, you can see that this Market had red accents. The inset shows the original price written in pencil on the handle.

K.   Pool Basket

22^{L} x 14.5^{W} x 6.25^{H}

J.W. made these baskets for the Dresden Pool to hold visitors' clothes. This basket still has the metal rings used to hold the basket in place.

Customized Baskets

In past years, The Longaberger Company® allowed customers to "customize" their baskets. Customizing meant they were able to special order baskets with special features. Between 1977 and 1978, almost any combination could be ordered for a basket – stained, natural, with or without color weaving, lid, no lid, handle, no handle, 1 handle, 2 handles, etc . . .. Because they were handmade and the orders were not as great as they are today, it was not hard to allow for this customizing policy.

In 1980, this policy was changed to only allow customers to choose between two special order options for an additional $5.00 charge: Natural or natural with color accent weave. The colors available for this option were:

BLUE GREEN BROWN RED YELLOW:

Only available as a choice for a short time prior to 1980.

Exceptions . . .

Most baskets were included for this option, with the following exceptions:

Not available with Color Weaving; Could Only be Special Ordered in Natural:

| Button | Cracker | Medium Vegetable |
| Bread | Small Vegetable | Wine |

Available **Stained Only**; No Special Order Options:

All promotional baskets

Available **Only** Natural or Natural with Color; Could Not be ordered Stained:

1984 – 1989 : Large (Infant) Cradle, Large Laundry

Discontinued option . . .

The entire customizing option was discontinued for all Regular Line baskets in 1986. The option continued for the Large Cradle and Large Laundry until August 1989.

How does this option affect the Market Value . . .

How this option affects the value of the basket is hard to determine. Start by determining the value as if it were not customized. Some collectors who like the Naturals might be willing to pay more for the option, others do not. It is reasonable to consider the option worth at least $5.00 more valuable because that was the original cost for the option. However, the buyer's preference will ultimately determine if the basket is worth that or not.

May Series™

Judy Holt
Manassas, Virginia

Judy uses her hall tree to showcase her baskets for all different seasons. The May Series™ displayed here is her favorite. Judy has been adding to her collection since 1989.

Features:

Named after Grandma Bonnie's Favorite Flowers

MARKET VALUES

Photo		Description	Original	Avg.	High
A.	1990	Violet™	24.95	**229**	**355**
		with **P**rotector	28.90	**228**	**365**
		with **L**iner	34.90	**285**	**365**
		Combo (**P/L**)	34.95	**348**	**525**
B.	1991	Rose™	29.95	**200**	**250**
		with **P**rotector	34.90	**213**	**250**
		with **L**iner	41.90	**213**	**285**
		Combo (**P/L**)	39.95	**256**	**400**
C.	1992	Pansy™	29.95	**94**	**135**
		with **P**rotector	34.90	**113**	**155**
		with **L**iner	41.90	**129**	**155**
		Combo (**P/L**)	39.95	**147**	**200**
D.	1993	Lily of the Valley™	28.95	**90**	**115**
		with **P**rotector	32.90	**92**	**126**
		with **L**iner	41.90	**92**	**126**
		Combo (**P/L**)	39.95	**107**	**129**
E.	1994	Lilac™	34.95	**90**	**115**
		with **P**rotector	39.95	**103**	**145**
		with **L**iner	47.90	**103**	**145**
		Combo (**P/L**)	42.95	**115**	**175**
E.	1994	Lilac™ Tie-On	5.95	**23**	**35**
F.	1995	Tulip™	42.95	**100**	**105**
		with **P**rotector	48.90	**103**	**110**
		with **L**iner	57.90	**103**	**110**
		Combo (**P/L**)	54.95	**120**	**140**
F.	1995	Tulip™ Tie-On	6.95	**20**	**35**
G.	1996	Sweet Pea™	45.95	**78**	**110**
		with **P**rotector	52.90	**80**	**130**
		with **L**iner	61.90	**80**	**130**
		Combo (**P/L**)	59.95	**95**	**141**
G.	1996	Sweet Pea™ Tie-On	6.95	**16**	**26**
H.	1997	Petunia™	45.95	**80**	**110**
		with **P**rotector	52.90	**88**	**125**
		with **L**iner	63.90	**88**	**125**
		Combo (**P/L**)	59.95	**90**	**140**
		Full Set (**C/Lid**)	88.90	**117**	**140**
H.	1997	Petunia™ Tie-On	6.95	**16**	**20**
I.	1998	Snapdragon™	47.00	**70**	**85**
		with **P**rotector	55.00	**75**	**85**
		with **L**iner	63.00	**75**	**90**
		Combo (**P/L**)	59.00	**78**	**110**
I.	1998	Snapdragon Tie-On	8.00	**14**	**25**
J.	1998	Grandma Bonnie's Print	48.00	**68**	**75**
K.	1999	Daisy™	39.00	**60**	**80**
		with **P**rotector	44.00	**63**	**85**
		with **L**iner	53.00	**63**	**85**
		Combo (**P/L**)	49.00	**68**	**92**
K.	1999	Daisy™ Tie-On	8.00	**15**	**23**
L.	2000	Morning Glory™	43.00	—	—
		with **P**rotector	49.00	—	—
		with **L**iner	60.00	—	—
		Combo (**P/L**)	59.00	—	—
	2000	Morning Glory Tie-On	8.00	—	—

A.　　　1990 Violet

5^L x 5^W x 4.5^H

Form No:　　　14000-BVS
No. Sold:　　　49,591

There were 28,791 Combos sold this year.

E.　　　1994 Lilac

6.5^{RD} x 6.5^H

Form No:　　　16209
Tie-On:　　　31291
No. Sold:

Tie-On sold separately

I.　　　1998 Snapdragon

7.5^{RD} x 9.25^H

Form No:　　　1086?
Tie-On:　　　3165?
No. Sold:

Tie-On sold separately

B.   1991 Rose

14.5^L x 7.5^W x 3.75^H

Form No: 4700-CSS
No. Sold:

C.   1992 Pansy

7RD x 4.5^H

Form No: 10006
No. Sold:

1993
D.   Lily of the Valley

5.5RD x 3.75^H

Form No: 15717
No. Sold:

3/8" Weaving. No color. Does not have an inverted bottom.

F.   1995 Tulip

14.25^L x 6.25^W x 3.25^H

Form No: 14648
Tie-On: 31542
No. Sold:

Tie-On sold separately.

G.   1996 Sweet Pea

8.25RD x 7^H

Form No: 14915
Tie-On: 32883
No. Sold: 156,288

Tie-On sold separately.

H.   1997 Petunia

9.5RD x 5^H

Form No: 12947
Tie-On: 34461
No. Sold:

Tie-On sold separately.

J.   "Grandma Bonnie's Favorites" Print

20^W x 24^H

Form No: 84999
No. Sold:

Frame not included.

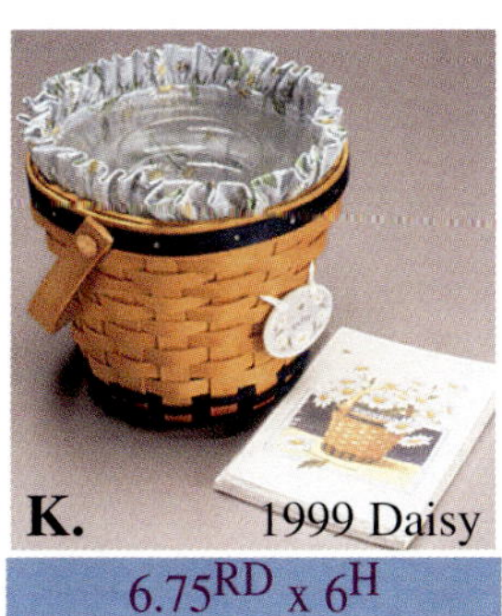

K.   1999 Daisy

6.75RD x 6^H

Form No: 13056
Tie-On: 36544
No. Sold:

Tie-On sold separately.

2000
L.   Morning Glory

7.5^L x 7.5^W x 4.75^H

Form No: 18899
No. Sold:

Grandma Bonnie's book, "Reflections on the Simple Life" included with every Combo. **145**

Basket Fun Fact

Top 10 Sellers of 1998

The Longaberger Company has reported the following baskets as Top Sellers in 1998.

Regular Line

Tea™

Small Spoon™

10" Generation™

Bread™

Tissue™

7" Generation™

Spring™

Cake™

Button™

Recipe™

Feature Baskets

Horizon of Hope™

25th Anniversary™

Green Glad Tidings™

Red Glad Tidings™

Rings & Things™

Hospitality™

Snapdragon™

Finder's Keepers™

Baker's Bounty™

Dash Away Sleigh™

Mother's Day™

Lisa Lahmon
Mount Vernon, Ohio

Lisa began collecting in 1987 when her Mother got her started. Her Mother's Day Collection is particularly special to her because it once belonged to her Mom. She was given the collection when her Mom passed away and has continued the tradition of collecting that series.

Features:
Pink Weave and Trim, except in 1993.

MARKET VALUES

Photo		Description	Original	Avg.	High
A.	1987	Large Peg™	26.95	**119**	160
B.	1988	Spring™	28.95	**130**	170
		Combo (**L**)	39.90	**137**	170
C.	1989	Mini Chore™	21.95	**85**	150
		Combo (**L**)	29.95	**108**	150
D.	1990	Small Oval™	28.95	**63**	100
		Combo (**L**)	36.95	**75**	100
E.	1991	Purse™	34.95	**95**	120
		with **Protector**	39.90	**108**	120
		with **Liner**	49.90	**108**	130
		Combo (**P/L**)	54.85	**121**	185
F.	1991	Potpourri™	21.95	**58**	80
		Combo (**L**)	30.90	**63**	100
G.	1992	Mother's Day™	34.95	**80**	125
		with **Protector**	40.90	**80**	125
		with **Liner**	50.90	**80**	125
		Combo (**P/L**)	49.95	**94**	150
H.	1993	Mother's Day™	44.95	**80**	115
		with **Protector**	50.90	**85**	115
		with **Liner**	59.90	**85**	115
		Combo (**P/L**)	57.95	**87**	130
I.	1994	Mother's Day™	37.95	**72**	95
		with **Protector**	42.90	**72**	100
		with **Liner**	50.90	**72**	100
		Combo (**P/L**)	49.95	**75**	115
I.	1994	Mother's Journal	5.95	**10**	21
J.	1995	Basket of Love™	37.95	**74**	85
		with **Protector**	43.90	**74**	85
		with **Liner**	52.90	**74**	85
		Combo (**P/L**)	49.95	**77**	110
J.	1995	Mother's Day Tie-On	6.95	**11**	23
K.	1996	Vanity™	44.95	**86**	105
		with **Protector**	56.90	**86**	105
		with **Liner**	60.90	**86**	105
		Combo (**P/L**)	59.95	**89**	125
		Full Set (**Combo/Lid**)	82.90	**107**	130
K.	1996	Mother's Day Tie-On	6.95	**12**	16
L.	1997	Timeless Memory™	49.95	**83**	95
		with **Protector**	59.90	**88**	100
		with **Liner**	69.90	**88**	100
		Combo (**P/L**)	69.95	**96**	130
		Full Set (**Combo/Lid**)	92.90	**114**	150
L.	1997	Mother's Day Tie-On	6.95	**10**	15

A. 1987 Large Peg

6.5^L x 6.5^W x 8^H

Form No: 11000-BPS
No. Sold:

E. 1991 Purse

9.5^L x 6^W x 6^H

Form No: 800-EPS
No. Sold:

I. 1994 Mother's Day

6.75^L x 9.25^W x 3.75^H

Form No: 16004
Journal: 72087
No. Sold:

Journal sold separately

B.   1988 Spring

11^L x 8^W x 5.5^H

Form No:	900-APS
No. Sold:	

Promotion did not include a Combo.

C.   1989 Mini Chore

7^L x 5^W x 3.5^H

Form No:	700-APS
No. Sold:	

Included note cards.

D.   1990 Small Oval

8.5^L x 5^W x 3.5^H

Form No:	33000-JPS
No. Sold:	

Promotion did not include a Combo.

F.   1991 Potpourri

5^L x 5^W x 2.5^H

Form No:	13000-APS
No. Sold:	

Hostess Only. Sold as the "Touch of Pink Potpourri". Does not have color on trim.

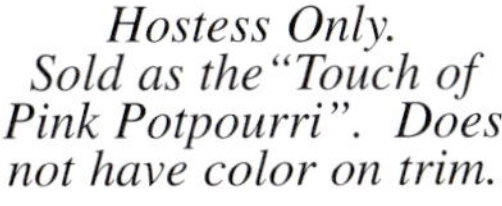

G.   1992 Mother's Day

10.5^L x 10.5^W x 4.5^H

Form No:	110-CPS
No. Sold:	

H.   1993 Mother's Day

8.5^L x 8^W x 6^H

Form No:	12904
No. Sold:	

3/8" Weaving. No color.

J.   1995 Basket of Love

8.5RD x 4^H

Form No:	18805
Tie-On:	31470
No. Sold:	
Tie-On:	90,515

Tie-On sold separately

K.   1996 Vanity

14.5^L x 7.5^W x 4.5^{FH} x 6.5^{BH}

Form No:	14753
Tie-On:	32328
No. Sold:	224,278

Tie-On & Lid sold separately. Divided protector came with Combo. A regular protector also available for $5.95.

L.   1997 Timeless Memory

11.25^L x 9.25^W x 5.75^H

Form No:	13030
Tie-On:	33995
No. Sold:	

Tie-On & Lid sold separately

Features:

These baskets are usually offered during March for Mother's Day gift giving.

MARKET VALUES

Photo		Description	Original	Avg.	High
M.	1998	Rings & Things™	34.00	—	—
		Combo (**Pouch**)	45.00	**54**	**80**
		with **P**rotector	40.00	—	—
		with **L**iner	48.00	—	—
		Combo2 (**P/L**)	54.00	**62**	**95**
M.	1998	Mother's Day Tie-On	8.00	**14**	**15**
N.	1999	Tea for Two™	39.00	**55**	**60**
		with **P**rotector	44.00	—	—
		with **L**iner	53.00	—	—
		Combo (**P/L**)	49.00	**61**	**72**
		Full Set (**Combo/Lid**)	68.00	**70**	**75**
N.	1999	Mother's Day Tie-On	8.00	**13**	**15**
O.	2000	Early Blossoms™	45.00	—	—
		with **P**rotector	50.00	—	—
		with **L**iner	60.00	—	—
		Combo2 (**P/L**)	56.00	—	—
O.	2000	Bonnet Tie-On	8.00	—	—

2000 was the first year for pottery items to be featured in the Mother's Day collection. While the pieces were sold separately, savings were offered to Hostesses who purchased the pottery along with the basket. Refer to the Pottery Collection on page 155 for more information on these pottery items.

M. 1998 Rings & Things

7RD x 3^H

Form No:	10383
Tie-On:	34002
No. Sold:	180,000

Combo included the basket and jewelry pouch (not pictured).

N. 1999 Tea for Two

7.75^L x 5.75^W x 3.25^H

Form No:	14931
Tie-On:	36251

Liner was offered in both White Vine™ and Mother's Day Floral fabric.

O. 2000 Early Blossoms

11^L x 7.25^W x 2.75^H

Form No:	19682
Tie-On:	37133

First ever 3-D tie-on from Longaberger. Pottery sold separately. See Pottery Collection for details.

Pewter Ornaments

Sarah Mueller

Tecumseh, Nebraska

Sarah has been collecting for 10 years. She really enjoys the pewter ornaments and displays them year round. Her other favorite collections include Shades of Autumn® and the Hostess Collection™.

Features:
Available individually or in sets of four.
Each ornament approximately 2" high.

MARKET VALUES

		Description	Original	Avg.	High
A.	*1993*	**Commemorative Santa Collection**			
		Father Christmas™	8.95	**10**	12
		Kriss Kringle™	8.95	**10**	12
		Santa Claus™	8.95	**10**	15
		St. Nick™	8.95	**10**	12
		SET of Four Gift Set	29.95	**60**	105
B.	*1994*	**Commemorative Baskets Collection**			
		1981 Candle™	8.95	**9**	9
		1982 Sleigh™	8.95	**10**	10
		1983 Bell™	8.95	—	—
		1984 Holly™	8.95	—	—
		SET of Four Gift Set	29.95	**44**	75
C.	*1995*	**Commemorative Baskets Collection**			
		1985 Cookie™	8.95	**13**	15
		1986 Candy Cane™	8.95	**13**	15
		1987 Mistletoe™	8.95	**13**	15
		1988 Poinsettia™	8.95	**13**	15
		SET of Four Gift Set	29.95	**36**	50
D.	*1996*	**Commemorative Baskets Collection**			
		1989 Memory™	8.95	—	—
		1990 Gingerbread™	8.95	**10**	10
		1991 Yuletide Traditions™	8.95	—	—
		1992 Season's Greetings™	8.95	—	—
		SET of Four Gift Set	29.95	**34**	55
E.	*1997*	**Commemorative Baskets Collection**			
		1993 Bayberry™	8.95	—	—
		1994 Jingle Bell™	8.95	—	—
		1995 Cranberry™	8.95	—	—
		1996 Holiday Cheer™	8.95	—	—
		SET of Four Gift Set	29.95	**30**	45
F.	*1998*	**Commemorative Angels Collection**			
		1993 Peace™	9.00	—	—
		1994 Hope™	9.00	—	—
		1995 Love™	9.00	—	—
		1996 Joy™	9.00	—	—
		SET of Four Gift Set	30.00	**34**	45
G.	*1999*	**Commemorative Angel Collection**			
		SET of Four Gift Set	30.00	**33**	35
H.	*1999*	**Commemorative Snowmen Collection**			
		SET of Two Gift Set	15.00	—	—

1993
A. Santa Ornaments

Form No:
Father Christmas	70653
Kriss Kringle	70637
Santa Claus	70629
St.Nick	70645
SET	70661

1997
E. Basket Ornaments

Form No:
Bayberry	71897
Jingle Bell	71960
Cranberry	71978
Holiday Cheer	71986
SET	71927

Last year for the Basket Ornaments.

B. Basket Ornaments — 1994

Form No:

Candle	72273
Sleigh	72281
Bell	72290
Holly	72303
SET	72311

C. Basket Ornaments — 1995

Form No:

Cookie	72141
Candy Cane	71838
Mistletoe	71943
Poinsettia	72460
SET	71803

D. Basket Ornaments — 1996

Form No:

Memory	71951
Gingerbread	72028
Yuletide Traditions	72001
Season's Greetings	71935
SET	71901

F. Angel Ornaments — 1998

Form No:

Peace	71765
Hope	71773
Love	71781
Joy	71790
SET	71757

First year for the Angel Ornaments.

G. Angel Ornaments — 1999

Form No:

Faith	
Friendship	
Gratitude	
Kindness	
SET	71072

Sold only as a set

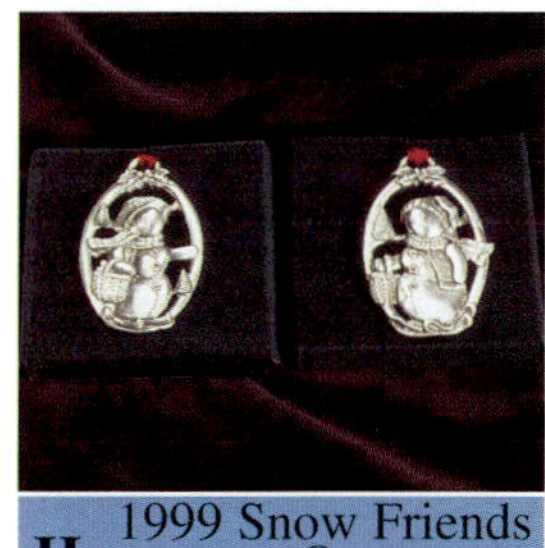

H. 1999 Snow Friends Ornaments

Form No:

Flurry	
Snowball	
SET	72800

Sold only as a set

Fun Fact

I spy . . . Longaberger!

On March 5, 1999, a Longaberger Mug showed up on *Live with Regis and Kathy Lee.*

Pottery Fun Fact

Introduction of Pottery . . .

The introduction of pottery to the Longaberger product line was a natural move for the company. The Longaberger family first made Ware Baskets for local pottery companies to use when carrying the pottery from the kilns. This introduction of pottery was promoted as "bringing two great American Classics back together again". The Roseville Pottery from 1990-1991was made by Friendship Pottery in Roseville, Ohio. The exclusive Woven Traditions design was hand decorated in <u>only</u> Classic Blue™. Each piece was dated and initialed. Due to problems in production, the production was moved to Sterling Pottery in East Liverpool, Ohio in late 1991. This pottery was not referred to as "Roseville Pottery" until after it was discontinued.

Roseville vs. Current Pottery. . .

The difference between the pottery is hard to see at first glance. The best way to determine if a piece is Roseville, is by turning it over and looking for the unique Roseville embossing on the bottom (see page 156 for picture). The Roseville Pottery was only available in the Classic Blue™ and is cream in color. The current line of pottery is available in Classic Blue™, Heritage Green™, Traditional Red™ and Heirloom Ivory™. The body is more white in color. There is no difference in the quality and attributes.

Embossing . . .

Current Longaberger Pottery® is made in East Liverpool, Ohio by Sterling Pottery and Hall China. This current pottery is neither signed nor dated. The only way to estimate its origination date is by its embossing. The original trademark reads "Made in East Liverpool, Ohio". Sometime between 1994 and 1995, the embossing was changed to read "Made in the U.S.A".

Starting with the Loaf Dish, released in August 1998, all pottery pieces now also have the product dimensions and capacity printed on the bottom of each piece.

Pottery attributes . . .

Longaberger Pottery® is American Vitrified China, which means that it has less than .05% absorption. To the consumer, this means that it won't pick up contamination. It also has high impact and ship resistibility, a high gloss glaze, a glazed foot for safe stacking and is freezer, oven, microwave, and dishwasher safe.

Pottery®

Theresa Drake
Lockport, Illinois

Theresa is not just a pottery fan! Her house is filled with baskets. She is a big believer in putting her baskets to use, using them for toy boxes or allowing her children to play with them. Her favorites are the Inaugural Baskets.

Roseville Embossing

Features:
Roseville: Produced by Friendship Pottery from 1990 – 91.

MARKET VALUES

Photo	Description	Original	Avg.	High
	Roseville Pottery – 1990–91			
A.	Small Mixing Bowl	17.95	**43**	**70**
A.	Medium Mixing Bowl	22.95	**48**	**65**
A.	Large Mixing Bowl	29.95	**57**	**75**
B.	Grandma Bonnie's Apple Pie Plate	23.95	**54**	**60**
C.	Small Juice Pitcher	21.95	**50**	**70**
C.	Large Milk Pitcher	27.95	**58**	**85**
	FULL SET		**225**	**250**
	Bricks			
D.	(91–98) Cracker	9.95	**10**	**10**
	Pottery, All-American			
E.	(98–00) Pie Plate	30.00	**35**	**40**
	Pottery, Christmas			
F.	(96–98) Casserole, 2Qt.	59.95	**—**	**—**
G.	(95–98) Covered Dish, Small	29.95	**33**	**40**
	(99–99) Plate, Snow Friends			
H.	(98) Cookies for Santa	40.00	**44**	**55**
I.	(99) Flurry & Snowball	29.00	**36**	**38**
J.	(95–98) Sauce Boat	24.95	**38**	**45**
K.	(97–98) Tea Pot	62.95	**79**	**117**

continued next page

Longaberger Pottery® was introduced in 1990 as the "Roseville Pottery", because it was made in Roseville, Ohio. The demand was high, but the production had some problems and was eventually moved to East Liverpool, Ohio in late 1991. The current line of pottery was reintroduced in 1991 in the Classic Blue™, Heritage Green™ and Traditional Red™. Heirloom Ivory™ joined the options in 1996.

D. 1991-98 Cracker Brick

9L x 2.25W

Form No: 30201
No. Sold:

H. 1998 Cookies for Santa

9RD / 8OZ

Form No: 36021
No. Sold:

Sold as a Set only. Available in Nov. & Dec 1998. Illustration by Richard Cowdrey.

A. Roseville Bowls

Form No:
Small: 30058
Medium: 30091
Large: 30023

B. Roseville Pie Plate

Form No: 30015
No.Sold:

Came with a box and a recipe for Grandma Bonnie's famous Apple Pie.

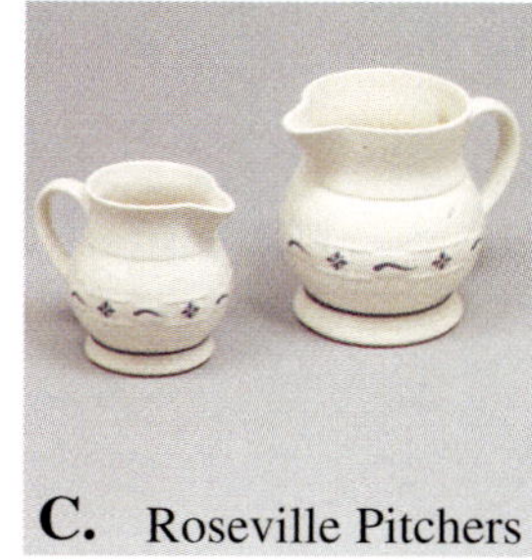

C. Roseville Pitchers

Form No:
Small: 30082
Large: 30031

E. 1998-00 Pie Plate

9RD x 2D

Form No: 35801/35807
No. Sold:

Red and blue design with stars around the edge. Only offered during the All-American campaign.

F. 1996-98 2 Qt. Casserole

10.5RD

Form No: 33162
No. Sold:

Traditional Holly.

G. 1995-98 Covered Dish

5.5RD

Form No: 31631
No. Sold:

Traditional Holly. Only offered during the Christmas promotional period.

I. 1999 Snow Friends

9RD

Form No: 36927
No. Sold:

Final year for the Snow Friends plate. Illustration by Richard Cowdrey.

J. 1995-98 Sauce Boat

12oz

Form No: 31569
No. Sold:

Traditional Holly. Only offered during the Christmas campaign.

K. 1997-98 Tea Pot

40oz

Form No: 31615
No. Sold:

Traditional Holly. Only offered during the Christmas campaign.

Features:

All Pottery pieces were originally sold with their own box and product card.

MARKET VALUES

Photo		Description	Original	Avg.	High
		Pottery, Feature			
L.	(99)	Candy Corn Crock	17.00	**26**	**30**
M.	(99)	Homestead Crock	45.00	**113**	**125**
		with Lid	66.00	**132**	**179**
N.	(00)	Early Blossoms Flower Pots & Tray	39.00	—	—
		Pottery, Fruit Medley[np]			
	(99)	Bowl, Pasta	69.00	—	—
	(99)	Mugs, set of 2	36.00	—	—
	(99)	Pitcher	49.00	—	—
	(99)	Ramekin	15.00	—	—
		Pottery, Regular Line			
O.	(94–98)	Bowl, Dessert	13.95	—	—
P.	(96–99)	Candlesticks	39.95	**45**	**75**
Q.	(97–98)	Flower Pot, Large	29.95	**41**	**50**
R.	(99–00)	Napkin Rings (2)	19.00	—	—
S.	(93–99)	Sauce Boat	24.95	**39**	**50**
T.	(96–98)	Spice Jars	19.95	**31**	**70**
		Tie-Ons			
U.	(96)	Baby	6.95	**8**	**10**
V.	(97)	Baby	6.95	**8**	**10**
W.	(98)	Baby	8.00	**12**	**20**
W.	(99)	Baby	8.00	—	—

continued next page

L. Candy Corn Crock
1 Pint

Form No: 37516

Only available during the Candy Corn campaign during August 1999.

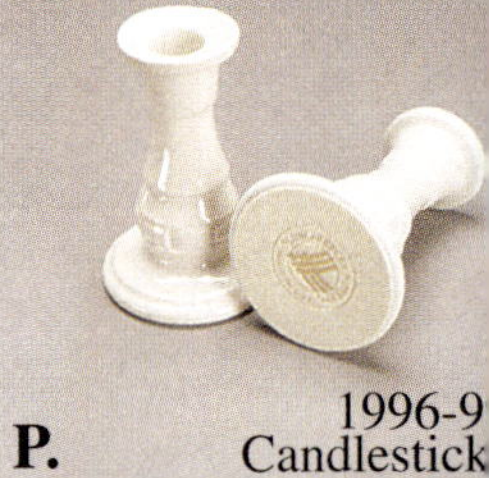

P. 1996-9 Candlestick

3.25RD x 5H

Form No: 32522/31/14 34037

Form numbers listed in order of blue, green, red and ivory. Sold as a Set of 2.

T. 1996-9 Spice Ja

4H

Form No: variou

Form numbers vary based on the color an the type of spice.

M. Homestead Crock — 1999

2 Quart

Form No:	37532
No. Sold:	

Features a sealable lid that sold separately.

N. Early Blossoms — 2000

Pots: 4RD x 3.5^{H}
Tray: 8.75^{L} x 5^{W} x 1.75^{H}

Form No:	38679

Featured during the 2000 Mother's Day campaign.

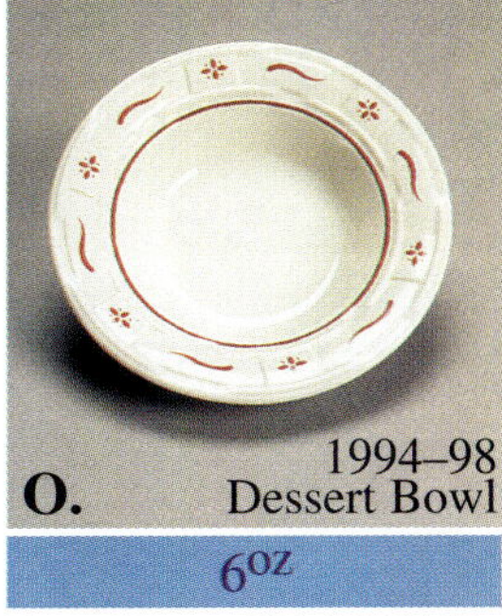

O. Dessert Bowl — 1994–98

6^{OZ}

Form No:	30147/30350
	30236/33278

Form numbers listed in order of blue, green, red and ivory.

Q. Large Flower Pot — 1997-98

6.5^{H}

Form No:	32816/24/32
	34444

Form numbers listed in order of blue, green, red and ivory.

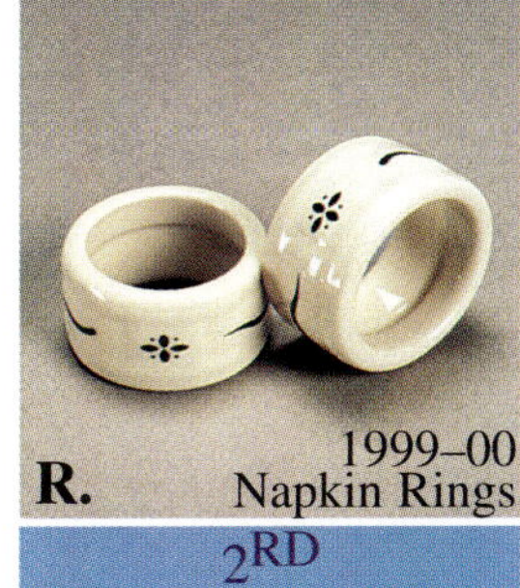

R. Napkin Rings — 1999–00

2RD

Form No:	37257/37265
	37273/37281

Form numbers listed in order of blue, green, red and ivory.

S. Sauce Boat — 1993-99

12^{OZ}

Form No:	30767/30601
	30929/34797

Form numbers listed in order of blue, green, red and ivory.

T. Baby Tie-On — 1996

2.5^{L} x 1.75^{W}

Form No:	32310

V. Baby Tie-On — 1997

2.5^{L} x 1.75^{W}

Form No:	30503

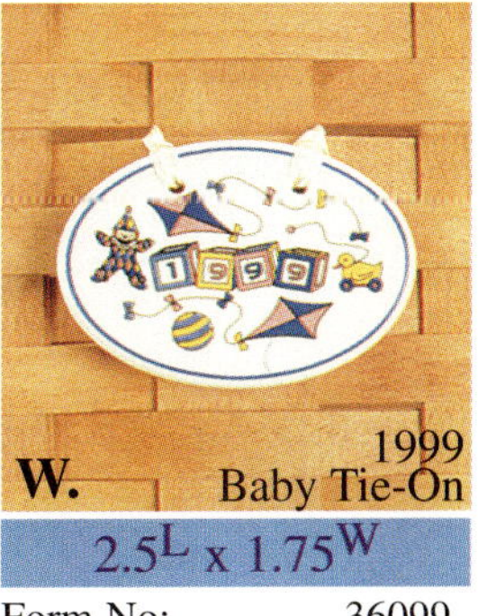

W. Baby Tie-On — 1999

2.5^{L} x 1.75^{W}

Form No:	36099

The 1998 Tie-On is the same design, except has "1998" in the center.

Features:

Most Pottery from the Regular Line was available in blue, green, red or ivory.

Photo	Description		MARKET VALUES		
			Original	Avg.	High
	Tie-Ons (con't)				
X.	(00) Baby		8.00	—	—
Y.	(96–97) Congratulations		6.95	**7**	**10**
	(96–98) Happy Birthday [np]		6.95	**8**	**14**
Z.	(96–98) Thank-You		6.95	**9**	**15**

[np] = Not Pictured

About the Red Pottery . . .

The Red Pottery was first introduced in 1992 but due to color problems was discontinued in 1993. After a short feature promotion later in 1993, a few pieces were reintroduced into the Regular Line in 1995. The balance of the pieces were brought back in 1996. Since this pottery is available again in the Regular Line, we do not currently consider it a part of the Secondary Market. A complete listing of <u>all</u> the pottery to help inventory your entire collection can be found in the Collector's Checklist.

X. 2000
Baby Tie-On

2RD

Form No: 36293

Y. 1996-9
Congratulation

2.5L x 1.75W

Form No: 3149(

Z. 1996-9
Thank Yo

2.5W x 1.75H

Form No: 32336

Paula Hawkins
Union Grove, Alabama

Paula didn't start collecting until February 1999, but she already has over 100 baskets! Her kids call her the "Basket Casket Lady", teasing her that she is so crazy for the baskets that they are going to bury her in one!! The May Series™ and the Christmas Collection™ are among her favorites.

Features:

These baskets were not declared a series until 1997 when the last items were introduced.

MARKET VALUES

Photo	Description			Original	Avg.	High
A.	1995	Pumpkin Basket™		47.95	**95**	**150**
		with **Protector**		54.90	**95**	**165**
		with **Liner**		64.90	**95**	**165**
		Combo (**P/L**)		59.95	**97**	**175**
		with **Lid**		72.90	**95**	**165**
		Full Set (**Combo/Lid**)		84.90	**131**	**200**
A.	1995	Pumpkin™ Tie-On		6.95	**14**	**25**
B.	1996	Small Pumpkin™		40.95	**77**	**110**
		with **Protector**		45.90	**77**	**110**
		with **Liner**		55.90	**77**	**110**
		Combo (**P/L**)		52.95	**89**	**135**
		with **Lid**		60.90	**89**	**110**
		Full Set (**Combo/Lid**)		72.90	**98**	**145**
C.	1997	Little Pumpkin™		34.95	**65**	**85**
		with **Protector**		39.90	**68**	**90**
		with **Liner**		49.90	**68**	**90**
		Combo (**P/L**)		46.95	**75**	**125**
		with **Lid**		52.90	**68**	**90**
		Full Set (**Combo/Lid**)		64.90	**105**	**185**
C.	1997	Pumpkin™ Tie-On		6.95	**13**	**20**
C.	1997	Large Pumpkin™				
		Combo (**P/L**)		117.95	**145**	**225**

A. 1995 Pumpkin

9.25^RD x 7.25^H

Form No:	19402
Tie-On:	31763
No. Sold:	

B. 1996 Small Pumpkin

7.25^RD x 5.25^H

Form No:	16012
No. Sold:	134,914

C. 1997 Pumpkin

Ltl: 5.75^RD x 4.25^H

Lg: 11.25^RD x 9^H

Form No:	
Little:	16021
No. Sold:	177,000
Large:	16039
No. Sold:	
Tie-On:	34517

The Large Pumpkin was available to Hostesses only.

Retired Baskets

Lois Bergman
Rantoul, Illinois

Lois is a big collector and thinks that the Market basket is the most useful. But, her favorite find has been one that she found at a garage sale painted white! She stripped it down and added it to her collection!

Features:

Offered at one time through the Regular Line. Baskets are listed in alphabetical order. The years offered are noted in parenthesis. Unless otherwise noted, the Original price listed is from the first year the basket was offered.

A. 1979–99 Berry Baskets
Small, Medium & Large

Form No:
Small: 11304/1300-O
Medium: 11410/1400-O
Large: 11509/1500-O

E. 1979–80 Canister Set
5", 7" & 9" Measuring

5" Measuring: $5^{RD} \times 4.5^H$
7" Measuring: $7^{RD} \times 6.5^H$
9" Measuring: $9^{RD} \times 8.5^H$

Only sold as a set. No handles, included lids.

I. 1979–93 Mini Cradle

$7^L \times 5^W \times 3.5^H$

Form No: 10715/700-K
No. Sold:

Had 2 wooden loops prior to 1984.

MARKET VALUES

Photo		Description	Original	Avg.	High
		Berry Baskets (no handles):			
A.	(79–99)	Berry, Large	8.95	**49**	**80**
A.	(79–99)	Berry, Medium	7.95	**43**	**65**
A.	(79–99)	Berry, Small	6.95	**34**	**50**
B.	(82–88)	Bread (Old)	11.95	**49**	**90**
C.	(79–94)	Cake (1st/h)	15.95	**105**	**150**
D.	(94)	Cake (Natural)	46.95	**62**	**105**
E.	(79–80)	Canister Set	39.95	**246**	**351**
		5" Measuring, w/lid			
		7" Measuring, w/lid			
		9" Measuring, w/lid			
F.	(79–94)	Corn	29.95	**140**	**275**
		with Protector	39.95	**145**	**300**
G.	(94)	Cracker (Natural)	20.95	**35**	**40**
		Cradles:			
	(79–86)	Cradle, Doll [pg.109]	25.95	**181**	**275**
	(79–86)	Cradle, Large [pg.109]	39.95	**340**	**475**
H.	(79–83)	Cradle, Medium	37.95	**—**	**200**
I.	(79–93)	Cradle, Mini	9.95	**85**	**120**
	(79–80)	Cradle, Small [np]	35.95	**—**	**105**
J.	(94)	Darning (Natural)	30.95	**64**	**110**
		Easter Baskets: (Renamed to Chore Baskets in 1987)			
	(79–87)	Easter, Baby (st/h) [np]	8.95	**50**	**70**
K.	(79–87)	Easter, Baby (sw/h)	9.95	**56**	**70**
L.	(79–87)	Easter, Large (st/h)	11.95	**71**	**80**
	(79–87)	Easter, Large (sw/h) [np]	12.95	**80**	**84**

(Easter Baskets continued next page)

[np] = Not Pictured

[pg.xx] = This item is also featured in another section. Go to the page noted for a photo.

B. 1982–88 "Old" Bread

15^L x 8^W x 2.25^H

Form No: 4600-OO
No. Sold:

Replaced by a deeper Bread basket in 1988.

C. 1979–94 Cake

12^L x 12^W x 6^H

Form No: 11002
No. Sold:

1 st/h, included divider.

D. 1994 Natural Cake

12^L x 12^W x 6^H

Form No: 16144
No. Sold:

Available from Feb. 1 through Aug. 31, 1994. Divider sold with basket.

F. 1979–94 Corn

17RD x 11.5^H

Form No: 14401
No. Sold:

Inverted bottom, two and slots. Reintroduced through the Hostess Collection with two braided ears in 1995.

G. 1994 Natural Cracker

11.5^L x 5^W x 3^H

Form No: 17198
No. Sold:

Available from Feb. 1 through Aug. 31, 1994.

H. 1979–83 Medium Cradle

28.5^L x 17.75^W x 9.75^H

Form No: 2700–M
No. Sold:

Doll: 19^L x 12^W x 6^H
Large: 30^L x 20^W x 10.5^H
Small: 24^L x 17^W x 10^H

J. 1994 Natural Darning

10RD x 4^H

Form No: 15521
No. Sold:

Available from Feb. 1 through Aug. 31, 1994.

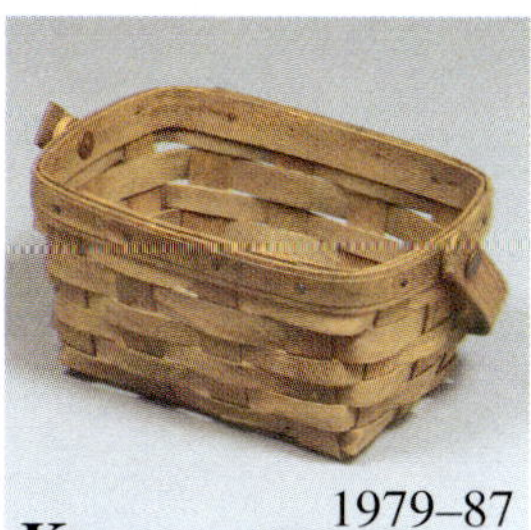

K. 1979–87 Baby Easter

7^L x 5^W x 3.5^H

Form No: 700-BO
No. Sold:

Also available with 1 st/h. (Form No. 700-AO)

L. 1979–87 Large Easter

14^L x 7.75^W x 5.25^H

Form No: 3600-AO
No. Sold:

Also available with 1 sw/h. (Form No. 3600-BO)

Features:

All baskets prior to 1985 will have the older, darker stain and all baskets after 1987 will have the newer, lighter stain. The stain was changed sometime between 1986 and 1987.

MARKET VALUES

Photo	Description	Original	Avg.	High
	(79–87) Easter, Med. (st/h) [np]	10.95	73	95
M.	(79–87) Easter, Med. (sw/h)	11.95	66	75
N.	(79–87) Easter, Small (st/h)	9.95	56	95
	(79–87) Easter, Small (sw/h) [np]	10.95	60	75
O.	(94–98) Flower Pot Basket	47.95	78	90
	Fruit Baskets – with Splint Hangers:			
P.	(79–80) Hanging, Large	21.95	100	140
P.	(79–80) Hanging, Medium	15.95	50	50
P.	(79–80) Hanging, Small	11.95	77	125
P.	(79–80) Hanging, Tall	18.95	—	—
Q.	(79–95) Fruit, Tall	15.95	76	110
	Gathering Baskets:			
R.	(83–93) Gathering, Lg. (1st/h)	26.95	84	110
S.	(79–94) Gathering, Lg. (2sw/h)	19.95	79	120
	(80–93) Gathering, Med. (1st/h)	41.95	77	120
T.	(86–93) Gathering, Sm. (1st/h)	22.95	74	100
	Hampers:			
	(79–86) Hamper, Lg. [pg.108]	59.95	236	300
	(79–86) Hamper, Sm./Med. [np]	31.95	140	175
U.	*Hanging Baskets – with Rawhide Hangers:*			
	(80–86) 5" Square bottom	14.95	37	45
	(80–86) 7" Square bottom	15.95	70	85
	(80–86) 9" Square bottom	22.95	40	40
	(80–86) 11" Square bottom	29.95	45	49
	(80–86) 13" Square bottom	35.95	40	40
V.	(79–86) Woven bottom	14.95	85	100
	Inverted Waste:			
	(79–84) Lg. Round (no/h) [np]	26.95	85	110
	(79–84) Lg. Round (1sw/h) [pg.81]	28.95	114	120
	(79–84) Sm. Round (no/h) [np]	21.95	90	100
W.	(79–84) Sm. Round (1sw/h)	23.95	—	125
X.	(94) Key, Tall (Natural)	31.95	58	70

[np] = Not Pictured

[pg.xx] = This item is also featured in another section. Go to the page noted for a photo.

M. 1979–87 Medium Easter

13L x 8W x 5H

Form No: 3500-BO
No. Sold:

*Also available with 1 st/h.
(Form No. 3500-AO)*

Q. 1979–95 Tall Fruit

8RD x 9H

Form No: 13307/3300-BO
No. Sold:

Inverted Bottom

U. 1980–86 Hanging Basket

5" :	5RD x 4.5H
7" :	7RD x 6.5H
9" :	9RD x 8.5H
11":	11RD x 10.5H
13":	13RD x 12.5H

N. 1979–87 Small Easter

10^L x 6^W x 4^H

Form No: 3400-AO
No. Sold:

Also available with 1 sw/h. (Form No. 3400-BO).

O. 1995–98 Flower Pot Basket

17^L x 7.5^W x 4.75^H

Form No: 16306
No. Sold:

Retired after 8/31/98, along with its liner, protector and riser.

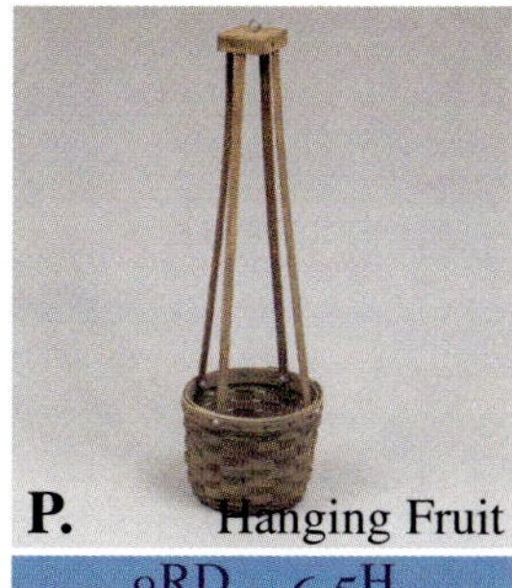

P. Hanging Fruit

8RD x 6.5^H

Small: 3000-P
Medium: 3100-P
Large: 3200-P
Tall: 3300-P

R. 1983–93 Large Gathering

19^L x 12^W x 6^H

Form No: 12505/2500-A
No. Sold:

<u>Medium</u>: 18^L x 11^W x 4.5^H
2408

All Gathering baskets with 1 st/h are currently retired.

S. 1979–94 Large Gathering

19^L x 12^W x 6^H

Form No: 12513/2500-C
No. Sold:

This basket was brought back into the regular line through the Hostess Collection in 1996.

T. 1986–93 Small Gathering

14^L x 9^W x 4.5^H

Form No: 12301/2300-AO
No. Sold:

Only the Small Gathering with 1 st/h has been retired. This basket with 2 sw/h is still available.

V. 1979–86 Woven bottom

8.25^{RD} x 7.75^H

Form No: 3700-PO
No. Sold:

W. 1979–84 Small Inverted

12.5^{RD} x 13.5^H

Form No: 1900-BO
No. Sold:

<u>Large</u>: 14RD x 16^H
2000-OO/BO

Both available with 1 sw/h or without a handle.

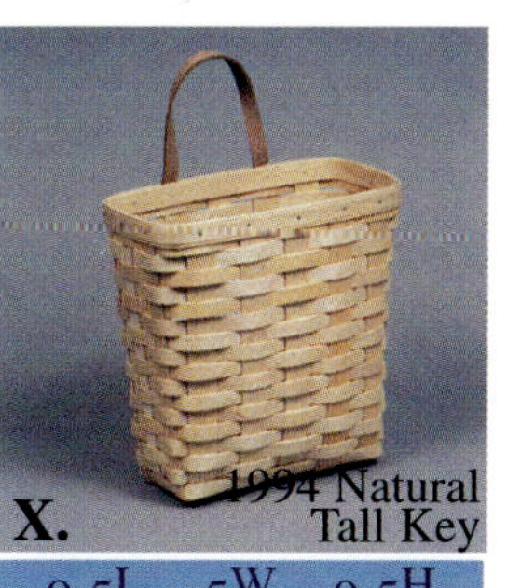

X. 1994 Natural Tall Key

9.5^L x 5^W x 9.5^H

Form No: 14630
No. Sold:

Available from Feb. 1 through Aug. 31, 1994.

Features:

From 1980 – 1986, most Regular Line baskets could be "customized" with color accent weaving and trim. See page 142 for more information.

MARKET VALUES

Photo	Description	Original	Avg.	High
	Laundry:			
	(79–86) Laundry, Large [pg. 109]	34.95	**268**	**300**
Y.	(79–83) Laundry, Medium	31.95	**—**	**150**
Z.	(79–98) Laundry, Small	29.95	**194**	**255**
	Magazine:			
A[1]	(79–95) Magazine (1sw/h, legs)	21.95	**90**	**100**
B[1]	(79–98) Magazine (1sw/h, legs, lid)	25.95	**87**	**125**
	Market:			
C[1]	(79–93) Market, Large (1st/h)	19.95	**103**	**110**
D[1]	(79–98) Market, Med (1st/h)	16.95	**56**	**70**
E[1]	(79–93) Market, Small (1st/h)	14.95	**101**	**140**
	Measuring:			
F[1]	(79–98) 5" Measuring	7.95	**44**	**68**
G[1]	(79–98) 7" Measuring	10.95	**54**	**65**
H[1]	(79–98) 9" Measuring	13.95	**65**	**81**
I[1]	(79–98) 11" Measuring	17.95	**78**	**100**
J[1]	(79–98) 13" Measuring	20.95	**88**	**135**

continued next page

Y. Medium Laundry 1979–83

28.5^L x 17.75^W x 9.75^H

Form No: 2700-O
No. Sold:

Large: 30^L x 20^W x 10.5^H
2800-OO

B[1] Large Market 1979–9

16^L x 11^W x 9^H

Form No: 10626/600-AC
No. Sold:

This basket is still available with 2 sw/h. Only the 1 sw/h option has been retired.

Fun Fact

J.W. Longaberger designed the Fruit Baskets in the early 20's for a local orchard owner. The unique inverted bottom allows the air to circulate around fruits and vegetables, thus making them an ideal basket for the fields.

G[1] 7" Measuring 1979–98

7RD x 6.5^H

Form No: 13901/3900-B
No. Sold:

Reintroduced into the Regular Line in 2000.

Z. 1979–98 Sm Laundry

24L x 17W x 10H

Form No: 12602
No. Sold:

A¹ 1979–95 Magazine

16L x 8W x 11H

Form No: 12122/2100-U
No. Sold:

1 sw/h, legs, no lid

B¹ 1979–98 Magazine

16L x 8W x 11H

Form No: 12214
No. Sold:

1 sw/h, legs, attached lid

D¹ 1979–98 Med Market

15L x 10W x 7.5H

Form No: 10529/500-AO
No. Sold:

This basket is still available with 2 sw/h. Only the 1 st/h option has been retired.

E¹ 1979–93 Small Market

15L x 9.5W x 5.5H

Form No: 10421/400-AO
No. Sold:

This basket is still available with 2 sw/h. Only the 1 st/h option has been retired.

F¹ 1979–98 5" Measuring

5RD x 4.5H

Form No: 13803/3800-B
No. Sold:

H¹ 1979–98 9" Measuring

9RD x 8.5H

Form No: 14001/4000-B
No. Sold:

Reintroduced into the Regular Line in 2000.

I¹ 1979–98 11" Measuring

11RD x 10.5H

Form No: 14109/4100-B
No. Sold:

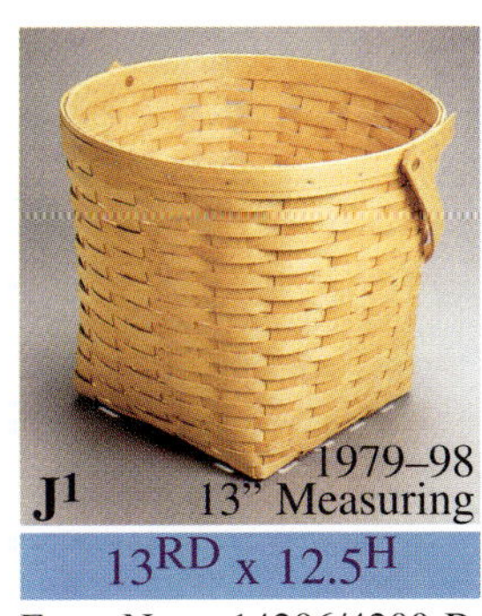

J¹ 1979–98 13" Measuring

13RD x 12.5H

Form No: 14206/4200-B
No. Sold:

Reintroduced into the Regular Line in 2000.

Features:

All baskets listed were offered at one time through the Regular Line.

MARKET VALUES

Photo	Description	Original	Avg.	High
	Peg Baskets:			
K[1]	(85–99) Peg, Large	19.95	**52**	75
K[1]	(85–99) Peg, Medium	17.95	**35**	48
K[1]	(85–99) Peg, Small	15.95	**38**	55
	Picnic:			
L[1]	(83–86) Picnic, Family	98.95	**326**	390
	with Liner	135.90	**346**	390
M[1]	(79–84) Picnic, Medium	26.95	**195**	240
	Planters:			
N[1]	(82–86) Fern, Lg. (w/feet)	27.95	**123**	180
	(79–86) Fern, Lg. (13" stand)[np]	23.95	**121**	200
	(79–86) Fern, Lg. (20" stand)[np]	26.95	**113**	130
O[1]	(82–86) Fern, Sm. (w/feet)	21.95	**97**	175
	(79–86) Fern, Sm. (13" stand)[np]	21.95	**115**	130
P[1]	(79–86) Fern, Sm. (20" stand)	24.95	**138**	150
	Purse:			
Q[1]	(94) Purse, Kiddie(Natural)	28.95	**51**	60
R[1]	(79–97) Purse, Medium	16.95	**58**	75
S[1]	(82–86) Purse, Med.(Split Lid)	24.95	**123**	255
T[1]	(96–99) Purse, Shoulder	84.95	**105**	140
U[1]	(79–99) Purse, Small	14.95	**47**	54
V[1]	(79–89) Purse, Tall	27.95	**74**	105

continued next page

[np] = Not Pictured

[pg.xx] = This item is also featured in another section. Go to the page noted for a photo.

K[1] 1985–99 Peg Baskets

Large: 6.5L x 6.5W x 8H
Medium: 5.5L x 5.5W x 6H
Small: 5L x 5W x 4.5H

Retired after 2/28/99, along with accessories.

O[1] 1982–86 Small Fern

8.5RD x 7.5H

Form No: 2900-RO
No. Sold:

These baskets are sometimes referred to as "Floor Planters" or planters with "feet".

S[1] 1982–86 Medium Purse

11L x 8W x 5.5H

Form No: 900-QO
No. Sold:

Split-lid option retired.

L[1] 1983–86 Family Picnic

24[L] x 17[W] x 10[H]

Form No: 2600-HO
No. Sold:

Red Gingham liner also available. Most Family Picnic Baskets will look darker than this one.

M[1] 1979–84 Medium Picnic

15[L] x 15[W] x 7.5[H]

Form No: 200-H
No. Sold:

N[1] 1982–86 Large Fern

13RD x 8.5[H]

Form No: 3200-RO
No. Sold:

P[1] 1979–86 Small Fern

8.5[RD] x 7.5[H] (20" stand)

Form No: 2900-TO
No. Sold:

Available for either Large or Small Fern baskets, 13" or 20" stand. No feet on baskets. Not available without a stand.

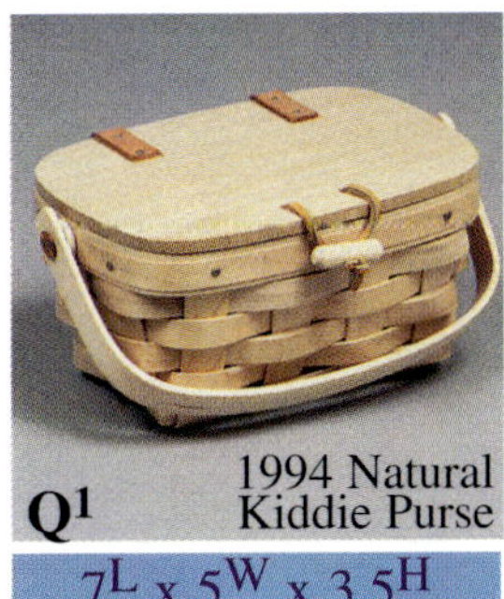

Q[1] 1994 Natural Kiddie Purse

7[L] x 5[W] x 3.5[H]

Form No: 17019
No. Sold:

Available from Feb. 1 through Aug. 31, 1994.

R[1] 1979–97 Medium Purse

11[L] x 8[W] x 5.5[H]

Form No: 10901/900-E
No. Sold:

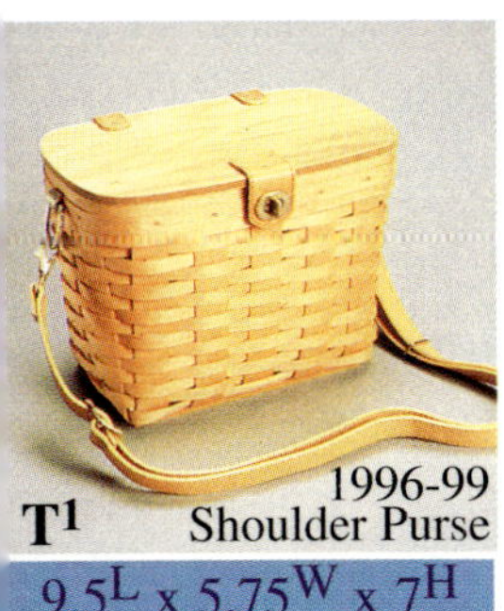

T[1] 1996-99 Shoulder Purse

9.5[L] x 5.75[W] x 7[H]

Form No: 18210
No. Sold:

U[1] 1979-99 Small Purse

9.5[L] x 6[W] x 6[H]

Form No: 10821 / 800-E
No. Sold:

V[1] 1979-89 Tall Purse

9.5[L] x 5[W] x 9.5[H]

Form No: 1000-EO
No. Sold:

Features:

Most of these baskets had a variety of accessories available, such as liners in many different fabrics, protectors, lids and garters.

MARKET VALUES

Photo	Description	Original	Avg.	High
	Sewing:			
W[1]	(78–86) Sewing, Round			
	with 13"stand	29.95	**217**	**300**
	without stand [pg.79]		**194**	**240**
X[1]	(78–83) Sewing, Rectangular	26.95	**381**	**400**
Y[1]	(79–94) Umbrella	18.95	**110**	**150**
	with Protector		**127**	**160**
Z[1]	(94) Vegetable, Medium (Natural)	38.95	**60**	**75**
	Waste			
A[2]	(79–00) Waste, Medium	21.95	**92**	**105**
A[2]	(79–00) Waste, Small	16.95	**56**	**75**
B[2]	(83-86) Wine, Large	29.95	**95**	**120**

W[1] 1978–86 Round Sewing

13RD x 8.5[H] (13" stand)

Form No: 3200-NO
No. Sold:

Split attached lid, 1 sw/h. Metal hinges changed to leather in 1979. Available with or without a stand.

A[2] 1979–00 Waste Baskets

Md: 13.5[L] x 13.5[W] x 16[H]
Sm: 9.5[L] x 9.5[W] x 12[H]

Med: 11703/1700-O
Small: 11801/1800-O

X[1] Rectangular Sewing — 1978–83

16ᴸ x 11ᵂ x 9ᴴ

Form No: 600-F
No. Sold:

Split attached lid, 2 sw/h. Had metal hinges in 1978, only.

Y[1] Umbrella — 1979–94

10ᴿᴰ x 17.5ᴴ

Form No: 11207/1200-OO
No. Sold:

Brought back in 1999 as a Hostess Only item.

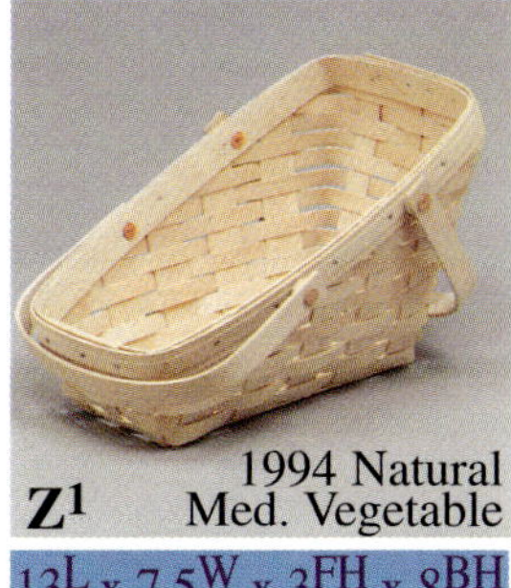

Z[1] Natural Med. Vegetable — 1994

13ᴸ x 7.5ᵂ x 3ᶠᴴ x 8ᴮᴴ

Form No: 15113
No. Sold:

Available from Feb. 1 through Aug. 31, 1994.

B[2] Large Wine — 1983–86

16ᴸ x 9ᵂ x 3.5ᶠᴴ x 9ᴮᴴ

Form No: 5200-CO
No. Sold:

Included dividers (wine rack).

Fun Fact

Up until 1989, handles on the baskets were made from oak. During 1989, oak handles were replaced with maple, with the exception of the J.W. Banker's Waste Basket.

J.W. hand-carved his own handles. These handles are easy to identify because they are very, very smooth.

Basket Fun Fact

Did the letters in the older form numbers stand for anything?

The letters in the older form numbers did stand for specific attributes of the baskets. They were set up to help customers visualize the baskets without seeing a picture or knowing its name. For example, when a customer saw the letter 'A' in a form number, they could tell that that basket had a stationary handle. The old form number system is depicted below.

The first letter immediately after the number in each code was used to identify different features of the basket. The remaining letters were specific manufacturing codes pertaining to color or stain. The following are meanings for the letter that appear **immediately after the numeral:**

Letter		Meaning	Example
A	=	1 st/h	[Candle: 1100-**AO**]
B	=	1 sw/h	[Poinsettia: 3900-**BRST**]
C	=	2 sw/h	[Yuletide Traditions: 5100-**CRST**]
D	=	Lid	[Large Hamper: 1600-**DO**]
E	=	1 sw/h & Lid	[Tall Purse: 1000-**EO**]
F	=	2 sw/h & Lid	[Rectangular Sewing: 600-**F**]
G	=	1 st/h & Divider	[Cake: 100-**GBRS**]
H	=	2 sw/h, Divider & Lid or, 2 sw/h & Split Lid	[Large Picnic: 300 **HBRS**]
I	=	Loop on Back & Metal Hook	[Small Key: 700-**IO**]
J	=	Ears	[Darning: 500-**JO**]
K	=	Rockers & Ears	[Mini Cradle: 700- **KO**]
L	=	2 sw/h & Rockers	[Doll Cradle: 2500-**LO**]
M	=	Rockers	[Large Cradle: 2800-**M**]
N	=	1 sw/h, Lid & Stand	[Round Sewing: 3200-**NO**]
O	=	Plain basket	[Bread: 4700-**OO**]
P	=	Large Hanger	[Hanging 13”: 4200-**PO**]
Q	=	1 st/h & Divided Lid	[Medium Purse: 900-**QO**]
R	=	Legs	[Patio Planter: 6000-**R**]
S	=	13-inch Stand	[Small Fern Planter, 13”: 2900-**SO**]
T	=	20-inch Stand	[Small Fern Planter, 20”: 2900-**TO**]
U	=	1 sw/h (lengthwise) & Legs	[Magazine: 2100-**U**]
V&W	=	1 sw/h (lengthwise), Legs & Lid	[Magazine: 2100-**V**]
X&Y	=	Woven Lid & 2 Swinging Handles	[Weekender: 200-**YO**]

Baskets with the same first numbers are made from the same form and have the same body dimensions. The differences can only be identified by the letters that follow. For example, Mini Cradle and the Small Key are both made with the same form (700); however, **KO** follows for the Mini Cradle while **IO** follows for the Small Key to distinguish their features.

Shades of Autumn ®

Peggy Herb
Halifax, Pennsylvania

This scene illustrates how Peggy enjoys display-ing her baskets. Her collection of 150+ baskets is displayed by series throughout her home. While her favorite collection is the Traditions Collection™, Peggy considers the Cake Basket™ to be the most useful basket.

Features:

Rust trim. Green, Rust and
Deep Blue weave.
Series completed in 1998.

A.　　　　　1990 Pie

12^L x 12^W x 4^H

Form No:　　2200-AGUBS
No. Sold:

MARKET VALUES

Photo		Description		Original	Avg.	High
A.	1990	Pie™		31.95	**95**	225
B.	1990	Small Vegetable™		35.95	**229**	325
C.	1991	Small Gathering™		36.95	**138**	185
		with **P**rotector		45.90	**140**	200
		with **L**iner		49.90	**140**	200
		Combo (**P/L**)		48.95	**146**	245
D.	1991	Acorn™		24.95	**132**	175
		with **P**rotector		28.90	**135**	175
		with **L**iner		35.90	**135**	175
		Combo (**P/L**)		35.95	**143**	192
E.	1992	Bittersweet™		24.95	**75**	120
		with **P**rotector		29.90	**80**	120
		with **L**iner		33.90	**80**	120
		Combo (**P/L**)		29.95	**81**	125
F.	1993	Harvest™		39.95	**101**	130
		with **P**rotector		45.90	**104**	130
		with **L**iner		52.90	**104**	130
		Combo (**P/L**)		49.95	**105**	160
F.	1993	Table runner		34.95	—	—
G.	1994	Recipe™		29.95	**90**	125
		with **P**rotector		34.90	**97**	135
		with **L**id		42.90	**97**	135
		with Recipe Card Set		35.90	—	—
		Combo (**P/Lid/Cards**)		44.95	**135**	145
H.	1995	Basket of Plenty™		53.95	**110**	150
		with **P**rotector		61.90	**110**	150
		with **L**iner		73.90	**110**	150
		Combo (**P/L**)		69.95	**117**	185
		Full Set (**Combo/Lid**)		101.85	**131**	200
H.	1995	Fall Foliage Tie-On		6.95	**11**	25
I.	1996	Maple Leaf™		40.95	**74**	90
		with **P**rotector		46.90	**75**	95
		with **L**iner		56.90	**75**	95
		Combo (**P/L**)		54.95	**78**	115
		Full Set (**Combo/Lid**)		74.90	**83**	120
I.	1996	Maple Leaf™ Tie-On		6.95	**11**	18
J.	1997	Bountiful Harvest™		44.95	**80**	110
		with **P**rotector		53.90	**85**	120
		with **L**iner		64.90	**85**	120
		Combo (**P/L**)		61.95	**90**	135
		Full Set (**Combo/Lid**)		86.90	**122**	175
K.	1998	Baker's Bounty™		39.00	**65**	75
		with **P**rotector		44.00	**66**	77
		with **L**iner		55.00	**66**	77
		Combo (**P/L**)		49.00	**72**	80
		Full Set (**Combo/Lid**)		71.00	**80**	90
K.	1998	Baker's Bounty Tie-On		8.00	**8**	10

E.　　　　　199
　　　　　Bitterswee

5.5^L x 5.5^W x 6^H

Form No:　　　　1080
No. Sold:

I.　　　1996 Maple Lea

7RD x 6.5^H

Form No:　　　　1393.
　Tie-On:　　　　3299
No. Sold:

B. 1990 Small Vegetable

0.5^L x 6.5^W x 3^{FH} x 7^{BH}

Form No: 5000-CGUBS
No. Sold:

Hostess Only

C. 1991 Small Gathering

14^L x 9^W x 4.5^H

Form No: 2300-CGUBS
No. Sold:

D. 1991 Acorn

7^L x 5^W x 3.5^H

Form No: 700-BGUBS
No. Sold:

F. 1993 Harvest

7^L x 4.75^W x 7.75^H

Form No: 14303
Tablerunner: 20150
No. Sold:

Liner is Autumn™. Reversible Table runner is Sunset™.

G. 1994 Recipe

8^L x 5.5^W x 4.5^{FH} x 6^{BH}

Form No: 17400
No. Sold:

Basket included set of Recipe Cards.

H. 1995 Basket of Plenty

12RD x 5.75^H

Form No: 15563
Tie-On: 31755
No. Sold:

Tie-On and Fabric Lid sold separately.

J. 1997 Bountiful Harvest

10.25^L x 10.25^W x 4.5^H

Form No: 12254
No. Sold:

Also promoted with 1 Quart Casserole Dish, which was then added to the regular line.

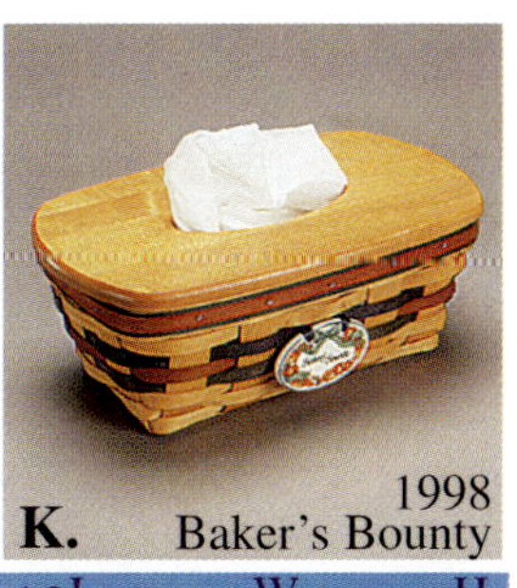

K. 1998 Baker's Bounty

10^L x 6.25^W x 3.75^H

Form No: 11771
Tie-On: 33669
No. Sold:

Promoted with the Loaf Dish, which was then added to the regular line.

Basket Fun Fact

With the help of a Massachusetts Consultant, Longaberger was represented at the 1999 Academy Awards. It is tradition to present lavish gifts to presenters and VIPs.

While Longaberger provided the basket, other upscale companies supplied jewelry and other gifts to fill the basket. The Hope Chest Basket™ was chosen because it needed to hold 97 pounds of gifts!

After sending out the baskets, the designer was so impressed with the beauty and quality, he refused to cover the baskets with cellophane, as he did in the past.

100 basketmakers were honored by their peers to make the gifts. Each was tagged with a brass tag that read "Longaberger – 71st Academy Awards – March 21, 1999".

Self addressed, postage-paid "Who Has My Basket" postcards were placed in each one. To date, postcards from Colin Powell, Andie McDowell, Andy Garcia, John Travolta, John Glenn and Peter Gabriel are among the ones returned.

Earlier this year, Longaberger was honored to be invited to *return* to the Oscars, this time sending the new Medium Wash Day Baskets™. Once again, 100 basketmakers were chosen for the honor and postcards were once again enclosed.

Denise Johnson
Santa Ynez, California

Denise's collection began in 1993. While she loves all of her 130+ baskets, she has a special love for the 1995 Family Traditions basket. It was in that year her Grandmother passed away and Denise purchased that basket in her honor. Now, every time she looks at it, it makes her smile.

Features:

Baskets produced in honor of a special event.
Listed by year within its own category.
Commemorative Tag.

MARKET VALUES

Photo	Description	Original	Avg.	High
	Bob & Dolores Hope:			
A.	1989 Bob & Dolores Hope	N/A	**667**	**700**
B.	1990 Bob & Dolores Hope	N/A	**557**	**600**
C.	1991 Bob & Dolores Hope	N/A	**544**	**600**
D.	1992 Bob & Dolores Hope	N/A	**543**	**600**
E.	1993 Bob & Dolores Hope	N/A	**575**	**625**
F.	1994 Bob & Dolores Hope	N/A	**600**	**750**
G.	1995 Bob & Dolores Hope	N/A	**613**	**625**
H.	1996 Bob & Dolores Hope	N/A	**600**	**650**
	[Series completed in 1996]			
	Inaugural:			
I.	1989 Inaugural™	19.89	**271**	**525** ✎
J.	1993 Inaugural™	24.95	**83**	**135**
	with **Protector**	28.90	**87**	**135**
	with **Liner**	34.90	**87**	**135**
	Combo (**P/L**)	34.95	**93**	**140**
K.	1997 Inaugural™	32.95	**60**	**75**
	with **Protector**	36.90	**65**	**75**
	with **Liner**	44.90	**65**	**85**
	Combo (**P/L**)	42.95	**65**	**110**
K.	1997 Inaugural™ Tie-On	6.95	**15**	**28**
	Miscellaneous Events:			
L.	1992 Discovery™	19.92	**62**	**95**
	Combo (**L**)	29.87	**80**	**125**

[continued next page]

✎ = With Signatures

A. 1989 Bob & Dolores Hope

11^L x 8^W x 5.5^H

Form No:	900-
No. Sold:	≈ 500

First Edition
Brown trim and center weave with blue shoe-string weave.

E. 1993 Bob & Dolores Hope

11^L x 8^W x 5.5^H

Form No:	900-
No. Sold:	≈ 500

Fifth Edition
Blue trim with brown, blue, brown center weave. No shoestring weaving.

I. 1989 Inaugural

5RD x 4.5^H

Form No:	3800-ABRST
No. Sold:	

In honor of President Bush's Inauguration

B. 1990 Bob & Dolores Hope

11^L x 8^W x 5.5^H

Form No: 900-
No. Sold: ≈ 500

Second Edition
Blue trim and center weave with brown shoestring weave.

C. 1991 Bob & Dolores Hope

11^L x 8^W x 5.5^H

Form No: 900-
No. Sold: ≈ 500

Third Edition
Blue trim with brown, blue, brown center weave. No shoestring weaving.

D. 1992 Bob & Dolores Hope

11^L x 8^W x 5.5^H

Form No: 900-
No. Sold: ≈ 500

Fourth Edition
Brown trim with blue, brown, blue center weave. No shoestring weaving.

F. 1994 Bob & Dolores Hope

11^L x 8^W x 5.5^H

Form No: 900-
No. Sold: ≈ 500

Sixth Edition
Blue trim and center weave. Brown shoestring weave.

G. 1995 Bob & Dolores Hope

11^L x 8^W x 5.5^H

Form No: 900-
No. Sold: ≈ 250

Seventh Edition
Blue trim and center weave. Brown shoestring weave.

H. 1996 Bob & Dolores Hope

11^L x 8^W x 5.5^H

Form No: 900-
No. Sold: ≈ 250

Eighth Edition
Blue trim and center weave. Brown shoestring weave.

J. 1993 Inaugural

5^L x 5^W x 4.5^H

Form No: 11461
No. Sold:

In honor of President Clinton's Inauguration.

K. 1997 Inaugural

5.5RD x 3.25^H

Form No: 15326
Tie-On: 71609
No. Sold: 298,318

In honor of President Clinton's Inauguration.

L. 1992 Discovery

5.5RD x 3.5^H

Form No: 5700-AO
No. Sold:

In honor of the Discovery of America. Does not have double weaving. Protector not offered.

M. 1996 Statehouse

11^L x 8^W x 5.5^H

Form No:	900-
No. Given:	400

Received at the Ohio Statehouse reopening in 1996.

Features:

This collection does not always have an addition each year. Only when The Company chooses to honor an event.

MARKET VALUES

Photo	Description	Original	Avg.	High
	[continued from previous page]			
M.	1996 Ohio Statehouse Opening	N/C	—	**80**
N.	1998 25th Anniversary™	49.95	**119**	**225**
	with **P**rotector	55.90	**119**	**250**
	with **L**iner	65.90	**119**	**250**
	Combo (**P/L**)	71.85	**128**	**300**
O.	1998 Barn Raising™		**173**	**260**
	with **P**rotector		**175**	**270**
	with **L**iner		**175**	**270**
	Combo (**P/L**)	59.95	**178**	**275**
	Full Set (**C/Lid**)	85.95	**215**	**300**
O.	1998 Barn Raising Tie-On	7.00	**18**	**25**
O.	1998 Barn Raising Magnet	N/C	—	—
	Heisey Horses:			
P.	1998 Red Heisey Horse	95.00	**1210**	**1300**
Q.	1999 Cobalt Heisey Horse	98.00	**152**	**268**
	Blue Balking Colt	50.00	**105**	**110**
	Blue Kicking Colt	50.00	**93**	**96**
	Blue Standing Colt	50.00	**88**	**90**
R.	2000 Emerald Heisey Horse	98.00	—	—
	Green Balking Colt	50.00	—	—
	Green Kicking Colt	50.00	—	—
	Green Standing Colt	50.00	—	—

Q. 199 Heisey Horse

6.5^W x 6.75^H

Form No:	unknown
Balking:	3.5
Kicking:	4
Standing:	5

Second in the series of three. First year for the Colts to be offered.

Jacob Birely – Iowa City, Now HE'S a Special Event

N. 25th Anniversary — 1997

8.75^L x 4.75^W x 6.5^H

Form No: 17612
No. Given:

Available to all customers in celebration of The Company's 25th Anniversary: 1973 – 1998.

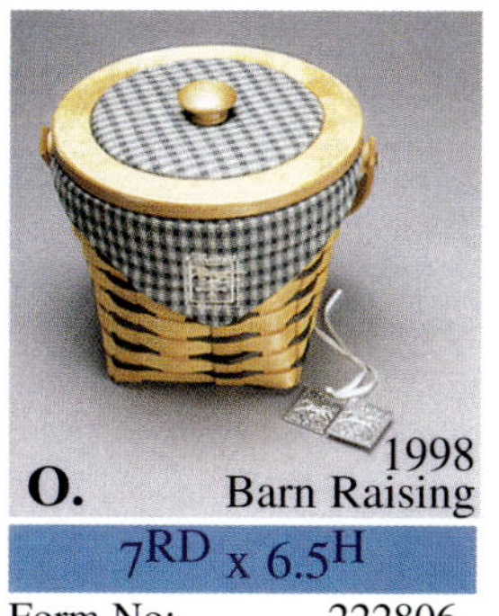

O. Barn Raising — 1998

7RD x 6.5^H

Form No: 222806
No. Given:

Sold at the Crawford Barn Raising Event. Sold only as a Combo. Other accessories offered through the mail. See page 96 for more information.

P. Heisey Horse — 1998

6.5^W x 6.75^H

Form No: unknown
No. Given: 900

This is the first of three horses that will be produced over the next 3 years.

O. Heisey Horse — 2000

6.5^W x 6.75^H

Form No: unknown
No. Given:

Last year for the Heisey Horse series.

Heisey Horses

Commissioned by the Heisey Glass Company for the Crawford Barn Raising Event in 1998. All pieces feature a maple leaf design on the leg to authenticate it as one of the Longaberger pieces. Product tags were also included, many of which in the market have been signed by Heisey Family Members who were in attendance at the Barn Raising.

Longaberger Homestead™

Why was it created?

Dave did not feel that Dresden had the infra-structure to accommodate the current number of guests, let alone the projections for the 21st Century. He also wanted to provide a one-stop touring, shopping and eating opportunity for collectors.

The Longaberger Homestead opened in June 1999. That first day, 60+ buses and over 60,000 visitors were in attendance.

From January – May, 1999, over 63,000 people visited the manufacturing campus. In June 1999, alone, more than 66,000 collectors walked through The Homestead.

Since its opening, they have sold over 2000 lbs. of fudge and handed out more than 200,000 shopping bags!

What's there?

Features the Crawford Barn, which has 20,000 square feet.

Family Members are now signing at the J.W. Workshop at The Homestead. Visitors permitted to bring two baskets to have signed between 10am – 4pm, Monday – Saturday. Family Members participating include Wendy (#2), Jerry (#3), Larry (#4), Mary (#7), Judy (#8), Carmen (#11), and Jeff (#12).

Homestead Hours

January – February
Mon – Sat, 9am – 5pm
Sun, Noon – 5pm

March – December
Mon – Sat, 8am – 6pm
Sun, Noon – 7:30pm

Sweetheart Baskets ®

Marsha Artis
Portsmouth, Ohio

Marsha started collecting in 1990 and has over 85 baskets in her collection. She thinks that she has always loved the Sweetheart Collection® because she is a "hopeless romantic"! Her love for the baskets does not end with just collecting. She hopes to soon become a Consultant.

Features:

Red Shoestring Weaving.
Red Ticking Liners Starting in 1993.

MARKET VALUES

Photo		Description	Original	Avg.	High
A.	1990	Sweetheart™	24.95	**116**	**180**
		Combo (L)	32.95	**140**	**230**
B.	1990	Getaway™	79.95	**158**	**225**
C.	1993	Sweetheart™	25.95	**74**	**160**
		with Protector	28.90	**74**	**160**
		with Liner	35.90	**74**	**160**
		Combo (P/L)	29.95	**78**	**175**
C.	1993	Pewter Tie-On	8.95	**27**	**50**
D.	1993	Getaway™	119.95	**150**	**175**
		with Protector	131.90	**155**	**190**
		with Liner	149.90	**155**	**190**
		Combo (P/L)	139.95	**159**	**200**
E.	1994	Be Mine™	27.95	**66**	**90**
		with Protector	32.90	**66**	**90**
		with Liner	39.90	**66**	**90**
		Combo (P/L)	36.95	**67**	**100**
F.	1994	Forever Yours™	109.95	**158**	**200**
		with Protector	123.90	**162**	**215**
		with Liner	139.90	**162**	**215**
		Combo (P/L)	139.95	**175**	**230**
E.	1994	Fabric Heart Tie-On	6.95	**13**	**18**
G.	1995	Sweet Sentiments™	28.95	**67**	**85**
		with Protector	31.90	**67**	**85**
		with Liner	38.90	**67**	**85**
		Combo (P/L)	33.95	**70**	**125**
G.	1995	Small Heart Tie-On	5.95	**14**	**23**
H.	1995	Precious Treasures™	89.95	**168**	**200**
		with Protector	100.90	**—**	**—**
		with Liner	116.90	**—**	**—**
		Combo (P/L)	99.95	**170**	**200**
		Full Set (C/Lid)	129.95	**—**	**—**
H.	1995	Large Heart Tie-On	6.95	**15**	**20**
I.	1996	Bouquet™	34.95	**65**	**75**
		with Protector	40.90	**69**	**89**
		with Liner	47.90	**69**	**89**
		Combo (P/L)	44.95	**70**	**100**
I.	1996	Bouquet™ Tie-On	6.95	**10**	**12**
J.	1997	Sweet Treats™	32.95	**53**	**88**
		with Protector	37.90	**55**	**88**
		with Liner	43.90	**55**	**88**
		Combo (P/L)	42.95	**58**	**90**
J.	1997	Sweet Treats Tie-On	6.95	**14**	**19**
J.	1997	Gourmet Gathering™	74.95	**90**	**98**
		with Protector	92.90	**95**	**105**
		with Liner	98.90	**95**	**105**
		Combo (P/L)	99.95	**124**	**168**
		Full Set (C/Lid)	144.90	**175**	**200**
K.	1997	Ticking Trivets	13.95	**18**	**20**

A. 1990 Sweetheart

5.75L x 3.75W x 3H

Form No: 45000-ARS
No. Sold:

E. 1994 Be Mine

8.5L x 5W x 3.5H

Form No: 18601
No. Sold:

I. 1996 Bouquet

6.5RD x 6.5H

Form No: 11240
Tie-On: 33596
No. Sold:

B. 1990 Getaway

17^L x 14^W x 11^H

Form No: 300-CRS
No. Sold:

Hostess Only

C. 1993 Sweetheart

5^L x 5^W x 2.5^H

Form No: 11347
Tie-On: 72036
No. Sold:

Tie-On sold separately.

D. 1993 Getaway

17^L x 14^W x 11^H

Form No: 10359
No. Sold:

Hostess Only

F. 1994 Forever Yours

20.5^L x 15^W x 10.5^H

Form No: 10367
Tie-On: 22659
No. Sold:

Hostess Only.
Tie-On sold separately.

G. 1995 Sweet Sentiments

4.25^L x 4.25^W x 3^H

Form No: 19046
Tie-On: 31780
No. Sold:

Tie-On sold separately.

H. 1995 Precious Treasures

13.25^L x 11.25^W x 9^H

Form No: 10456
Tie-On: 31798
No. Sold:

Hostess Only.
Tie-On sold separately.

J. 1997 Sweet Treats & Gourmet Gathering

<u>Sm:</u> 8^L x 5^W x 3^H

<u>Lg:</u> 18^L x 11^W x 4.5^H

Form No:	Small	Large
Red	15938	15946
Green	15962	16063
Blue	15954	16055
Purple	15971	16071
Tie-On:		71617

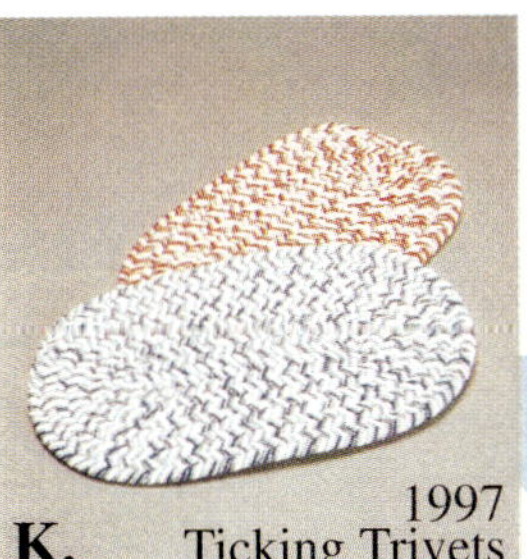

K. 1997 Ticking Trivets

14^L x 9^W

Form No:
Red: 2366390
Green: 2366391
Blue: 2366392
Purple: 2366393

Promoted along with
the Gourmet Gathering.

Sweetheart & Friends

Starting in 1997, Longaberger introduced colors to the Sweetheart Collection. Baskets and Ticking liners were available in red, green, blue, purple or even classic stain (in 1998 only). These options were promoted as "Sweetheart & Friends", but did not reappear with the 1999 Sweetheart baskets.

Features:

In 1997, the Sweetheart Collection was extended to include green, blue or purple shoestring weaving, along with matching ticking liners.

MARKET VALUES

Photo	Description	Original	Avg.	High
L.	1998 Picture Perfect™	39.00	**48**	**67**
	with **P**rotector	43.00	**50**	**70**
	with **L**iner	54.00	**50**	**80**
	Combo (**P/L**)	49.00	**66**	**90**
	Full Set(**C/HTie**)	55.00	**75**	**115**
L.	1998 Pewter Lapel Pin/Tie-On	8.00	**10**	**13**
L.	1998 Cherished Memories™	89.00	**120**	**150**
	with **P**rotector	99.00	**125**	**150**
	with **L**iner	118.00	**130**	**155**
	Combo (**P/L**)	119.00	**140**	**160**
	Full Set(**C/Lid/HT**)	153.00	—	—
L.	1998 Pewter Frame/Tie-On	10.00	**14**	**15**
M.	1999 Love Letters™	44.00	**66**	**95**
	with **P**rotector	49.00	—	—
	with **L**iner	61.00	—	—
	Combo (**P/L**)	56.00	—	—
	Full Set(**C/Lid**)	82.00	**97**	**101**
M.	1999 Love Tie-On	8.00	**10**	**12**
M.	1999 Love Treasures™	68.00	—	—
	with **P**rotector	84.00	—	—
	with **L**iner	90.00	—	—
	Combo (**P/L**)	89.00	**101**	**110**
	Full Set(**C/Lid**)	137.00	**141**	**158**
M.	1999 Love Stationary	14.00	—	—

1998
L. Sweetheart Baskets

Sm: 7.25^L x 4^W x 4.5^H
Lg: 14.25^L x 6.25^W x 9.5^H

Form No:	Small	Large
Red	17523	17531
Blue	16250	16268
Green	16357	16365
Purple	16454	16462
Classic	16551	16560
Lapel Pin:		72761
Frame:		72770

1999
M. Sweetheart Baskets

Sm: 8.75^L x 7.75^W x 2.75^H
Lg: 13.25^L x 12.5^W x 4.25^H

Form No:	
Small:	12963
Large:	13064
Tie-On:	37184
Stationary:	73245

Elaine Renner
Eaton, Ohio

This is the second year that Elaine has been chosen as a Nationwide Photo Search Winner! She just loves the Baskets AND the Pottery. Her favorite addition to her collection has been her Barn Raising Basket™. She just enjoyed the whole experience of the Barn Raising event!

Features:

The only baskets that cannot be purchased through a Consultant. Available only in Dresden or Hartville. Brass Tag with date.

MARKET VALUES

Photo	Description	Original	Avg.	High
A.	*Dresden:*			
	1988 Tour™		—	—
	1989 Tour™		**58**	**70**
	1990 Tour™		**70**	**70**
	1991 Tour™		**78**	**85**
	1992 Dresden Tour™		**49**	**60**
	1993 Dresden Tour™	24.95	**53**	**60**
	with Protector	30.90	**63**	**80**
	1994 Dresden Tour™	29.95	**50**	**55**
	with Protector	35.90	**50**	**60**
	1995-99 Dresden Tour™	34.95	**66**	**90**
	with Protector	40.90	**72**	**95**
B.	*Dresden II:*			
	1996-99 Dresden Tour II™	29.95	**55**	**65**
	with Protector	33.90	**64**	**80**
C.	*Hartville:*			
	1995-99 Hartville Tour™	34.95	**50**	**60**
	with Protector	40.90	**60**	**60**
D.	*Hartville II:*			
	1996-99 Hartville Tour II™	29.95	—	**45**
	with Protector	33.90	—	—
	Miscellaneous:			
E.	1997-99 20th Century™	49.95	**75**	**90**
	with Protector	55.90	**83**	**125**
	with Liner	64.95	**83**	**125**
	Combo (P/L)	70.90	**118**	**175**
F.	2000 Homestead Tie-On	0.00	--	—
	Woven Memories:			
G.	1999 Blue Basket	39.95	—	—
	with Protector	45.90	—	—
	with Liner	55.95	—	—
	Combo (P/L)	61.90	**174**	**239**
H.	2000 Burgundy Basket	39.95	—	—
	with Protector	45.90	—	—
	with Liner	55.95	—	—
	Combo (P/L)	61.90	—	—

A. Dresden Tour

8.75^L x 4.75^W x 6.5^H

Form No: 5600-BO / 1560

Basket pictured is the actual first Tour Basket ever sold in Dresden in 1988.

E. 20th Century

8.75^L x 4.75^W x 6.5^H

Form No: 17575
No.Sold:

First offered in at the 199 Bee General Session. More than 9,500 were sol prior to being available t the public. In Sept. 1998 it was moved to the Baske Village Preview Center fo sale to the public. All 199 baskets are marked as "First Edition". Starting 1998, this notation was removed from the tag.

B.　　Dresden Tour II

7^L x 3.5^W x 4.75^H

Form No:　　　　　15814

*This new form first
appeared in Dresden &
Hartville stores in Jan. 96.*

C.　　Hartville Tour

8.75^L x 4.75^W x 6.5^H

Form No:　　　　　15661

*Same as the Dresden Tour,
except different tag. First
appeared in the Hartville
factory store in 1995.*

D.　　Hartville Tour II

7^L x 3.5^W x 4.75^H

Form No:　　　　　15814

E.　Homestead Tie-On　2000

2RD x 1.5^H

Form No:　　　　unknown

*Postcards were sent to
Collectors Club Members
and Consultants inviting
them to visit the Homestead.
For a limited time on their
visit, they could redeem the
postcard for this free Tie-On.*

F.　Woven Memories　1999

10^L x 6^W x 4^H

Form No:　　　　unknown

*Available in both
Classic Stain or with
blue accent weaving.
Accessories sold
separately.*

G.　Woven Memories　2000

10^L x 6^W x 4^H

Form No:　　　　unknown

*Also available in Classic
stain. Accessories sold
separately. Inset picture
shows the special
embroidered liner that
was available.*

Fun Facts

If you own a 20th Century Basket, you helped preserve
American History. The Longaberger Company donated $1
from each 20th Century Basket sale to the preservation of
American History. A lump sum donation of $50,000 was
given by The Company to launch the commitment. The
20th Century Basket was available through the end of 1999.

The Big Basket Office

In 1998, The Longaberger Home Office moved to Newark, Ohio into the "Big Basket". A visit to this unique building does nothing short of leave you speechless.

This seven-story building sits on 25 acres and is 160 times the size of the original Medium Market Basket. It has 180,000 square feet and weighs 9,000 tons. The two swinging handles overhead are heated to prevent ice from forming and are attached to the building with two replica copper/wooden rivets. This extraordinary replica is topped off with two Longaberger "brass tags" measuring 25' x 7' x 3' and weighing over 725 pounds each.

A 20-foot brick replica of the Longaberger logo laid into the walkway at the front entrance welcomes you into the amazing lobby. While the outside appearance speaks for itself, the 30,000 square foot atrium is not without its own statement.

In order to allow everyone to enjoy the sunlight, the atrium is open to all seven stories. The beautiful foyer features all cherry woodwork and trim, much of which was harvested during the construction of the Longaberger Gold Course. A grand staircase is definitely a highlight of the entrance, where during the Christmas season, The Company invites many local groups and choirs to perform.

This unique structure has been recognized as one of the 140th national finalist in the American Consulting Engineer Council's Engineering Award Competition. Not only is it worthy of awards, it is definitely a must see on your next trip to Dresden!

Traditions Collection™

Kristin Anderson
Mackinaw, Illinois

GRAND PRIZE WINNER

Even though Kristin has only been collecting for less than two years, she definitely has an appreciation for how beautiful these baskets are! In her own words, she has "fallen head-over-heels in love" with the baskets. She even has her children using them!

Features:

Heritage Green™ Weave and Trim.
Commemorative Brass Tag.
Series completed in 1999.

MARKET VALUES

Photo	Description	Original	Avg.	High
A.	1995 Family™	89.95	**193**	**270**
	Combo (P)	95.95	**204**	**285**
	with Liner (1996)	119.90	**204**	**285**
	Full Set (P/L)	125.90	**229**	**300**
B.	1996 Community™	84.95	**149**	**200**
	with Protector	93.95	**150**	**200**
	with Liner	114.90	**150**	**200**
	Combo (P/L)	109.95	**168**	**225**
	Full Set (C/Div)	117.90	**156**	**225**
C.	1997 Fellowship™	69.95	**103**	**135**
	with Protector	81.90	**114**	**138**
	with Liner	92.90	**114**	**138**
	Combo (P/L)	89.95	**125**	**175**
	Full Set: (C/Lid/Grip)	129.95	**138**	**183**
D.	1998 Hospitality™	89.00	**100**	**110**
	with Protector	110.00	**130**	**150**
	with Liner	115.00	**130**	**150**
	Combo (P/L)	114.00	**138**	**200**
E.	1999 Generosity™	119.00	**140**	**150**
	with Protector	150.00	**150**	**160**
	with Liner	147.00	**150**	**160**
	Combo (P/L)	159.00	**190**	**200**
	Full Set (C/Lid)	218.00	**240**	**295**

A. 1995 Family

15.25^L x 11^W x 7.75^H

Form No: 19101
No. Sold:

3/8" Weaving. Liner added in 1996, not originally available.

B. 1996 Community

14.75^L x 13.5^W x 6.25^H

Form No: 19119
No. Sold: 171,381

Divider sold separately.

C. 1997 Fellowship

12.5^L x 6.5^W x 7.75^H

Form No: 15920
No. Sold:

Handle Gripper not shown.

D. 1998 Hospitality

18.5^L x 13.5^W x 5.25^H

Form No: 10669
No. Sold:

E. 1999 Generosity

19.25^L x 13.5^W x 7.75^H

Form No: 13358
No. Sold:

Tree-Trimming®

Ruth Libey

Angola, Indiana

There are over 21 Booking Baskets, plus the Collectors Club Miniatures on this tree. These, along with her Christmas and Inaugural Baskets, are Ruth's favorites in her collection of 70+.

Features:

Smaller replica versions of the Christmas Collection Baskets. Collection designed to decorate a Christmas tree.

A. 1999 Peppermint

5.5RD x 2.75^H

Form No: 19364/16837
No.Sold:

*Available in red or green. Comes with a box and burned-in logo on **inside** of basket.*

MARKET VALUES

	Description	Original	Avg.	High
A.	Peppermint™	45.00	**50**	**55**
	with **P**rotector	48.00	**60**	**65**
	with **L**iner	56.00	**60**	**65**
	Combo (**P/L**)	59.00	**68**	**80**

This special burned-in logo is present on the *inside* of all Tree-Trimming Baskets, authenticating the collection.

Jean Greiner
Belleville, Illinois

The variey of baskets shown here come from Jean's collection of about 75 baskets. She has only been collecting since 1995. Among her favorite baskets are the two that her husband has woven himself at the Make-A-Basket Shop during their trips to Dresden.

Features:
Decorative handcrafted Wood Products.
Years listed in parenthesis are the years
the items were available.

MARKET VALUES

Photo	Description	Original	Avg.	High
	Cupboards:			
A.	(80) 2-Door (Pine)		**480**	**500**
B.	(84–85) 1-Door (Maple)	119.95	**350**	**400**
C.	(84–85) 2-Door (Oak)	189.95	**467**	**500**
D.	(85–86) 1-Door (bottom shelf)	139.95	**425**	**500**
	Dividers:			
	(99) 4-way, Ntrl (Spring)[np]	12.00	—	—
E.	(92-99) 6-way (Chore, Med.)	18.00	—	—
F.	(92-99) 6-way (Gathering, Med)	20.00	—	—
G.	(92-99) 8-way (Pantry)	19.00	—	—
	(99) 8-way, Ntrl (Pantry)[np]	19.00	—	—
	Lids:			
H.	(95-99) Corn Lid	37.95	**48**	**60**
	(95-98) Fabric Lids:			
I.	Cake	24.95	**31**	**32**
J.	Fruit, Large	24.95	—	—
J.	Fruit, Medium	21.95	—	—
J.	Fruit, Small	19.95	—	—
J.	Magazine	21.95	—	—
J.	Sewing	24.95	**30**	**48**
K.	(83–86) Measuring Baskets:			
	5" Measuring	6.95	—	**13**
	7" Measuring	7.95	—	—
	9" Measuring	8.95	—	—
	11" Measuring	9.95	—	**15**
	13" Measuring	10.95	—	**20**
L.	(97–98) Measuring Baskets:			
	5" Measuring	13.95	—	—
	11" Measuring	34.95	—	—

[continued next page]

[np] = Not Pictured

A. 1980 Pine Cupboard

15.5^L x 5^W x 32.75^H

Form No: unknown
No. Sold:

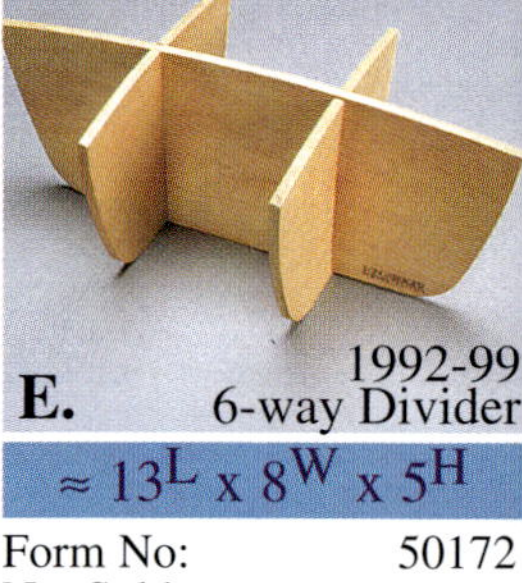

E. 1992-99 6-way Divider

≈ 13^L x 8^W x 5^H

Form No: 50172
No. Sold:

Fits the Medium Chore.

I. 1995-98 Cake Fabric Lid

12^L x 12^W

Form No: 51021
No. Sold:

*All regular line fabrics
offered.*

B. 1984–85 Maple Cupboard

27.5^L x 13^W x 5.25^H

Form No: 8101-OO
No. Sold:

C. 1984–85 Oak Cupboard

22.5^L x 17.5^W x 6.25^H

Form No: 8100-O
No. Sold:

D. 1985–86 Cupboard

27.25^L x 15.5^W x 5.25^H

Form No: 8100-OO
No. Sold:

Also featured in 1988

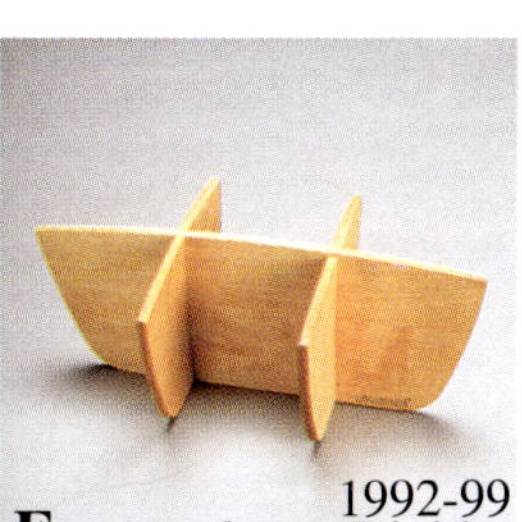

F. 1992-99 6-way Divider

≈ 18^L x 11^W x 4.5^H

Form No: 50920
No. Sold:

Fits the Medium Gathering Basket.

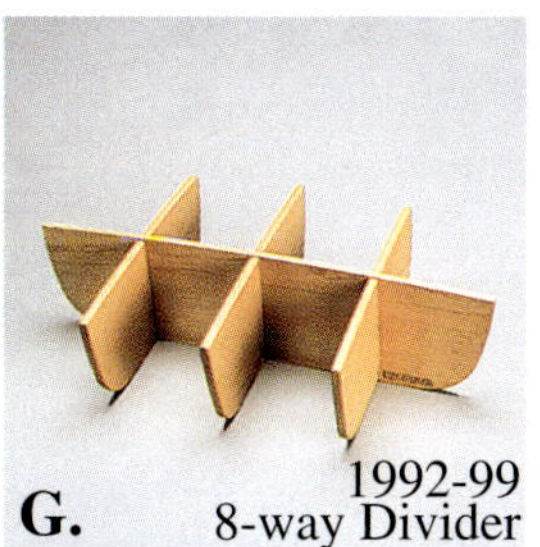

G. 1992-99 8-way Divider

≈ 14^L x 9^W x 4.5^H

Form No: 50164
No. Sold:

Fits either the Pantry or Small Gathering.

H. 1995-99 Corn Lid

17RD

Form No: 54429
No. Sold:

J. 1995-98 Fabric Lids

Left to right, back row first

Sewing	53210
Fruit, Large	53236
Fruit, Small	53015
Fruit, Medium	53112
Magazine	52108

All regular line fabrics offered. The Sewing lid has a quilted underside, to be used as a pin cushion.

K. 1983–86 Measuring Lids

5", 7", 9", 11", 13"

5" Lid	8300-OO
7" Lid	8301-OO
9" Lid	8302-OO
11" Lid	8303-OO
13" Lid	8304-OO

L. 1997–98 Measuring Lids

5", 7", 9", 11", 13"

5" Lid	53848
11" Lid	53864

7", 9", and 13" lids returned to the Regular Line in 2000.

Features:

The WoodCrafts® lids have been offered in a variety of ways: center wood or painted knobs, no knobs or covered in fabric.

MARKET VALUES

Photo	Description	Original	Avg.	High
	Lids (con't):			
	Natural Lids			
M.	(99-P) Spoon, Medium	16.00	—	—
	Paddles:			
	Butter Paddles:			
	(83–85) 28^L x 4.5^W [np]	14.95	**33**	**55**
N.	(85–94) 28^L x 6.25^W	16.95	**40**	**52**
O.	**Stencil-Cut Paddles:**			
	(87–88) Heart™	14.95	**63**	**75**
	(87–88) Goose™	14.95	**35**	**40**
	(87–88) Gingerbread Man™	14.95	**56**	**75**
	Wall Hangings:			
	Rectangular, with shelf:			
P.	(79–84) 10^L x 14^H	16.95	**100**	**110**
Q.	(85–86) 12^L x 16^H	39.95	**145**	**175**
	(79–80) 12^L x 24^H [np]	21.95	**150**	**180**
	Square, with shelf:			
R.	(79–80) Square, 20"	26.95	**168**	**180**
S.	(79–80) Square, 10"	12.95	**75**	**75**
	Triangle, with shelf:			
	(79–80) Triangle, 12^L x 10^H [np]	15.95	**130**	**180**
T.	(79–80) Triangle, 24^L x 21^H	23.95	**95**	**125**
	Wall Brackets:			
U.	(79–85) Large	6.95	**33**	**33**
V.	(79–85) Small	5.95	**30**	**30**
	(85–86) Small [np]	12.95	**18**	**20**
	Miscellaneous Hangings:			
W.	(80) Cathedral Mirror		**263**	**300**

[continued next page]

[np] = Not Pictured

M. 1999-P Med. Spoon Lid

6.5^L x 6.5^W

Form No: 58611
No. Sold:

Fits Medium Spoon and all other baskets with its form, such as Large Peg.

Q. 1985–86 Rectangular

12^L x 16^H

Form No: 7800-O
No. Sold:

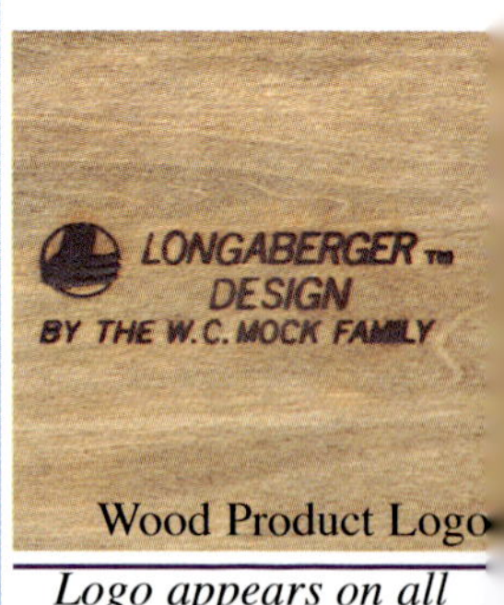

Wood Product Logo

Logo appears on all wood products starting in 1985. Unknown when the logo was changed to the current WoodCrafts® logo.

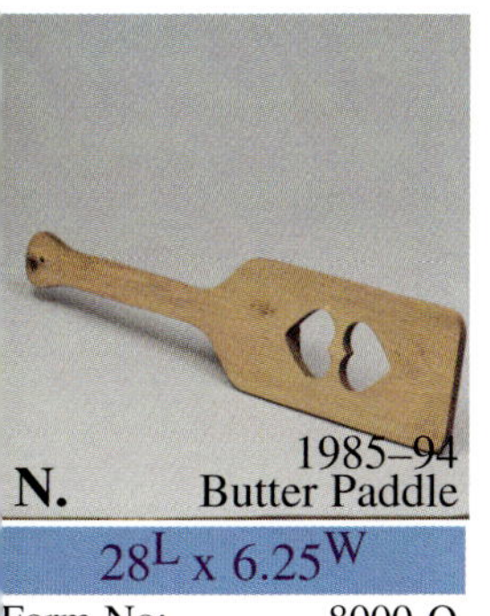

N. 1985–94 Butter Paddle

28^L x 6.25^W

Form No: 8000-O
No. Sold:

1983–85 Butter Paddle
28L x 4.5W   8010-O

O. 1987–88 Stencil Paddles

12.5^L x 4.5^H

Form No:
Heart   8020-OO
Goose   8030-OO
Gingerbread   8040-OO

P. 1979–84 Rectangular

10^L x 14^H

Form No: 7800-OO
No. Sold:

12^L x 24^W 7801-O
Same style as the one
above, only larger.

R. 1979–80 Square

20^L x 20^H

Form No: 7701-O
No. Sold:

S. 1979–80 Square

10^L x 10^H

Form No: 7700-O
No. Sold:

T. 1979–80 Triangular

24^L x 21^H

Form No: 7901-O
No. Sold:

12^L x 10^W 7900-OO
Same style as the one
above, only smaller.

U. 1979–85 Wall Brackets

Lg: 4.5^W x 13.5^H x 11.5^{EXT}
Sm: 4.5^W x 8^H x 6.5^{EXT}

Form No:
Large: 8902-O
Small: 8900-O

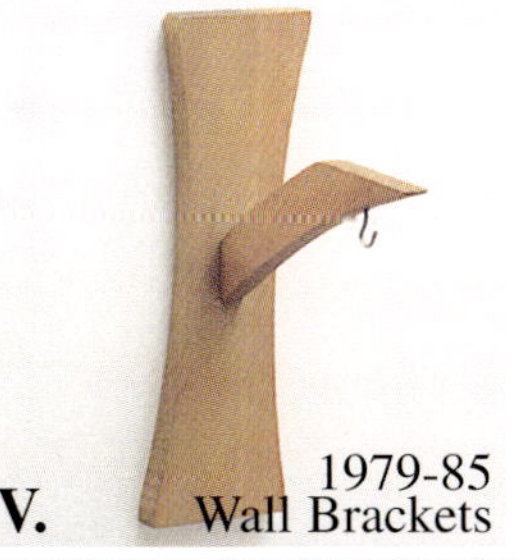

V. 1979-85 Wall Brackets

*Both the "X" shaped brackets to
the left and the "Hourglass"
design above were offered from
the company. When the change
in design occurred is unknown.
It was redesigned again in 1985,
shaped like an upside down "L".*

W. 1980 Cathedral Mirror

9^W x 25^H

Form No: unknown
No. Sold:

Features:

While lids are made from hardwood maple, to match the baskets, the other wood crafts were made from hardwood poplar.

MARKET VALUES

Photo		Description	Original	Avg.	High
		Wall Hangings: (con't)			
X.	(80)	Framed Clock	39.95	**437**	**450**
	(80)	Framed Mirror[np]	32.95	**383**	**400**
Y.	(N/A)	Nail Board		—	—
Z.	(80)	Picture Frame	29.95	—	**325**
A[1]	(85–94)	Peg Board	21.95	**37**	**50**
B[1]	(94–99)	Peg Board	39.95	**40**	**50**
C[1]	(94-97)	Wood Shelf	89.95	**112**	**114**
		Misc. Wood Crafts:			
D[1]	(80)	Bread Box	N/A	**300**	**375**
E[1]	(80)	Carpenter Box	N/A	**135**	**165**
F[1]	(80)	Cheese Board	N/A	—	—
G[1]	(80)	Cookbook Nook	N/A	**172**	**210**
H[1]	(79–82)	Toilet Paper Holder	6.95	**48**	**50**
I[1]	(79–80)	Towel Holder, 12"	8.95	**48**	**50**
	(79–80)	Towel Holder, 18"[np]	10.95	**35**	**35**
	(79–80)	Towel Holder, 21"[np]	11.95	—	—
	(79–80)	Towel Holder, 24"[np]	12.95	—	—

[continued next page]

X. 1980 Framed Clock

20L x 20H

Form No: 7701-X

8 x 10 face.

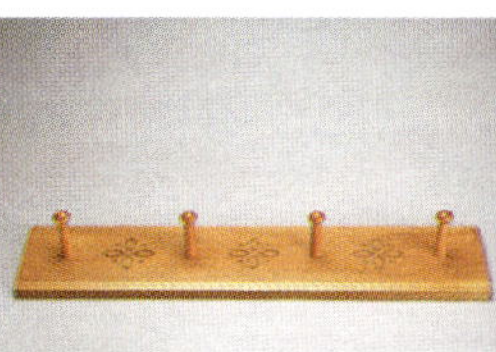

B[1] 1994-99 Peg Board

23.5L x 5H x 3.5H

Form No: 51101

Made of hardwood poplar.

F[1] Cheese Board

15L x 10W

Form No: unknown
No. Sold:

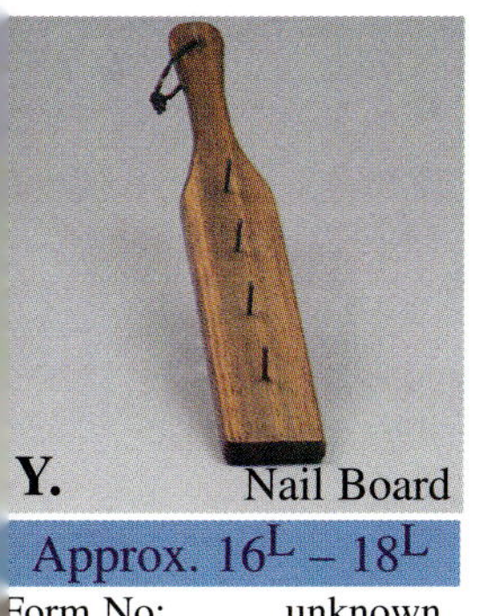

Y. Nail Board

Approx. 16L – 18L

Form No: unknown
No. Sold:

Z. 1980
Picture Frame

20L x 20H

Form No: 7701-Z

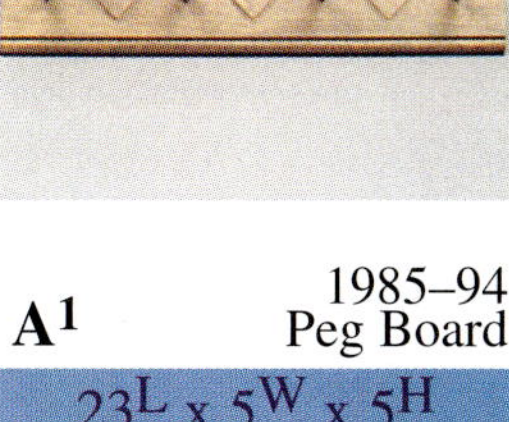

A¹ 1985–94
Peg Board

23L x 5W x 5H

Form No: 7900-

Often promoted along with the Peg Baskets.

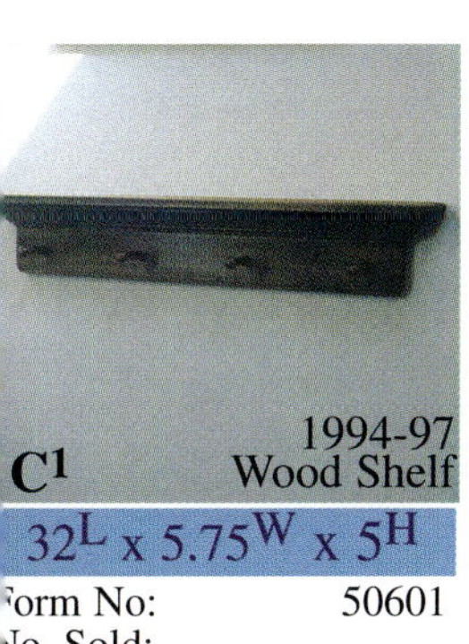

C¹ 1994-97
Wood Shelf

32L x 5.75W x 5H

Form No: 50601
No. Sold:

Made of hardwood poplar.

D¹ 1980
Bread Box

18.5L x 12.75W x 13.5H

Form No: unknown
No. Sold:

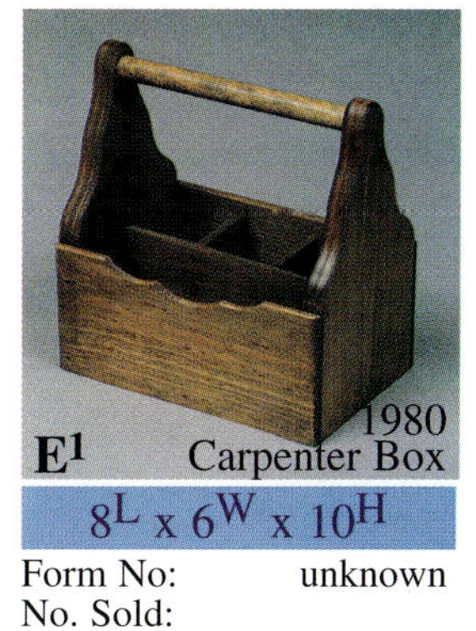

E¹ 1980
Carpenter Box

8L x 6W x 10H

Form No: unknown
No. Sold:

Came with divider

G¹ 1980
Cookbook Nook

13W x 17H

Form No: unknown
No. Sold:

H¹ 1979–82 Toilet
Paper Holder

8L x 3.5W

Form No: 8800-O
No. Sold:

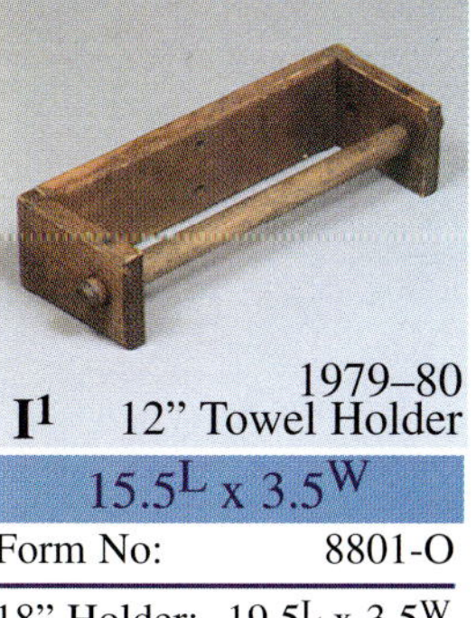

I¹ 1979–80
12" Towel Holder

15.5L x 3.5W

Form No: 8801-O

18" Holder: 19.5L x 3.5W
8802-O
 21" Holder: 22.5L x 3.5W
8803-O
 24" Holder: 25.5L x 3.5W
8804-O

Features:

Many of the earlier wood crafts were made by a Dresden, family-owned cabinet company called Mock Woodworking.

MARKET VALUES

Photo	Description	Original	Avg.	High
	Misc. Wood Crafts (con't):			
J1	(94-97) Wood Mug Tree	34.95	**35**	**45**
K1	(81) Wood Scoop	N/A	—	—

J1   1994-97 Mug Tree

14.75H

Form No: 51306
No. Sold:

Made of hardwood poplar.

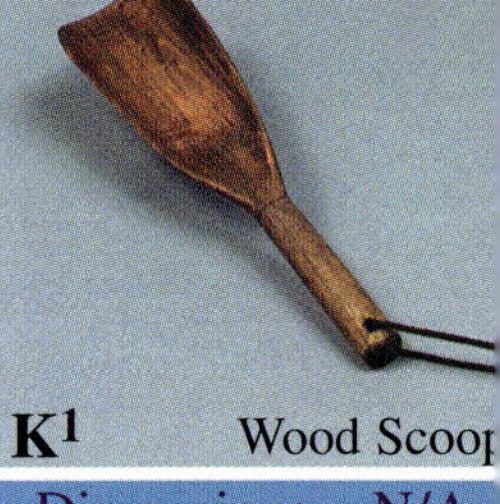

K1   Wood Scoop

Dimensions – N/A

Form No: unknown
No. Sold:

Fun Fact

Because each basket is handmade, some WoodCrafts® lids may fit more tightly than others. Most lids fit the basket in only one way. If it does not seem to fit in one direction, simply rotate it until you are able to find the best fit.

The Company recommends cleaning your WoodsCraft® items with a clean cloth and occasionally with furniture polish.

Woven Traditions®

Julie Kokoszka
Issaquah, Washington

Julie's home and office have been referred to as "Basketville"! She has been a Consultant for almost 2 years and has more than 150 baskets.

Features:

Red, blue, green shoestring weaving.
Series created in 1992.

MARKET VALUES

Photo		Description	Original	Avg.	High
A.	(92-97)	Berry, Large™	30.95	**45**	65
B.	(95-99)	Peg, Large™	39.95	**48**	65
C.	(1994)	Pie™	37.95	**65**	90
		with **Protector**	45.90	**70**	90
		with **Liner**	55.90	**70**	90
		Combo **(P/L/Plate)**	79.95	**80**	95
D.	(95-97)	Spring™	41.95	**60**	65
E.	(95–99)	Tea™	28.95	**31**	85
F.	(95-99)	Vegetable, Small™	35.95	**44**	50

A. 1992-97 Large Berry

8.5^L x 8.5^W x 5^H

Form No: 11533
No. Sold:

One of the original three pieces introduced during the 1992 Holiday Season.

E. 1995-99 Tea

7^L x 5^W x 3.5^H

Form No: 10710
No. Sold:

Retired after 8/31/99.

Collection Fun Fact

The Woven Traditions Collection® was
introduced during the Holiday season
1992. Three baskets began the series:

Large Berry™

Cracker™

Bread™

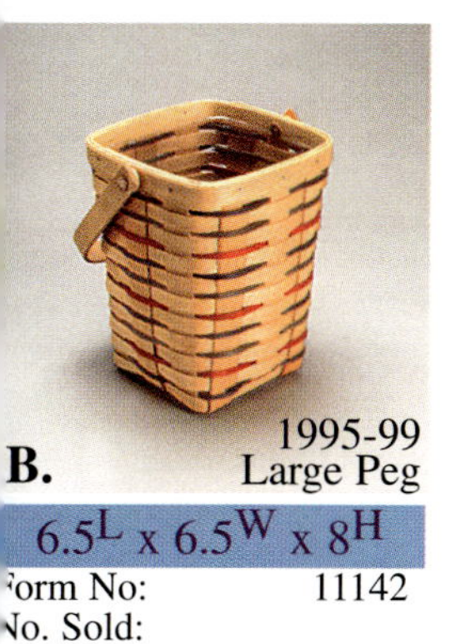

B. 1995-99
Large Peg

6.5^L x 6.5^W x 8^H

Form No: 11142
No. Sold:

Retired after 2/28/99 long with its accessories.

C. 1994 Pie

12^L x 12^W x 4^H

Form No: 12211
No. Sold:

Combo included Liner, Protector and Pie Plate. Featured in 1994.

D. 1995-97 Spring

11^L x 8^W x 5.5^W

Form No: 10936
No.Sold:

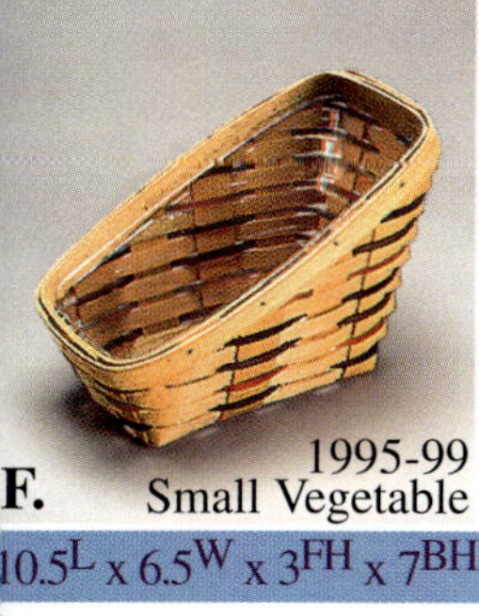

F. 1995-99
Small Vegetable

10.5^L x 6.5^W x 3^{FH} x 7^{BH}

Form No: 15016
No.Sold:

Retired after 2/28/99.

Weaving Techniques

There are many different weaving techniques, some of which have become popular in the secondary market. While it is hard to determine if there is an added value for these features, it is becoming a trend that some Collectors are starting to look specifically for these unique features, and thus are willing to pay a premium for them.

Continuous Weaving:

This is the practice of using the same splint to weave the entire basket. While it makes the basket very strong, it is a very time-consuming and difficult technique. It was one of J.W. Longaberger's trademarks and was a common feature for Longaberger Baskets, until sometime after May 1989. It is evident on a basket by a split upsplint which was done to allow for the weave pattern to continue.

Left-handed Weaving:

This feature is evident by looking at the trim strip. When you hold the basket in front of you, with the end of the trim strip facing up, look at which direction the trim "turn" is pointing. If it is pointing towards your left hand, it is a left-handed basket, meaning that a left-handed weaver made the basket. If the turn points towards your right hand, it was made by a more common right-hander.

Hardest Baskets to Make

According to a few weavers, the hardest baskets to make are the small baskets with inverted bottoms, such as the Button or Tree-Trimming. The most difficult one, before the new Founder's Basket, was the 1992 Discovery Basket. Because the basket was not made with double splints, if a mistake was made, it was difficult to correct.

# ★ Quick Find Index ★

How To Use:

This quick-reference index was designed to help collectors easily find information concerning their baskets.

The *"Quick Find"* Index has been divided into six columns; **Basket, Collections (Year), Original Price, Market Value, Page in Guide, Form No., and Other Baskets Using Same Form**. Across the top of the right-hand page is also a quick index of which baskets are listed on that page of the index.

Basket

Each basket is listed alphabetically by name, not by collection. For example, the *J.W. Corn®* basket is found under *'C'* for *Corn*, <u>not</u> *"J"* for the *J.W. Collection®*. If you want to see the baskets by collection, the front part of the Guide is what you should use. Also listed in this column are the basket's dimensions.

Collections

This column lists all the different collections of which the basket has been a part. The number in parenthesis represents the year(s) that the basket was available. The letter 'P' in this parenthesis stands for 'Present' and means that the item is still available directly from the Company.

Original Price

The price that the basket originally sold for is listed in this column. The values listed are for **Basket Only**, unless otherwise noted by the following letters: **C** (Combo), **B** (basket only), **L** (basket sold with liner), **P** (basket sold with protector), or **F** (full set).

Market Price

Both the *Average and the High Market Values* are listed in this column. In addition, if a collection has ** listed, this indicates that the basket may have several different market values, usually dependent on the year it was produced. When this notation is used, you will need to go to its location in the Guide or Checklist to find its value. If this column has been left blank or has dashes, a market value has not been determined.

Page in Guide

Refer to the listed page number or reference in order to obtain additional information on the basket or to find a picture of the basket. If 'checklist' is noted, this item is still available directly in the Regular Line and can only be found in the checklist. If the page number is blue in color, a picture is not featured in the Guide.

Form No./Other Baskets Using Same Form

Listed is the basket's form number(s) and then a compilation of the different baskets made with this same form and the same dimensions. This information is very useful when trying to identify what basket you have or when looking for an accessory to fit a discontinued basket.

Disclaimer

All basket names listed in this index are trademarks registered and owned by The Longaberger Company® and J. Phillip Inc. has no interest therein.

Basket	Collection (Year)	Orig.Price	AVG	HIGH
Acorn 7^L x 5^W x 3.5^H	Shades of Autumn (91)	24.95	132	175
Address 8.25^L x 6.25^W x 3.75^H	Father's Day (96) Regular Line (98-P)	29.95 34.00	60 34	80 34
Advisor Recognition 14^L x 9^W x 4.5^H	Incentive (86)	N/A	87	95
All-Star Trio 5.75^L x 3.75^W x 3^H	Feature (93)	29.95	57	95
Ambrosia 5.5^L x 4^W x 4^H	Booking (92-96) Employee Christmas (95)	22.95 N/A	42 92	60 100
American Beauty 13.5^L x 8.25^W x 5.25^H	Incentive (97)	N/A	—	140
Apple see **Large Fruit** 13RD x 8.5^H	J.W. Collection (85)	45.95	631	850
Apple, Miniature 5.25^{RD} x 3.25^H	Collectors Club (98)	139.95	165	200
Associate Homestead Tour 13RD x 8.5^H	Incentive (00-P)	N/A	—	—
Associate Producer 5.5^{RD} x 2.5^H	Incentive (96)	N/A	128	130
Baker's Bounty 10^L x 6.25^W x 3.75^H	Shades of Autumn (98)	39.00	65	75

KEY:
Values listed are for **BASKET ONLY, unless otherwised noted, (-P)** = to present

Page in Guide	Form No.	Other Baskets Using Same Form
page 176	700-BGUBS	Basket of Thanks, Mini Berry, Mini Chore, Mistletoe, Mini Cradle, Baby Easter, 91 Hostess Easter, 93 Small Easter, 94 Employee Christmas, Kiddie Purse, Star Team, Small Key, Tea, Patriot
page 70 checklist	12611 18546	None
page 120	2300-	92 Bee, 90 Employee Christmas Small Gathering, Tray, Pantry
page 74	64408	89 Employee Birthday, Keepsake, Paint the Town, 90 Recruit, Shining Star, Rosemary, Sugar and Spice, 90 Sweetheart, Treasure Chest, 95 Horizon of Hope, 98 Hostess Appreciation, 00 Branch Sales
page 28 page 66	10120 10120	97 Horizon of Hope, Thanks-A-Million
page 130	unknown	94 Easter
page 136	3200-BT	Large Fruit
page 42	13749	None
page 122	unknown	Homestead
page 130	unknown	None
page 176	11771	None

Basket	Collection(Year)	Orig.Price	AVG	HIGH
Bakery	Feature[87]	19.95	**48**	50
	Heartland[90-P]	30.95	**40**	40
14.5^L x 7.5^W x 3.75^H				
Baking	Crisco® [93]	39.95	**105**	120
14.5^L x 7.5^W x 3.75^H				
Banker's Waste	J.W. Collection[89]	59.95	**308**	575
	Regular Line, Hostess[99-P]	119.00	**119**	199
12.5RD x 13.5^H				
Barbeque Buddy	Good Ol' Summertime[00]	49.00	—	—
12^L x 5.25^W x 3^H				
Barn Raising	Special Event [98]	59.95 C	**178**	275 C
7RD x 6.5^H				
Basket Bin, Large	Regular Line[00-P]	79.00	**79**	79
16.5^L x 12.5^W x 5^{FH} x 7.75^{BH}				
Basket Bin, Small	Regular Line[00-P]	54.00	**54**	54
12^L x 11.75^W x 3^{FH} x 5.55^{BH}				
Basket O' Luck	Feature[90]	N/A	**110**	150
5.5RD x 3.75^H				
Basket of Love	Mother's Day [95]	37.95	**74**	85
8.5RD x 4^H				
Basket of Plenty	Shades of Autumn[95]	53.95	**110**	150
12RD x 5.75^H				
Basket of Thanks	Incentive[93]	N/A	**72**	115
7^L x 5^W x 3.5^H				
Bayberry	Christmas[93]	42.95	**73**	125
9^L x 9^W x 4.5^H				
Be Mine	Sweetheart[94]	27.95	**66**	90
8.5^L x 5^W x 3.5^H				

KEY:
Values listed are for BASKET ONLY, unless otherwised noted, (-P) = to present

Page in Guide	Form No.	Other Baskets Using Same Form
page 80 checklist	4700-JO 14711	Bread (new), Breakfast, Baking, Rose
page 74	14745	Bakery, Bread (new), Breakfast, Rose
page 136 checklist, Hostess	1900-BBST 14761	Master Employee, Waste (Small Round Inverted), Tree Trimming
page 92	16284	None
page 182	222806	7" Hanging, 7" Measuring, 90 Bee, 92 Sponsor (Lg), Maple Leaf, Poinsettia, 97 Perfect Attendance, Canister Set
checklist	17850	None
checklist	17752	None
page 74	17000-AGS	Laurel
page 148	18805	Best Supporting Role, 98 Renewal
page 176	15563	High Achiever, Quilting
page 122	700-	Acorn, Mini Berry, Mini Chore, Tea Mistletoe, Mini Cradle, Patriot, Baby Easter, 91 Hostess Easter, 93 Small Easter, 94 Employee Christmas, Kiddie Purse, Star Team, Small Key, 99 Branch Excellence
page 36	11584^R/11592^G	98 Large Easter
page 186	18601	92 Regional Sponsored Award, Small Oval, 93 Sponsor (Large), 97 Small Easter, Rose Petal

Basket	Collection(Year)	Orig.Price	AVG	HIGH
Beachcomber 10.5^L x 9^W x 8^H	Good Ol' Summertime$^{(99)}$	67.00	—	—
Bed 11.5^L x 5^W x 3^H	Feature$^{(89)}$	18.95	85	105
Bee, Large **1988** 14^L x 7.75^W x 5.25^H	Bee$^{(88)}$	N/A	145	165
Bee, Medium **1988** 13^L x 8^W x 5^H	Bee$^{(88)}$	N/A	100	100
Bee **1989** 8.75^L x 4.75^W x 6.5^H	Bee$^{(89)}$	N/A	145	180
Bee **1990** 7RD x 6.5^H	Bee$^{(90)}$	19.90	69	100
Bee **1991** 8.5^L x 8.5^W x 5^H	Bee$^{(91)}$	19.91	82	165
Bee **1992** 14^L x 9^W x 4.5^H	Bee$^{(92)}$	20.00	89	155
Bee **1993** 13^L x 8^W x 5^H	Bee$^{(93)}$	25.00	100	125
Bee **1994** 6.5^L x 6.5^W x 8^H	Bee$^{(94)}$	25.00	167	270
Bee **1995** 10^L x 6^W x 4^H	Bee$^{(95)}$	25.00	190	250
Bee **1996** 8.5^L x 8.5^W x 5^H	Bee$^{(96)}$	25.00	90	205

KEY:
Values listed are for BASKET ONLY, unless otherwised noted, (-P) = to present

Page in Guide	Form No.	Other Baskets Using Same Form
page 92	15342	Weekender, Remembrance, Top Performer
page 82	4500-AO	Liberty, Cracker, Muffin, Herb, 96 Employee Christmas
page 22	3600-AO	Large Chore, 88 Large Easter
page 22	3500-AN	Medium Chore, 88 Medium Easter, 93 Bee
page 22	5600-BRST	Dresden, Tour, Hartville, Memory, 92 Employee Birthday, Sophomore – Senior Recognition, 20th Century, 25th Anniversary (Sm)
page 22	3900-AO	7" Hanging, 7" Measuring, Barn Raising, Poinsettia, 92 Sponsor (Lg), Maple Leaf, 97 Perfect Attendance
page 22	1500-	Large Berry, 88-89 Sponsor, 96 Bee 98 Regional Sales Excellence
page 22	12335	Advisor Recognition, Tray, Pantry 90 Employee Christmas, Small Gathering
page 22	13501	Medium Chore, Medium Easter 88 Medium Bee
page 22	unknown	Large Peg, Medium Spoon, 96 Sponsor, 98 Perfect Attendance
page 24	unknown	93 Lg Easter, 88 Sm Easter, Gingerbread, 91 Regional Sponsored, $500 Million, Small Chore, Woven Memories
page 24	unknown	91 Bee, 88-89 Sponsor, Large Berry 98 Regional Sales Excellence

Basket	Collection (Year)	Orig. Price	AVG	HIGH
Bee 1997 5.5[L] x 5.5[W] x 6[H]	Bee (97)	27.95	85	135
Bee 1998 5.25[L] x 5.25[W] x 4[H]	Bee (98)	25.00	75	80
Bee 1999 7[L] x 3[W] x 4.75[H]	Bee (99)	29.00	81	100
Bee, Speaker 1988 15[L] x 10[W] x 7.5[H]	Incentive (88)	N/A	—	—
Bee, Speaker 1990 16[L] x 9[W] x 6[H]	Incentive (90)	N/A	120	130
Bee, Speaker 1991-P 11[L] x 8[W] x 5.5[H]	Incentive (91-P)	N/A	**	**
Bell 6.5[RD] x 7[H]	Christmas (83)	22.95	690	915
Berry, Large 8.5[L] x 8.5[W] x 5[H]	Feature (1st/h) (85, 88)	18.95	44	60
	Feature (Natrl) (99)	28.00	—	—
	J.W. Collection (90)	48.95	214	290
	Regular Line (1sw/h) (79-P)	10.95	35	45
	Retired (no/h) (79-99)	8.95	49	80
	Woven Traditions (92-97)	30.95	45	65
Berry, Medium 7.5[L] x 7.5[W] x 3.5[H]	All-American (87)	19.95	122	155
	Feature (1st/h) (85, 88)	17.95	35	45
	Feature (96-97)	29.95	41	50
	Regular Line (1sw/h) (79-P)	9.95	29	35
	Retired (no/h) (79-99)	7.95	43	65
Berry, Mini (see Tea) 7[L] x 5[W] x 3.5[H]		7.95	85	85

KEY:
Values listed are for **BASKET ONLY**, unless otherwised noted, (-P) = to present

Page in Guide	Form No.	Other Baskets Using Same Form
page 24	unknown	Bittersweet, Carry Along, Medium Peg, Small Spoon, 96 Sponsor, Shaker Peg
page 24	unknown	None
page 24	unknown	Tour II, 98 Flag Sponsoring, Hartville II
page 124	500-	87 Employee Christmas, Heirloom, Medium Market, 77-87 Tenth Anniversary, 99 Team Excellence, Founder's
page 124	3700-	Harvest, Original Easter, Senior Employee
page 124	900-	Bob and Dolores Hope, Boo Basket, 91 Customer Easter, Medium Purse, Red Pottery Thank You, Spring, 96 Statehouse, 99 Perfect Attendance, Sparkler
page 34	4901-OO	None
page 78	1500-AO	91 Bee, 88-89 Sponsor, 96 Bee, 98 Regional Sales Excellence
page 84	19844	
page 136	1500-BBST	
checklist	11517/1500-BO	
page 164	11509/ 1500-OO	
page 206	11533	
page 16	1400-ABRS	95 Regional Sponsored
page 78	1400-AO	
page 74	16241/25/33	
checklist	11428/1400-AO	
page 164	11410/1400-O	
checklist		Renamed Tea as of May 1, 1991

Basket	Collection (Year)	Orig.Price	AVG	HIGH
Berry, Small	Employee Christmas (98)	N/A	71	115
	Feature(1st/h) (85, 88)	16.95	38	45
	Feature (Natrl) (00)	22.00	—	—
	Regular Line(1sw/h) (79-P)	8.95	27	35
6.5^L x 6.5^W x 3^H	Retired (no/h) (79-99)	6.95	34	50 B
Best Supporting Role 8.5RD x 4^H	Incentive (96)	N/A	105	150
Bittersweet 5.5^L x 5.5^W x 6^H	Shades of Autumn (92)	24.95	75	120
Blue Ribbon Bread 10.5^L x 8.75^W x 4^H	All-American (99)	39.00	54	70
Bob and Dolores Hope 11^L x 8^W x 5.5^H	Special Events (89-96)	N/A	**	**
Boo 11^L x 8^W x 5.5^H	Feature (94)	34.95	93	135
Bountiful Harvest 10.25^L x 10.25^W x 4.5^H	Shades of Autumn (97)	44.95	80	110
Bouquet 6.5RD x 6.5^H	Sweetheart (96)	34.95	65	75
Branch Basket 15.75^L x 6.5^W x 11^H	Incentive (88-P)	N/A	300	312
Branch Bouquet 10.5^L x 6^W x 4^H	Incentive (97)	N/A	138	140
Branch Excellence 1998 6.5^L x 6.5^W x 3^H	Incentive (98)	N/A	92	110
Branch Excellence 1999 7^L x 5^W x 3.5^H	Incentive (99)	N/A	83	90

KEY:
Values listed are for **BASKET ONLY**, unless otherwised noted, **(-P)** = to present

Page in Guide	Form No.	Other Baskets Using Same Form
page 66	unknown	Spare Change, 98 Branch Excellence
page 78	1300-AO	
page 86	17841	
checklist	11312/1300-AO	
page 164	11304/1300-O	
page 130	unknown	Basket of Love, 98 Renewal
page 176	10804	Carry Along, Md Peg, Sm Spoon 97 Bee, Shaker Peg, 96 Sponsor
page 18	14346	None
page 180	900-	91-P Bee Speaker, Boo Basket, 91 Customer Easter, Medium Purse, Red Pottery Thank You, Spring, 96 Statehouse, 99 Perfect Attendance, Sparkler
page 74	10987	91-P Bee Speaker, Bob & Dolores Hope, 91 Customer Easter, Medium Purse, Red Pottery Thank You, Spring, 96 Statehouse, 99 Perfect Attendance, Sparkler
page 176	12254	None
page 186	11240	Lilac
page 126	unknown	Director Basket, Regional Basket
page 124	unknown	None
page 126	unknown	Small Berry, Spare Change
page 126	unknown	Basket of Thanks, Mini Berry, Mini Chore, Mistletoe, Mini Cradle, Baby Easter, 91 Hostess Easter, 93 Small Easter, 94 Employee Christmas, Kiddie Purse, Star Team, Small Key, Tea, Patriot

Basket	Collection (Year)	Orig.Price	AVG	HIGH
Branch Sales	Incentive (00)	N/A	—	—
5.75^L x 3.75^W x 3^H				
Branch Sponsoring, 1999	Incentive (99)	N/A	70	85
9.5^L x 6^W x 6^H				
Branch Sponsoring, 2000	Incentive (00)	N/A	—	—
7.75^L x 3.75^W x 4.5^H				
Bread (new)	Incentive (86)	N/A	145	175
	Feature, WT(Natrl) (00)	33.00	—	—
	Regular Line (88-P)	20.95	34	60
	Regular Line (Natrl) (99-P)	34.00	34	34
14.5^L x 7.5^W x 3.75^H	Woven Traditions (92-P)	36.95	39	48
Bread (old)	Retired (82-88)	11.95	46	90
15^L x 8^W x 2.25^H				
Bread & Milk	Feature (81)	unknown	675	800
16^L x 8^W x 11^H	J.W. Collection (87)	43.95	393	600
Bread & Milk Miniature	Collectors Club (00)	130.00	—	—
6^L x 3.25^W x 4.5^H				
Breakfast	Feature (89)	24.95	85	110
14.5^L x 7.5^W x 3.75^H				
Business Card	Father's Day (94)	22.95	88	150
	Incentive (99-P)	N/A	—	75
	Regular Line (97-P)	22.95	27	27
4.75^L x 3.75^W x 2.25^H				
Button	Booking (xx-84)	6.43	58	65
	Employee Christmas (93)	N/A	95	125
	Heartland (94-P)	22.95	33	35
	Regular Line (84-P)	24.95	27	45
	Regular Line (Natrl) (99-P)	27.00	27	27
7RD x 3^H	Woven Traditions (99-P)	33.00	33	33

220 **KEY:**
Values listed are for BASKET ONLY, unless otherwised noted, (-P) = to present

Page in Guide	Form No.	Other Baskets Using Same Form
page 126	unknown	Rosemary, All-Star Trio, Keepsake, Sugar and Spice, 95 Horizon of Hope, 98 Hostess Appreciation, Treasure Chest, 90 Sweetheart, Paint the Town, Shining Star, 89 Employee Birthday
page 126	unknown	Small Purse, Season's Greetings, 94 Regional Sponsored
page 126	unknown	None
page 120	4700-AO	Bakery, Breakfast, Crisco Baking, Rose
page 86	18031	
checklist	14702/4700-OO	
checklist	14974	
checklist, WT	14737	
page 164	4600-OO	Holly, Garden
page 78	2100-	Magazine, 25th Anniversary (Lg)
page 136	2100-ABT	
page 44	13391	None
page 82	4700-AO	Bakery, Bread (new), Crisco Baking, Rose
page 70	17477	Star Bound
page 122	17361	
checklist	17361	
page 28	5400-JO	Stitching, Cookie, Show Star, Rings & Things
page 66	5400-	
checklist, HL	15423	
checklist	15407	
checklist	19526	
checklist, WT	12971	

Basket	Collection(Year)	Orig.Price	AVG	HIGH
Cake	All-American[88]	39.95	155	225
	Employee [92]	N/A	—	150
	Employee Christmas[88]	N/A	143	180
	Feature[83-84]	20.95	—	—
	Feature(Natrl) [98]	43.95	—	—
	Heartland [99-P]	62.00	64	64
	J.W. Collection[92]	55.95	167	290
	J.W. Originals	N/A	—	—
	Regular Line (2sw/h)[85-P]	26.95	56	70
	Retired (1st/h)[79-94]	15.95	105	150
	Retired (Natrl)[94]	46.95	62	105
12^L x 12^W x 6^H	Woven Traditions [96-P]	59.95	64	64
Candle	All-American[94]	34.95	70	85
	Booking[84-90]	N/A	45	76
	Christmas[81]	14.95	737	950
	Employee Christmas[89]	N/A	132	150
9^L x 5^W x 5^H	Regular Line [99-P]	36.00	36	36
Candy Cane 5^L x 5^W x 4.5^H	Christmas[86]	26.95	173	280
Candy Corn 7.75^L x 4^W x 3.75^H	Feature[99]	29.00	46	53
Canister Set Set of 3 Baskets	Retired [79-80]	39.95	246	351set
Carry Along 5.5^L x 5.5^W x 6^H	All-American[95]	34.95	70	90
Catch-All 7.25^{RD} x 2.25^H	Regular Line[00-P]	32.00	32	32
Century Celebration 10.5^L x 6.25^W x 4.75^H	Collectors Club[00]	59.00	—	—
Century Celebration **Hostess Appreciation** 7.5^L x 4.5^W x 3.5^H	Feature[00]	44.00	—	—
Cheers 7.5^L x 4.5^W x 3.5^H	Feature[00]	39.00	61	70

KEY:
Values listed are for BASKET ONLY, unless otherwised noted, (-P) = to preser

Page in Guide	Form No.	Other Baskets Using Same Form
page 16	100-GBRS	Crisco Pie, Oak Lid Picnic,
page 62	100-	Small Picnic
page 64	100-	
page 78	100-CO	
page 82	10481	
checklist, HL	15148	
page 136	100-CBST	
page 140	unknown	
checklist	11011/100-GO	
page 164	11002/100-A	
page 164	16144	
checklist, WT	11657	
page 18	11134	90 Sponsor, Medium Key, 96 Perfect
page 28	1100-AO	Attendance, 89 Employee Christmas,
page 34	1100-	97 Collectors Club Renewal
page 64	1100-	
checklist	19739	
page 34	14000-ART/AGT	93 Inaugural, Violet, Small Peg, 96 Recruit, Teaspoon
page 76	14354	None
page 164	4700/4800/4900-O	See Measuring (5", 7" and 9")
page 18	14656	Bittersweet, Med Peg, Small Spoon 96 Sponsor, 97 Bee, Shaker Peg
checklist	15083	None
page 44	15385	None
page 78	13498	Cheers
page 78	18945	Century Celebration (Hostess)

Basket	Collection(Year)	Orig.Price	AVG	HIGH
Cherished Memories 14.25^L x 6.25^W x 9.5^H	Sweetheart [98]	89.00	120	150
Chives 4^L x 4^W x 4^H	Employee Christmas [97] Regular Line [96-P]	N/A 25.95	115 27	130 45
Chore, Large 14^L x 7.75^W x 5.25^H	Feature [86]	23.95	51	60
Chore, Medium 13^L x 8^W x 5^H	Easter [87] Feature [86] Heartland [88-97] Regular Line [86-P]	28.95 18.95 36.95 40.95	246 53 50 43	326 55 90 65
Chore, Mini 7^L x 5^W x 3.5^H	Heartland [89-97] Mother's Day [89]	19.95 21.95	40 85	75 150
Chore, Small 10^L x 6^W x 4^H	Feature [86] Heartland [89-97]	17.95 22.95	55 43	60 55
Christmas Sponsoring 10^L x 9.25^W x 6.5^H	Incentive [97]	N/A	127	150
Community 14.75^L x 13.5^W x 6.25^H	Traditions [96]	84.95	149	200
Cookie 7RD x 3^H	Christmas [85]	24.95	200	340
Cookie, Crisco 10RD x 4^H	Crisco® [92]	29.95	128	175
Corn 17RD x 11.5^H	Hostess Collection [95-99] J.W. Collection [91] J.W. Originals Retired [79-94]	139.95 89.95 N/A 29.95	142 334 -- 140	250 470 — 275
Coverlet 16^L x 16^W x 8^H	Incentive [88]	N/A	—	—

KEY:
Values listed are for **BASKET ONLY, unless otherwised noted**, (-P) = to prese[r]

Page in Guide	Form No.	Other Baskets Using Same Form
page 188	17531^R/16268^B 16365^G/16462^P/16560^C	None
page 66 checklist, Booking	unknown 15211	None
page 80	3600-CO	88 Large Bee, 88 Large Easter,
page 56 page 80 page 94 checklist	3500-CX 3500-CO 13528 /3500-CCS 13510 /3500-CO	93 Bee, 88 Medium Easter, 88 Medium Bee
page 94 page 148	10758 /700-ACS 700-APS	Acorn, Basket of Thanks, Tea, Mini Berry, Mistletoe, Mini Cradle, Baby Easter, 91 Hostess Easter, 93 Small Easter, 94 Employee Christmas, Patriot, Kiddie Purse, Star Team, Small Key, 99 Branch Excellence
page 80 page 94	3400-CO 13404 / 3400-ACS	93 Lg Easter, 88 Sm Easter, 95 Bee Gingerbread, 91 Regional Sponsored, $500 Million, Woven Memories
page 114	unknown	Snowflake (Small)
page 194	19119	None
page 34	5400-AR / G	Stitching, Button, 93 Employee Christmas, Rings & Things
page 74	10081	Daisy, Darning, 89 Easter 96 Regional Sponsored
page 110 page 136 page 140 page 164	14443 4400-JBST unknown 14401 /4400-OO	None
page 118	unknown	None

Basket	Collection (Year)	Orig.Price	AVG	HIGH
Cracker	Employee Christmas (96)	N/A	80	100
	Regular Line (83-P)	9.95	25	50
	Retired (Natrl) (94)	20.95	35	40
$11.5^L \times 5^W \times 3^H$	Woven Traditions (92-P)	26.95	31	35
Cradle, Doll	Feature (91)	69.95	—	—
	Hostess (86-90)	44.95	183	240
$19^L \times 12^W \times 6^H$	Retired (79-86)	25.95	181	275
Cradle, Large	Hostess (86-90)	109.95	357	400
(Infant)	Retired (79-86)	39.95	340	475
$30^L \times 20^W \times 10.5^H$				
Cradle, Medium	Retired (79-83)	37.95	—	200
$28.5^L \times 17.75^W \times 9.75^H$				
Cradle, Mini	Retired (79-93)	9.95	85	120
$7^L \times 5^W \times 3.5^H$				
Cradle, Small	Retired (79-80)	35.95	—	105
$24^L \times 17^W \times 10^H$				
Cranberry	Christmas (95)	47.95	82	105
$8.5^L \times 8.5^W \times 7^H$				
Daisy	May (99)	39.00	60	80
$6.75^{RD} \times 6^H$				
Daisy	Feature(Stained) (86, 87)	25.95	68	95
$10^{RD} \times 4^H$	Feature(Natrl) (86)	27.95	63	70
Darning	Feature (Natrl) (99)	31.00	—	—
	Heartland (96-P)	39.95	44	44
	Regular Line (83-P)	15.95	38	60
	Retired(Natrl) (94)	30.95	64	110
$10^{RD} \times 4^H$	Woven Traditions (94-P)	39.95	44	44
Dash Away Sleigh	Feature (98-P)	36.00	50	75
$7.75^L \times 4.5^W \times 2.25^{FH} \times 4.5^{BH}$				
Director Basket	Incentive (88-P)	N/A	—	—
$15.75^L \times 6.5^W \times 11^H$				

KEY:
Values listed are for **BASKET ONLY, unless otherwised noted, (-P)** = to present

Page in Guide	Form No.	Other Baskets Using Same Form
page 66	4500-	Liberty, Bed, Muffin, Herb
checklist	14508 /4500-OO	
page 164	17198	
checklist, WT	14532	
page 82	2500-LO	Large Gathering
page 108	2500-LO	
page 164	2500-LO	
page 108	2800-M	Large Laundry
page 164	2800-MO	
page 164	2700-M	Medium Laundry
page 164	10715/700-K	Acorn, Basket of Thanks, Tea, Mini Berry, Mini Chore, Mistletoe, Baby Easter, 91 Hostess Easter, 93 Small Easter, 94 Employee Christmas, Kiddie Purse, Star Team, Small Key, Patriot, 99 Branch Excellence
page 164	2600-M	Small Laundry, Family Picnic
page 36	19500^R / 19518^G	None
page 144	13056	None
page 80	5500-AO	Crisco Cookie, Darning, 89 Easter
page 80	5500-AN	96 Regional Sponsored
page 84	19640	Crisco Cookie, Daisy (Feature),
checklist, HL	15598	96 Regional Sponsored, 89 Easter
checklist	15504 /500-JO	
page 164	15521	
checklist, WT	15539	
page 76	13943	Summertime
page 126	unknown	Branch Basket, Regional Basket

Basket	Collection[(Year)]	Orig.Price	AVG	HIGH
Director Sales Excellence 1998 $12^L \times 12^W \times 4^H$	Incentive[(98)]	N/A	—	125
Director Sales Excellence 1999 $16^L \times 11^W \times 9^H$	Incentive[(99)]	N/A	—	—
Director Sponsoring Excellence 1998 $12^L \times 12^W \times 4^H$	Incentive (Natrl) [(98)]	N/A	—	—
Director Sponsoring Excellence 1999 $16^L \times 11^W \times 9^H$	Incentive (Natrl) [(99)]	N/A	—	—
Director Sponsored 2000 $14.5^L \times 5.5^W \times 9.5^H$	Incentive[(00)]	N/A	—	—
Discovery $5.5^{RD} \times 3.5^H$	Special Event [(92)]	19.92	62	95
Dresden Basket see **Tour** $8.75^L \times 4.75^W \times 6.5^H$			**	**
Dresden Basket II see **Tour II** $7^L \times 3.5^W \times 4.75^H$		29.95	55	65
Early Blossoms $11^L \times 7.25^W \times 2.75^H$	Mother's Day [(00)]	45.00	—	—
Easter (1989) $10^{RD} \times 4^H$	Easter [(89)]	29.95	**	**
Easter (1992) $10.5^L \times 7.5^W \times 4.5^H$	Easter [(92)]	27.95	50	75
Easter (1994) $13.5^L \times 8.25^W \times 5.25^H$	Easter [(94)]	49.95	51	75
Easter (1995) $10.75^L \times 8.75^W \times 5.25^H$	Easter [(95)]	49.95	65	90

KEY:
Values listed are for BASKET ONLY, unless otherwised noted, (-P) = to present

Page in Guide	Form No.	Other Baskets Using Same Form
page 132	unknown	Pie, Director Sponsoring Excellence
page 132	unknown	Large Market, Rectangular Sewing 99 Director Sponsoring Excellence
page 132	unknown	Pie, Director Sales Excellence
page 132	unknown	Large Market, Rectangular Sewing 99 Director Sales Excellence
page 132	unknown	None
page 180	5700-AO	None
page 190	100114/5600-	89 Bee, 92 Employee Birthday, Sophomore - Senior Recognition, Tour, Memory, 25th Anniversary (Sm), Hartville, 20th Century
page 190	unknown	Tour II
page 150	19682	None
page 56	5500-ABS/AO/APS	Crisco Cookie, Daisy, Darning 96 Regional Sponsored
page 58	34000-APVCNK	None
page 58	$16926^S/34^U/00/18$	American Beauty
page 58	18708	None

Basket	Collection[(Year)]	Orig.Price	AVG	HIGH
Easter (1996) 7.5[L] x 5[W] x 6[H]	Easter [(96)]	39.95	60	83
Easter, Baby 7[L] x 5[W] x 3.5[H]	Easter [(88)] Retired(1st/h) [(79-87)] Retired(1sw/h) [(79-87)]	18.95 8.95 9.95	74 50 56	117 70 70
Easter, Customer (1991) 11[L] x 8[W] x 5.5[H]	Easter [(91)]	26.95	53	75
Easter, Hostess (1991) 7[L] x 5[W] x 3.5[H]	Easter [(91)]	21.95	39	60
Easter, Large 14[L] x 7.75[W] x 5.25[H]	Easter [(88)] Retired(1st/h) [(79-87)] Retired(1sw/h) [(79-87)]	32.95 11.95 12.95	87 71 80	110 80 84
Easter, Large (1990) 9.5[RD] x 5[H]	Easter [(90)]	43.95	63	110
Easter, Large (1993) 10[L] x 6[W] x 4[H]	Easter [(93)]	27.95	60	80
Easter, Large (1997) 12[L] x 7[W] x 4.5[H]	Easter [(97)]	42.95	55	60
Easter, Large (1998) 9[L] x 9[W] x 4.5[H]	Easter [(98)]	43.95	—	—
Easter, Large (1999) 7.5[L] x 7.5[W] x 3.75[H]	Easter [(99)]	39.00	50	55

KEY:
Values listed are for BASKET ONLY, unless otherwised noted, (-P) = to present

Page in Guide	Form No.	Other Baskets Using Same Form
page 58	12912^S/12939^U	None
page 56 page 164 page 164	700-AN 700-AO 700-BO	Acorn, Basket of Thanks, Tea, Mini Berry, Mini Chore, Mistletoe, Small Key, Mini Cradle, 91 Hostess Easter, 93 Small Easter, Kiddie Purse, Patriot, 94 Employee Christmas, Star Team, 99 Branch Excellence
page 58	900-ATMS/ATMN	91-P Bee Speaker, Bob & Dolores Hope Boo Basket, Medium Purse, Red Pottery Thank You, Spring, 96 Statehouse, 99 Perfect Attendance, Sparkler
page 58	700-ATMS/ATMN	Acorn, Basket of Thanks, Tea, Mini Berry, Mini Chore, Mistletoe, Mini Cradle, Baby Easter, 93 Small Easter, Patriot, 94 Employee Christmas, Kiddie Purse, Star Team, Small Key, 99 Branch Excellence
page 56 page 164 page 164	3600-AN 3600-AO 3600-BO	88 Large Bee, Large Chore
page 56	41000-APVBS	Petunia
page 58	13439^S/13412^U	Gingerbread, Small Chore, 88 Small Easter, 91 Regional Sponsored, 95 Bee, $500 Million, Woven Memories
page 58	13447^S/13455^U	Rose Garden
page 58	11851^S/11860^U	Bayberry
page 60	14061^S / 14265^U	None

Basket	Collection(Year)	Orig.Price	AVG	HIGH
Easter, Large (2000) 12.5RD x 6^H	Easter (00)	65.00	—	—
Easter, Medium 13^L x 8^W x 5^H	Easter (88)	28.95	84	105
	Retired(1st/h) (79-87)	10.95	73	95
	Retired(1sw/h) (79-87)	11.95	66	75
Easter, Medium (1990) 8RD x 4.5^H	Easter (90)	38.95	55	100
Easter, Small 10^L x 6^W x 4^H	Easter (88)	22.95	68	90
	Retired(1st/h) (79-87)	9.95	56	95
	Retired(1sw/h) (79-87)	10.95	60	75
Easter, Small (1993) 7^L x 5^W x 3.5^H	Easter (93)	24.95	44	60
Easter, Small (1997) 8.5^L x 5^W x 3.5^H	Easter (97)	29.95	47	70
Easter, Small (1998) 6^L x 6^W x 3^H	Easter (98)	32.95	45	55
Easter, Small (1999) 5.75^L x 5.75^W x 3^H	Easter (99)	33.00	50	60
8 x 8 Basket 9.5^L x 9.5^W x 2.75^H	Regular Line(99-P)	37.00	37	37
Envelope 12^L x 5.25^W x 3.75^{FH} x 5^{BH}	Regular Line(99-P)	43.00	43	43
Evergreen 15.5^L x 15.5^W x 12.25^H	Holiday Hostess (95)	139.95	180	225

Everything's Coming Up Roses (small)
    see **Rose Bud**

KEY:
Values listed are for BASKET ONLY, unless otherwised noted, (-P) = to present

Page in Guide	Form No.	Other Baskets Using Same Form
page 60	19283^S / 19186^U	None
page 56	3500-AN	93 Bee, Medium Chore, 88 Md Bee
page 166	3500-AO	
page 166	3500-BO	
page 56	40000-APVBS	None
page 56	3400-AN	Gingerbread, Small Chore, 95 Bee
page 166	3400-AO	93 Lg Easter, 91 Regional Sponsored
page 166	3400-BO	$500 Million, Woven Memories
page 58	10774^S/10766^U	Acorn, Basket of Thanks, Tea, Mini Berry, Mini Chore, Mistletoe, Mini Cradle, Baby Easter, Patriot, 91 Hostess Easter, 94 Employee Christmas, Kiddie Purse, Star Team, Small Key, 99 Branch Excellence
page 58	63541^S/63550^U	Be Mine, 93 Sponsor (All-Star), 92 Regional Sponsored Award, Small Oval, Rose Petal
page 58	11959^S/11967^U	None
page 60	14052^S/14168^U	None
checklist	15393	Picnic Pal
checklist	14311	Picnic Pal
page 100	19607^R/19615^G	None
page 130	unknown	93 Recruit, 93 Sponsor (Small), Lavender, 94 Hostess Appreciation

KEY: In blue = Not pictured in the Guide. **S** = Stained, **U** = Unstained
HL = Heartland® Collection, **WT** = Woven Traditions®, **R** = Red, **G** = Green

Basket	Collection (Year)	Orig.Price	AVG	HIGH
Everything's Coming Up Roses (medium) see **Rose Petal**				
Everything's Coming Up Roses (large) see **American Beauty**				
Family $15.25^L \times 11^W \times 7.75^H$	Traditions [95]	89.95	193	270
Fellowship $12.5^L \times 6.5^W \times 7.75^H$	Traditions [97]	69.95	103	135
File $20^L \times 17.5^W \times 12.5^H$	Regular Line, Hostess [99-P]	189.00	189	200
Finders' Keepers $6^L \times 6^W \times 4.25^{FH} \times 5.25^{BH}$	Father's Day [97]	34.00	48	65
$500 Million $10^L \times 6^W \times 4^H$	Incentive [97]	N/A	194	275
Flag $10.75^L \times 5.75^W \times 7.5^H$	Incentive [89]	N/A	—	—
Flag Recruit $7^L \times 3.5^W \times 4.75^H$	Incentive [98]	N/A	192	200
Flag Sponsoring $7^L \times 3.5^W \times 4.75^H$	Incentive [98]	N/A	200	250
Flower Pot Basket $17^L \times 7.5^W \times 4.75^H$	Retired [95-98]	47.95	78	90
Flower Pot Basket, Small $14^L \times 6^W \times 3^H$	Regular Line [96-P]	34.95	35	50
Forever Yours $20.5^L \times 15^W \times 10.5^H$	Sweetheart [94]	109.95	158	200

<u>**KEY:**</u>
Values listed are for BASKET ONLY, unless otherwised noted, (-P) = to present

Page in Guide	Form No.	Other Baskets Using Same Form
page 130	unknown	Small Oval, Be Mine, 93 Sponsor (All-Star), 92 Regional Sponsored Award, 97 Small Easter
page 130	unknown	94 Easter
page 194	19101	None
page 194	15920	None
checklist, Hostess	12769	None
page 70	12777	None
page 122	900-	Gingerbread, 95 Bee, 93 Lg Easter, 88 Sm Easter, 91 Regional Sponsored, Small Chore, Woven Memories
page 118	unknown	None
page 114	unknown	Tour II, Hartville II
page 114	unknown	Tour II, Hartville II
page 166	16306	None
checklist	18414	Personal Organizer
page 186	10367	Gift Giving

Basket	Collection (Year)	Orig.Price	AVG	HIGH
Forget-Me-Not 5RD x 4.5^H	Booking (86-87)	N/A	60	90
Founder's 15^L x 10^W x 7.5^H	Feature (00)	189.00	—	—
Friendship 5.5^L x 5.5^W x 2.5^H	Feature (89)	21.95	55	80
Fruit, Large (Apple) 13RD x 8.5^H	Holiday Hostess (89)	49.95	121	172
	Incentive, Recruit (88)	N/A	—	—
	Incentive, N.Sales (93)	N/A	—	—
	Regular Line (79-P)	18.95	68	135
	Retired, hanging (79-80)	21.95	100	140
Fruit, Medium 8RD x 6.5^H	Incentive, Recruit (88)	N/A	—	165
	Incentive, N.Sales (93)	N/A	—	135
	Regular Line (79-P)	12.95	37	65
	Retired, hanging (79-80)	15.95	50	50
Fruit, Small 6.5^{RD} x 5^H	Feature (00)	25.00	—	—
	Incentive, Recruit (88)	N/A	—	140
	Incentive, N.Sales (93)	N/A	—	190
	Regular Line (79-P)	9.95	31	50
	Retired, hanging (79-80)	11.95	77	125
Fruit, Tall 8RD x 9^H	Retired, hanging (79-80)	18.95	—	—
	Retired (79-95)	15.95	76	110
Garden 15^L x 8^W x 2.25^H	Feature (86)	N/A	83	110
	Incentive (88)	N/A	80	80
Gathering, Large 19^L x 12^W x 6^H	Holiday Hostess (90)	65.95	127	165
	Hostess Collection (96-99)	89.95	103	120
	Incentive, N.Sponsor (93-98)	N/A	**	**
	Retired(1st/h) (83-93)	26.95	84	110
	Retired(2sw/h) (79-94)	19.95	79	120

KEY:
Values listed are for BASKET ONLY, unless otherwised noted, (-P) = to present

Page in Guide	Form No.	Other Baskets Using Same Form
page 28	3800-AO	89 Inaugural, 88 Employee Birthday, 5" Hanging, 92 Sponsor (Small), 92 Employee Christmas, Resolution, 5" Measuring, 92 Recruit, Watch Your Business Bloom, 5" Canister, 99 Recruit
page 86	500-	Medium Market, 87 Employee Christmas, Heirloom, 77-87 Tenth Anniversary, 99 Team Excellence, 88 Bee Speaker
page 82	13100-JO	91 Employee Birthday, Ivy, 96 Hostess Appreciation
page 98	3200-BGRS	Apple
page 112	3200-BO	
page 118	3200-	
checklist	13200/3200-BO	
page 166	3200-P	
page 112	3100-BO	Master Employee2 (97-P)
page 118	3100-	
checklist	13102/3100-BO	
page 166	3100-P	
page 86	17671	
page 112	3000-BO	94 Perfect Attendance, Senior Employee2
page 118	3000-	
checklist	13005/3000-BO	
page 166	3000-P	
page 166	3300-P	None
page 166	13307/3300-BO	
page 80	4600-AO	Bread (old), Holly
page 122	4600-	
page 98	2500-CGRS	Doll Cradle
page 110	12564	
page 114	2500-	
page 166	12505/2500-A	
page 166	12513/2500-CO	

Basket	Collection (Year)	Orig.Price	AVG	HIGH
Gathering, Medium	Feature (Natrl) [87]	41.95	70	85
	Holiday Hostess [89]	40.95	104	135
	Incentive, N.Sponsor [93-98]	N/A	**	**
	J.W. Collection [88]	36.95	300	550
	J.W. Original	N/A	—	—
	Regular Line(2sw/h) [79-P]	17.95	64	64
18^L x 11^W x 4.5^H	Retired(1st/h) [80-93]	41.95	77	120
Gathering, Small	Easter [87]	28.95	167	205
	Employee Christmas [90]	N/A	110	140
	Feature [98]	39.95	—	—
	Incentive, N.Sponsor [93-98]	N/A	**	**
	Regular Line(2sw/h) [79-P]	15.95	50	50
	Retired(1st/h) [86-93]	22.95	74	100
14^L x 9^W x 4.5^H	Shades of Autumn [91]	36.95	138	185
Gathering, XLarge 23^L x 15^W x 8^H	Incentive [96-98]	N/A	**	**
Generations, 7" 7^L x 6.75^W x 3^H	Regular Line [98-P]	28.95	29	29
Generations, 8" 8^L x 7.75^W x 3.5^H	Regular Line [98-P]	35.00	35	45
Generations, 10" 10^L x 9.25^W x 4^H	Regular Line [98-P]	38.95	39	39
Generations, 12" 12^L x 11^W x 4.5^H	Regular Line [98-P]	54.00	54	54
Generations, 14" 14^L x 12.75^W x 5^H	Regular Line [98-P]	57.95	58	58
Generosity 19.25^L x 13.5^W x 7.75^H	Traditions [99]	119.00	140	150
Getaway	Heartland [90]	65.95	140	200
	Sweetheart [90]	79.95	158	225
17^L x 14^W x 11^H	Sweetheart [93]	119.95	150	175
Gift Giving 20.5^L x 15^W x 10.5^H	Holiday Hostess [92]	124.95	158	200
Gingerbread 10^L x 6^W x 4^H	Christmas [90]	32.95	89	130

KEY:
Values listed are for BASKET ONLY, unless otherwised noted, (-P) = to presen

Page in Guide	Form No.	Other Baskets Using Same Form
page 80	2400-C	Gourmet Gathering
page 98	2400-AGRS	
page 114	2400-	
page 136	2400-ABT	
page 140	unknown	
checklist	12416/2400-CO	
page 166	12408/2400-AO	
page 56	2300-AX	Advisor Recognition, 92 Bee, Tray,
page 64	2300-	Pantry, 90 Employee Christmas
page 82	12572	
page 114	2300-	
checklist	12319/2300-CO	
page 166	12301/2300-AO	
page 176	2300-CGUBS	
page 114	unknown	None
checklist	13757	None
checklist	13765	None
checklist	13773	None
checklist	13790	None
checklist	13781	None
page 194	13358	None
page 94	300-CCS	Large Picnic
page 186	300-CRS	
page 186	10359	
page 98	12700^R /12718^G	Forever Yours
page 34	3400-ARST/AGST	88 Sm Easter, 93 Lg Easter, Small Chore, 91 Regional Sponsored, 95 Bee, $500 Million, Woven Memories

Basket	Collection (Year)	Orig. Price	AVG	HIGH
Glad Tidings 8.75^L x 6^W x 2^{FH} x 5.5^{BH}	Christmas (98)	49.00	64	75
Gold Nugget 4.5^{RD} x 3^H	Incentive (94)	N/A	178	235
Gold Rush 6.5^{RD} x 4.75^H	Incentive (94)	N/A	178	270
Gourmet Gathering 18^L x 11^W x 4.5^H	Sweetheart (97)	74.95	90	98
Grandad's Sleigh 9.25^L x 5.5^W x 2^{FH} x 5.5^{BH}	Christmas (82)	19.95	790	950
Growing Strong Together 9.5^L x 5^W x 9.5^H	Incentive (96-97) Incentive (97-P)	N/A N/A	— —	— —
Hamper, Large 16.5^L x 16.5^W x 21.5^H	Feature (86) Feature (93-94) Feature, SOA (91) Hostess (86-90) Retired (79-86)	79.95 179.95 149.95 109.95 59.95	223 235 227 241 236	295 275 295 305 300
Hamper, Large (1995 – P) 17^L x 17^W x 22^H	Regular Line, Hostess (95-P)	219.95	227	295
Hamper, Medium 12^L x 12.25^W x 16.25^H	Hostess (86-90) Retired (79-86)	69.95 31.95	131 140	175 175
Hamper, Small 12^L x 12.25^W x 16.25^H	Feature, SOA (91)	99.95	153	165
Hanging, 13" Sq. Bottom 13RD x 12.5^H	Retired (80-86)	35.95	40	40
Hanging, 11" Sq. Bottom 11RD x 10.5^H	Retired (80-86)	29.95	45	49

KEY:
Values listed are for **BASKET ONLY, unless otherwised noted**, **(-P)** = to preser

Page in Guide	Form No.	Other Baskets Using Same Form
page 36	12386^R /12394^G	None
page 128	unknown	Thyme
page 128	unknown	None
page 186	15946^R/16063^G 16055^B/16071^P	Medium Gathering
page 34	4900-Z	None
page 122 page 122	unknown unknown	Tall Key, MBA, Tall Purse, Two-Quart, Membership, 91 Employee Christmas
page 80	1600-OO	90-91 Sponsor
page 82	11622	
page 82	1600-DS	
page 108	1600-DO	
page 166	1600-DO	
checklist, Hostess	11631	None
page 108 page 166	1700-DO 1700-DO	Small Hamper, 90-91 Recruit, 90-91 Sponsor (Superstar),
page 82	1700-DS	Medium Hamper, 90-91 Recruit, 90-91 Sponsor (Superstar),
page 166	4200-PO	13" Measuring
page 166	4100-PO	11" Measuring

Basket	Collection (Year)	Orig.Price	AVG	HIGH
Hanging, 9" Sq. Bottom 9RD x 8.5^H	Retired (80-86)	22.95	40	40
Hanging, 7" Sq. Bottom 7RD x 6.5^H	Retired (80-86)	15.95	70	85
Hanging, 5" Sq. Bottom 5RD x 4.5^H	Retired (80-86)	14.95	37	45
Hanging, Woven Bottom 8.25RD x 7.75^H	Retired (79-86)	14.95	85	100
Harbor 10^L x 8.25^W x 8.25^H	Collectors Club (98)	85.00	107	165
Hartville Basket see **Tour** 8.75^L x 4.75^W x 6.5^H		34.95	50	60
Hartville II Basket see **Tour II** 7^L x 3.5^W x 4.75^H		29.95	—	45
Harvest 16^L x 9^W x 6^H	Hostess (90-92)	54.95	96	122
Harvest (1993) 7^L x 4.75^W x 7.75^H	Shades of Autumn (93)	39.95	101	130
Hearthside 11.75RD x 6.5^H	Hostess (90-92)	59.95	87	130
Heirloom 15^L x 10^W x 7.5^H	Hostess (90-92)	87.95	110	150

KEY:
Values listed are for BASKET ONLY, unless otherwised noted, (-P) = to present

Page in Guide	Form No.	Other Baskets Using Same Form
page 166	4000-PO	9" Measuring, 9" Canister
page 166	3900-PO	90 Bee, Poinsettia, 7" Measuring, 92 Sponsor (Large), Maple Leaf, 97 Perfect Attendance, 7" Canister, Barn Raising
page 166	3800-PO	88 Employee Birthday, Resolution 92 Employee Christmas, Forget-Me-Not, 5" Hanging, 5" Measuring, 92 Recruit, 92 Sponsor (Small), Watch Your Business Bloom, 5" Canister, 99 Recruit
page 166	3700-PO	None
page 42	10677	None
page 190	15661	Tour, 89 Bee, 92 Employee Birthday Sophomore - Senior Recognition, 20th Century, Dresden Basket, Memory, 25th Anniversary (Sm)
page 190	15814	Tour II, 98 Flag Sponsoring, 99 Bee
page 108	3700-AOS	Original Easter, Senior Employee, 90 Bee Speaker
page 176	14303	None
page 108	42000-AOS	None
page 108	500-HOS	88 Bee Speaker, 87 Employee Christmas, Medium Market, 99 Team Excellence, (77-87) Tenth Anniversary, Founder's

Basket	Collection (Year)	Orig.Price	AVG	HIGH
Herb 11.5L x 5W x 3H	Feature (86) Incentive (87-88)	32.90 set N/A	72 80	100 80
High Achiever 12RD x 5.75H	Incentive (95-96)	N/A	**	**
Holiday Cheer 12L x 8W x 4.25H	Christmas (96)	47.95	64	100
Holiday Sleigh 13L x 7.5W x 3FH x 8BH	Feature (97-P)	47.95	90	100
Holly 15L x 8W x 2.25H	Christmas (84)	24.95	325	475
Homecoming 15L x 15W x 7.5H	Holiday Hostess (93) Regular Line, Hostess (99-P)	109.95 99.00	140 99	200 99
Homestead 10RD x 6.25H	Collectors Club (99) Feature (99)	79.00 59.00	— —	— —
Hope Chest 23L x 14W x 11.25H	Regular Line, Hostess (98-P)	189.00	189	360
Horizon of Hope (1995) 5.75L x 3.75W x 3H	Feature (95)	28.95	75	95
Horizon of Hope (1996) 6.75L x 4.75W x 2.25H	Feature (96)	28.95	63	80
Qorizon of Hope (1997) 5.5L x 4W x 4H	Feature (97)	28.95	50	60
Horizon of Hope (1998) 4L x 4W x 5.5H	Feature (98)	31.00	50	75
Horizon of Hope (1999) 6.25L x 5.25W x 3H	Feature (99)	31.00	60	75

KEY:
Values listed are for **BASKET ONLY, unless otherwised noted**, **(-P)** = to present

Page in Guide	Form No.	Other Baskets Using Same Form
page 80	4500-AO	Liberty, Bed, Cracker, Muffin
page 122	4500-	96 Employee Christmas
page 130	unknown	Basket of Plenty, Quilting
page 36	18511^R / 18520^G	None
page 76	16811	Medium Vegetable, Yuletide Traditions
page 34	4600-AZ	Bread (old), Garden
page 100	12084^R / 12092^G	Medium Picnic
checklist, Hostess	13081	
page 44	13871	Associate Homestead Tour
page 76	6609596	
checklist, Hostess	18431	None
page 104	17124	All-Star Trio, Keepsake, Paint the Town, 90 Recruit, Shining Star, Rosemary, Sugar and Spice, Treasure Chest, 90 Sweetheart, 95 Horizon of Hope, 98 Hostess Appreciation, 00 Branch Sales
page 104	15911	None
page 104	18724	Ambrosia, Thanks-A-Million
page 104	10472	None
page 104	14150	None

Basket	Collection[(Year)]	Orig.Price	AVG	HIGH
Hospitality $18.5^L \times 13.5^W \times 5.25^H$	Traditions [(98)]	89.00	**100**	**110**
Hostess Appreciation (94) $8^L \times 4^W \times 2^H$	Feature [(94)]	N/A	**62**	**125**
Hostess Appreciation (96) $5.5^L \times 5.5^W \times 2.5^H$	Feature [(96)]	N/A	**50**	**70**
Hostess Appreciation (98) $5.75^L \times 3.75^W \times 3^H$	Feature [(98)]	29.95	**56**	**85**
Inaugural, (1989) $5^{RD} \times 4.5^H$	Special Event [(89)]	19.89	**271**	**525**
Inaugural, (1993) $5^L \times 5^W \times 4.5^H$	Special Event [(93)]	24.95	**83**	**135**
Inaugural, (1997) $5.5^{RD} \times 3.25^H$	Special Event [(97)]	32.95	**60**	**75**
Ivy $5.5^L \times 5.5^W \times 2.5^H$	Booking [(90-92)] Employee [(91)]	N/A N/A	**52** **90**	**80** **130**
JAM 2000 $5.5^{RD} \times 3.75^H$	Incentive[(00)]	N/A	—	—
Jelly Bean $5.5^{RD} \times 3.75^H$	Easter [(00)]	34.00	—	—
Jingle Bell $8^{RD} \times 6^H$	Christmas [(94)]	47.95	**90**	**125**

KEY:
Values listed are for BASKET ONLY, unless otherwised noted, (-P) = to present

Page in Guide	Form No.	Other Baskets Using Same Form
page 194	10669	None
page 82	unknown	93 Recruit, 93 Sponsor (Small), Lavender, Rose Bud
page 82	unknown	Ivy, 91 Employee Birthday, Friendship
page 82	unknown	All-Star Trio, 89 Employee Birthday, Keepsake, Paint the Town, 00 Branch Sales, Reach for the Stars (Med), Sugar and Spice, 90 Sweetheart, Treasure Chest, 95 Horizon of Hope Rosemary, 98 Hostess Appreciation
page 180	3800-ABRST	88 Employee Birthday, 92 Sponsor (Small), 92 Employee Christmas, Forget-Me-Not, 5" Hanging, 5" Measuring, 92 Recruit, Resolution, Watch Your Business Bloom, 5" Canister, 99 Recruit
page 180	11461	Candy Cane, Violet, Small Peg 96 Recruit, Teaspoon
page 180	15326	None
page 28 page 62	13100-JOS 13100-	91 Employee Birthday, Friendship, 96 Hostess Appreciation
page 122	unknown	Lily of the Valley, Pot of Gold, Jelly Bean
page 60	19488	Lily of the Valley, Pot of Gold, JAM 2000
page 36	17906[R] / 17914[G]	None

Basket	Collection (Year)	Orig.Price	AVG	HIGH
Junior Recognition	Employee (xx-97)	N/A	79	85
8.75^L x 4.75^W x 6.5^H				
Keepsake	Booking (88-90)	16.95	52	85
5.75^L x 3.75^W x 3^H				
Key, Medium	Feature (94)	29.95	37	55
	Heartland (88-97)	26.95	44	60
	Regular Line (79-P)	9.95	32	55
9^L x 5^W x 5^H				
Key, Small	Feature (94)	27.95	40	55
	Heartland (94-97)	21.95	37	50
	Regular Line (79-P)	7.95	26	50
7^L x 5^W x 3.5^H				
Key, Tall	Employee Christmas (91)	N/A	108	140
	Feature (94)	40.95	55	80
	Heartland (88-97)	34.95	54	75
	Holiday Hostess (88)	30.95	92	125
	Regular Line (79-P)	11.95	42	70
	Retired (Natrl) (94)	31.95	58	70
9.5^L x 5^W x 9.5^H				
Laundry, Large	Hostess (86-90)	96.95	242	300
	Retired (79-86)	34.95	268	300
30^L x 20^W x 10.5^H				
Laundry, Medium	Retired (79-83)	31.95	—	150
	J.W. Original	N/A	—	—
28.5^L x 17.75^W x 9.75^H				
Laundry, Small	Holiday Hostess (88)	67.95	240	342
	Retired (79-98)	29.95	194	255
24^L x 17^W x 10^H				
Laurel	Booking (90-92)	N/A	52	70
5.5RD x 3.75^H				

KEY:
Values listed are for BASKET ONLY, unless otherwised noted, (-P) = to present

Page in Guide	Form No.	Other Baskets Using Same Form
page 62	unknown	89 Bee, Dresden Basket, Tour, 92 Employee Birthday, Memory, Sophomore – Senior Recognition, Hartville, 25th Anniversary (Sm), 20th Century
page 28	45000-IO	All-Star Trio, 89 Employee Birthday Paint the Town, 90 Recruiting, Shining Star, Rosemary, Sugar and Spice, 90 Sweetheart, Treasure Chest, 95 Horizon of Hope, 98 Hostess Appreciation, 00 Branch Sales
page 74 page 94 checklist	$15172^R/99^B/81^G$ 11118/1100-ICS 11100/1100-IO	Candle, Collectors Club 97 Renewal, 89 Employee Christmas, 90 Sponsor, 96 Perfect Attendance
page 74 page 94 checklist	$17078^R/51^B/60^G$ 10782 10723/700-IO	Acorn, Basket of Thanks, Tea, Mini Berry, Mini Chore, Mistletoe, Mini Cradle, Tea, Baby Easter, 91 Hostess Easter, 93 Small Easter, 94 Employee Christmas, Kiddie Purse, Star Team, Patriot, 99 Branch Excellence
page 64 page 74 page 94 page 98 checklist page 166	1000- $14672^R/99^B/81^G$ 11061/1000-ICS 1000-IRGS 11053/1000-IO 14630	MBA, Tall Purse, Two-quart, Collectors Club Membership, 91 Employee Christmas
page 108 page 168	2800-O 2800-OO	Large Cradle
page 168 page 140	2700-O unknown	Medium Cradle
page 98 page 168	2600-ORGS 12602 /2600-OO	Family Picnic, Small Cradle
page 28	17000-JOS	Basket 'O Luck

Basket	Collection (Year)	Orig.Price	AVG	HIGH
Lavender 8^L x 4^W x 2^H	Booking (92-99)	22.95	32	53
Liberty 11.5^L x 5^W x 3^H	All-American (93)	29.95	70	95
Lilac 6.5RD x 6.5^H	May (94)	34.95	90	115
Lily of the Valley 5.5RD x 3.75^H	May (93)	28.95	90	115
Little Joy 5^L x 3.75^W x 4.5^H	Feature (99)	38.00	65	80
Loaf, Small 7.5^L x 4.75^W x 2.5^H	Regular Line (99-P)	32.00	32	32
Lots of Luck 4.25^L x 4.25^W x 3^H	Feature (99)	29.00	90	130
Love Letters 8.75^L x 7.75^W x 2.75^H	Sweetheart (99)	44.00	66	95
Love Treasures 13.25^L x 12.5^W x 4.25^H	Sweetheart (99)	68.00	—	—
Magazine 16^L x 8^W x 11^H	Employee (92)	N/A	—	—
	Holiday Hostess (89)	53.95	122	160
	Regular Line(2sw/h) (79-P)	21.95	75	75
	Retired(1sw/h, legs) (79-98)	25.95	87	125
	Retired(1sw/h, legs, no lid) (79-95)	21.95	90	100
Mail 12^L x 8^W x 11.5^H	Hostess (92-96)	79.95	118	140
Maple Leaf 7RD x 6.5^H	Shades of Autumn (96)	40.95	74	90
Market, Large 16^L x 11^W x 9^H	Feature (96-97)	77.95	104	110
	Holiday Hostess (88)	49.95	114	161
	Regular Line(2sw/h) (83-P)	29.95	78	78
	Retired(1st/h) (79-93)	19.95	103	110

KEY:
Values listed are for BASKET ONLY, unless otherwised noted, **(-P)** = to present

Page in Guide	Form No.	Other Baskets Using Same Form
page 30	10138	94 Hostess Appreciation, 93 Recruit 93 Sponsor (Small)
page 18	14541	Bed, Cracker, Herb, Muffin, 96 Employee Christmas
page 144	16209	Bouquet
page 144	15717	Pot of Gold, JAM 2000, Jelly Bean
page 76	19445	None
checklist	12823	None
page 76	18465	None
page 188	12963	None
page 188	13084	None
page 62	12106	Bread & Milk, 25th Anniversary (Lg)
page 98	2100-CGRS	
checklist	12106/2100-CO	
page 168	12114/2100-W	
page 168	12122/2100-U	
page 108	10600	None
page 176	13935	7" Measuring, 90 Bee, Poinsettia, 92 Sponsor (Large), 7" Hanging, 7" Canister, 97 Perfect Attendance, Barn Raising
page 76	16641^R/24^B/32^G	Rectangular Sewing, 99 Director Sales & Sponsoring Excellence
page 98	600-ARGS	
checklist	10634/600-CO	
page 168	10626/600-AO	

Basket	Collection (Year)	Orig.Price	AVG	HIGH
Market, Medium	Employee Christmas (87)	N/A	248	310
	Feature (Natrl) (87)	41.95	—	—
	Feature (Natrl) (98)	53.95	—	—
	Heartland (89-97)	43.95	74	90
	J.W. Collection (83)	32.95	1346	1800
	J.W. Originals	N/A	—	—
	Regular Line (2sw/h) (83-P)	24.95	68	70
15L x 10W x 7.5H	Retired (1st/h) (79-98)	16.95	56	70
Market, Miniature 5.75L x 4W x 3H	Collectors Club (96)	125.00	340	400
Market, Small	All-American (92)	39.95	100	140
	Regular Line(2sw/h)(93-P)	45.95	53	53
15L x 9.5W x 5.5H	Retired(1st/h)(79-93)	14.95	101	140
Master Employee 12.5RD x 13.5H	Employee (xx-97)	N/A	232	275
Master Employee2 8RD x 6.5H	Employee (97-P)	N/A	—	—
MBA Basket 9.5L x 5W x 9.5H	Incentive (88-P)	N/A	198	220
Meadow Blossoms Pottery	Incentive (85)	N/A	**	**
Measuring, 13"	Holiday Hostess (90)	69.95	123	155
	Incentive, N.Sales (98)	N/A	—	—
	Regular Line (00-P)	89.00	89	89
13RD x 12.5H	Retired (79-98)	20.95	88	135
Measuring, 11" 11RD x 10.5H	Incentive, N.Sales (94-98)	N/A	**	**
	Retired (79-98)	17.95	78	100
Measuring, 9"	Incentive, N.Sales (94-98)	N/A	**	**
	Regular Line (00-P)	56.00	56	56
9RD x 8.5H	Retired (79-98)	13.95	65	81
Measuring, 7"	Incentive, N.Sales (94-98)	N/A	**	**
	Regular Line (00-P)	44.00	44	44
7RD x 6.5H	Retired (79-98)	10.95	54	65

KEY:
Values listed are for BASKET ONLY, unless otherwised noted, (-P) = to present

age in Guide	Form No.	Other Baskets Using Same Form
page 64	500	88 Bee Speaker, Heirloom,
page 80	500-	77-87 Tenth Anniversary,
page 82	10588	87 Employee Christmas, 99 Team
page 94	10545/500-ACS	Excellence, Founder's
page 136	500-AT	
page 140	unknown	
checklist	10537	
page 168	10529/500-AO	
page 40	15024/150240	None
page 16	10707	Welcome Home, 99 Regional
checklist	10430/400-CO	Sales & Sponsoring Excellence
page 168	10421/400-AO	
page 62	1900-	Banker's Waste, Waste (Inverted, Small Round) , Tree-Trimming
page 62	unknown	Medium Fruit
page 124	1000-FO	91 Employee Christmas, Tall Key, Tall Purse, Two-Quart, Growing Strong Together, Membership
page 120	unknown	None
page 98	4200-CGRS	13" Hanging
page 120	unknown	
checklist	19968	
page 168	14206/4200-B	
page 118, 120	unknown	11" Hanging
page 168	14109/4100-B	
page 118, 120	unknown	9" Hanging, 9" Canister
checklist	19763	
page 168	14001/4000-B	
page 118, 120	unknown	90 Bee, Maple Leaf, Poinsettia,
checklist	19861	92 Sponsor (Large), 7" Hanging,
page 168	13901/3900-B	97 Perfect Attendance, 7" Canister, Barn Raising

Basket	Collection (Year)	Orig.Price	AVG	HIGH
Measuring, 5"	Booking (xx-84)	N/A	30	35
	Employee Birthday (88)	N/A	77	105
	Employee Christmas (92)	N/A	94	120
	Incentive, N.Sales (94-98)	N/A	**	**
5RD x 4.5H	Retired (79-98)	7.95	44	68
Membership	Collectors Club (95-96)	75.00	105	178
	Collectors Club (97-P)	75.00	—	—
9.5L x 5W x 9.5H				
Memory	Christmas (89)	34.95	94	135
	Feature (88-89)	39.95	132	165
8.75L x 4.75W x 6.5H				
Mistletoe	Christmas (87)	19.95	100	155
7L x 5W x 3.5H				
Morning Glory 7.5L x 7.5W x 4.75H	May (00)	43.00	—	—
Mother's Day (1992) 10.5L x 10.5W x 4.5H	Mother's Day (92)	34.95	80	125
Mother's Day (1993) 8.5L x 8W x 6H	Mother's Day (93)	44.95	80	115
Mother's Day (1994) 6.75L x 9.25W x 3.75H	Mother's Day (94)	37.95	72	95
Muffin 11.5L x 5W x 3H	Heartland (90-P)	25.95	31	40
National High Sales Level 1 5RD x 4.5H	Incentive (99-P)	N/A	**	**
National Sponsoring Large unknown	Incentive (99-P)	N/A	**	**

KEY:
Values listed are for BASKET ONLY, unless otherwised noted, (-P) = to prese

Page in Guide	Form No.	Other Baskets Using Same Form
Page 28	3800-BO	89 Inaugural, Forget-Me-Not,
Page 62	3800-	5" Hanging, 92 Recruit, Resolution,
Page 64	3800-	92 Sponsor (Small), 5" Canister,
Page 118, 120	unknown	Watch Your Business Bloom,
Page 168	13803/3800-B	99 Recruit
Page 40	62839	91 Employee Christmas, MBA,
Page 40	62839	Tall Purse, Two-Quart, Tall Key,
		Growing Strong Together
Page 34	5600-BRST/BGST	89 Bee, Dresden Basket, Hartville,
Page 74	5600-BBS	Tour, 92 Employee Birthday,
		Sophomore - Senior Recognition,
		25th Anniversary(Sm), 20th Century
Page 34	700-ART/AGT	Acorn, Basket of Thanks, Tea, Mini
		Berry, Mini Chore, Patriot, Mini Cradle,
		Baby Easter, 91 Hostess Easter, Small
		Key, 93 Small Easter, 94 Employee
		Christmas, Kiddie Purse, Star Team, 99
		Branch Excellence
Page 144	18899	None
Page 148	110-CPS	None
Page 148	12904	None
Page 148	16004	None
Checklist, HL	14516/4500-JCS	Liberty, Bed, Cracker, Herb,
		96 Employee Christmas
Page 120	unknown	None
Page 114	unknown	None

Basket	Collection(Year)	Orig.Price	AVG	HIGH
National Sponsoring Medium unknown	Incentive(99-P)	N/A	**	**
National Sponsoring Small 14^L x 9^W x 4.25^H	Incentive(99-P)	N/A	**	**
Newspaper 15.75^L x 10.5^W x 2.75^H	Regular Line(99-P)	124.00	124	124
9 x 13 Basket 9.5^L x 14.5^W x 2.75^H	Regular Line(99-P)	49.00	49	49
Note Pal 7.5^L x 5.5^W x 2^{FH} x 3.5^{BH}	Regular Line(00-P)	32.00	32	32
Odds & Ends 18.75^L x 9^W x 12.75^{FH} x 5.25^{BH}	Regular Line, Hostess(95-P)	149.95	154	200
Oregano 5^L x 3^W x 3.5^H	Regular Line, Booking(98-P)	27.00	27	38
Original Easter 16^L x 9^W x 6^H	J.W. Collection (93)	65.95	165	225
Our Business is Show Busines (small) see **Associate Producer**				
Our Business is Show Busines (medium) see **Show Star**				
Our Business is Show Busines (large) see **Best Supporting Role**				
Over the Rainbow (small) see **Gold Nugget**				
Over the Rainbow (medium) see **Pot of Gold**				
Over the Rainbow (large) see **Gold Rush**				
Paint the Town	Incentive (93)	N/A	100	150

5.75^L x 3.75^W x 3^H

KEY:
Values listed are for **BASKET ONLY, unless otherwised noted**, (**-P**) = to prese...

Page in Guide	Form No.	Other Baskets Using Same Form
page 114	unknown	None
page 114	unknown	None
checklist	17329	None
checklist	15491	None
checklist	11606	Paper
checklist, Hostess	18902	None
checklist, Booking	13145	None
page 136	13722	Harvest, Senior Employee, 90 Bee Speaker
page 130	unknown	None
page 130	unknown	Button, Stitching, Rings & Things, Cookie, 93 Employee Christmas
page 130	unknown	Basket of Love, 98 Renewal
page 128	unknown	None
page 128	unknown	Lily of the Valley, Jelly Bean, JAM 2000
page 128	unknown	None
page 128	45000-	All-Star Trio, 89 Employee Birthday, Keepsake, 90 Recruit, Shining Star, Rosemary, Sugar and Spice, 90 Sweetheart, Treasure Chest, 95 Horizon of Hope, 98 Hostess Appreciation, 00 Branch Sales

Basket	Collection (Year)	Orig.Price	AVG	HIGH
Pansy 7RD x 4.5^H	May $^{(92)}$	29.95	94	135
Pantry	Feature $^{(85)}$	21.95	62	70
	Feature $^{(96-97)}$	46.95	59	80
	Heartland $^{(98-P)}$	53.00	53	53
	Regular Line $^{(86-P)}$	21.95	45	65
14^L x 9^W x 4.5^H	Woven Traditions $^{(98-P)}$	53.00	53	53
Paper	Father's Day $^{(92)}$	23.95	105	130
	Incentive $^{(92-98)}$	N/A	65	75
	Incentive $^{(99-00)}$	N/A	—	—
7.5^L x 5.5^W x 2^{FH} x 3.5^{BH}				
Paper Tray **(Bottom)** 12^L x 14.5^W x 3^H	Regular Line $^{(99-P)}$	50.00	50	50
Paper Tray **(Tapered)**	Incentive $^{(99-00)}$	N/A	—	—
	Regular Line $^{(99-P)}$	55.00	55	55
12^L x 14.5^W x 3^{FH} x 5.5^{BH}				
Parsley 6^L x 4.5^W x 2.5^H	Regular Line, Booking $^{(99-P)}$	27.00	27	35
Patriot	All-American $^{(97)}$	32.95	55	70
7^L x 5^W x 3.5^H				
Peg, Large	Bee $^{(88)}$	N/A	—	—
	Heartland $^{(89-97)}$	28.95	52	70
	Mother's Day $^{(87)}$	26.95	119	160
	Retired $^{(85-99)}$	19.95	52	75
6.5^L x 6.5^W x 8^H	Woven Traditions $^{(95-99)}$	39.95	48	65
Peg, Medium	Bee $^{(88)}$	N/A	—	—
	Feature (shaker) $^{(84)}$	14.95	45	60
5.5^L x 5.5^W x 6^H	Retired $^{(85-99)}$	17.95	35	48
Peg, Small	Bee $^{(88)}$	N/A	—	—
	Retired $^{(85-99)}$	15.95	38	55
5^L x 5^W x 4.5^H				

KEY:
Values listed are for **BASKET ONLY**, unless otherwised noted, **(-P)** = to present

Page in Guide	Form No.	Other Baskets Using Same Form
page 144	10006	95 Perfect Attendance
page 78	2300-JO	Advisor Recognition, 92 Bee,
page 74	16446^R/20^B/38^G	90 Employee Christmas, Tray,
checklist, HL	13951	Small Gathering
checklist	12327/ 2300-JO	
checklist, WT	13854	
page 70	16000	Note Pal
page 122	16000	
page 122	16000	
checklist	18961	None
page 122	19062	None
checklist	19062	
checklist, Booking	12882	None
page 18	10651	Acorn, Basket of Thanks, Mini Berry, Mini Chore, Mistletoe, Mini Cradle, Baby Easter, 91 Hostess Easter, 93 Small Easter, Star Team, 94 Employee Christmas, Kiddie Purse, Small Key, Tea, 99 Branch Excellence
page 22	11000-AO	Medium Spoon, 94 Bee, 96 Large
page 94	11177/11000-ACS	Sponsor, 98 Perfect Attendance
page 148	11000-BPS	
page 170	11151 /11000-AO	
page 206	11142	
page 22	10000-AO	Bittersweet, Carry Along, Small
page 78	10000-AO	Spoon, 96 Sponsor, 97 Bee
page 170	11070 /10000-AO	Shaker Peg
page 22	14000-AO	93 Inaugural, Candy Cane, Violet
page 170	11452 /14000-ART	96 Recruit, Teaspoon

Basket	Collection (Year)	Orig.Price	AVG	HIGH
Pen Pal 4RD x 4.25^H	Regular Line (00-P)	29.00	**29**	**29**
Pencil 4RD x 4.25^H	Father's Day (92)	20.95	**110**	**170**
	Incentive (92-98)	N/A	**74**	**90**
	Incentive (99-00)	N/A	—	—
Peppermint 5.5^{RD} x 2.75^H	Tree-Trimming (99)	45.00	**50**	**55**
Perfect Attendance (1994) 6.5^{RD} x 5^H	Employee (94)	N/A	**433**	**475**
Perfect Attendance (1995) 7RD x 4.5^H	Employee (95)	N/A	**425**	**475**
Perfect Attendance (1996) 9^L x 5^W x 5^H	Employee (96)	N/A	**400**	**425**
Perfect Attendance (1997) 7RD x 6.5^H	Employee (97)	N/A	--	—
Perfect Attendance (1998) 6.5^L x 6.5^W x 8^H	Employee (98)	N/A	--	—
Perfect Attendance (1999) 11^L x 8^W x 5.5^H	Employee (99)	N/A	--	—
Personal Organizer 14^L x 6^W x 3^H	Father's Day (97)	39.95	**66**	**80**
Petunia 9.5^{RD} x 5^H	May (97)	45.95	**80**	**110**
Picnic, Family 24^L x 17^W x 10^H	Retired (83-86)	98.95	**326**	**390**

KEY:
Values listed are for **BASKET ONLY**, unless otherwised noted, **(-P)** = to present

Page in Guide	Form No.	Other Baskets Using Same Form
checklist	11541	Pencil
page 70	15000	Pen Pal
page 122	15000-	
page 122	15000-	
page 196	19364^R/16837^G	None
page 64	unknown	Small Fruit, Senior Employee2
page 64	unknown	Pansy
page 64	unknown	Candle, 90 Sponsor, Medium Key, 97 Collectors Club Renewal, 89 Employee Christmas
page 64	unknown	90 Bee, Maple Leaf, Poinsettia, 92 Sponsor (Large), 7" Hanging, 7" Canister, 7" Measuring, Barn Raising
page 64	unknown	Large Peg, Medium Spoon, 94 Bee, 96 Sponsor
page 64	unknown	Spring, Bob & Dolores Hope, 91-P Bee Speaker, Sparkler, Boo, Red Pottery Thank You, 91 Customer Easter, Medium Purse, Ohio Statehouse, Sparkler
page 70	13137	Flower Pot (Small)
page 144	12947	90 Large Easter
page 170	2600-HO	Small Laundry, Small Cradle

Basket	Collection (Year)	Orig.Price	AVG	HIGH
Picnic, Family Collectors Club 20^L x 14^W x 9.5^H	Collectors Club (99)	255.00	288	300
Picnic, Gourmet 13.25^L x 11.25^W x 9^H	Hostess (92-95)	99.95	130	170
Picnic, Large 17^L x 14^W x 11^H	All-American (87)	64.95	255	365
	Feature (Natrl) (99)	89.00	—	—
	Regular Line (79-P)	29.95	106	130
Picnic, Medium 15^L x 15^W x 7.5^H	Retired (79-84)	26.95	195	240
Picnic, Oak Lid 12^L x 12^W x 6^H	Feature (82)	N/A	536	600
Picnic Pal 9.5^L x 9.5^W x 2.75^H	Good Ol' Summertime (98)	37.00	50	60
Picnic, Small 12^L x 12^W x 6^H	All-American (88)	65.95	144	215
	Feature (Natrl) (00)	59.00	—	—
	Regular Line (79-P)	21.95	71	82
Picture Perfect 7.25^L x 4^W x 4.5^H	Sweetheart (98)	39.00	48	67
Pie 12^L x 12^W x 4^H	All-American (98)	55.00	75	105
	Easter (87)	28.95	233	375
	Feature (85)	19.95	—	50
	Feature (Natrl) (99)	39.00	41	60
	Regular Line (86-P)	22.95	47	57
	Shades of Autumn (90)	31.95	95	225
	Woven Tradition (94)	37.95	65	90
Pie, Crisco 12^L x 12^W x 6^H	Crisco® (91)	79.95	355	500
Pinecone 13RD x 6.25^H	Holiday Hostess (99)	99.00	—	—
Planter, Large Fern 13RD x 8.5^H	Feature(feet) (88)	42.95	140	140
	Retired(feet) (82-86)	27.95	123	180
	Retired(13") (79-86)	23.95	121	200
	Retired(20") (79-86)	26.95	113	130

KEY:
Values listed are for BASKET ONLY, unless otherwised noted, (-P) = to present

Page in Guide	Form No.	Other Baskets Using Same Form
page 44	13561	None
page 108	10413	Precious Treasures
page 16 page 84 checklist	300-HBRS 19755 10324 /300-HO	Getaway
page 170	200-H	Homecoming
page 78	unknown	Cake, Crisco Pie, 88 Employee Christmas, Small Picnic
page 92	18643	8 x 8 Basket
page 16 page 86 checklist	100-HBRS 18040 10324 /300-HO	Cake, Crisco Pie, 88 Employee Christmas, Oak Lid Picnic
page 188	17523^R/16250^B 16357^G/16454^P/16551^C	None
page 18 page 56 page 84 page 78 checklist page 176 page 206	12289 2200-AX 2200-AO 19941 12203 /2200-AO 2200-AGUBS 12211	Director Sales Excellence, Director Sponsoring Excellence
page 74	100-DBRS	Cake, 88 Employee Christmas, Small Picnic, Oak Lid Picnic
page 100	15253^R/15164^G	None
page 80 page 170 page 170 page 170	3200-RO 3200-RO 3200-SO 3200-TO	Sewing (Round)

Basket	Collection (Year)	Orig.Price	AVG	HIGH
Planter, Patio 10RD x 5.5^{H}	Feature (84)	21.95	90	135
Planter, Sleeve 31.5^{RD} x 18^{H}	Incentive (91)	N/A	445	500
	Incentive (25th) (98)	N/A	—	—
Planter, Small Fern 8.5^{RD} x 7.5^{H}	Feature(feet) (88)	35.95	125	140
	Retired(feet) (82-86)	21.95	97	175
	Retired(13") (79-86)	21.95	115	130
	Retired(20") (79-86)	24.95	138	150
Poinsettia 7RD x 6.5^{H}	Christmas (88)	26.95	99	155
Pool 22^{L} x 14.5^{W} x 6.25^{W}	J.W. Originals	N/A	—	—
Popcorn 10.5^{RD} x 5^{H}	Christmas (99)	59.00	—	—
Pot of Gold 5.5^{RD} x 3.75^{H}	Incentive (94)	N/A	91	160
Potpourri 5^{L} x 5^{W} x 2.5^{H}	Booking (85-90)	3.00	45	95
	Employee Birthday (90)	N/A	75	100
	Mother's Day (91)	21.95	58	80
Precious Treasures 13.25^{L} x 11.25^{W} x 9^{H}	Sweetheart (95)	89.95	168	200
Pumpkin 9.25^{RD} x 7.25^{H}	Pumpkin (95)	47.95	95	150
Pumpkin, Large 11.25^{RD} x 9^{H}	Pumpkin (97)	117.95	145	225 C
Pumpkin, Little 5.75^{RD} x 4.25^{H}	Pumpkin (97)	34.95	65	85
Pumpkin, Small 7.25^{RD} x 5.25^{H}	Pumpkin (96)	40.95	77	110

KEY:
Values listed are for **BASKET ONLY**, unless otherwised noted, **(-P)** = to present

Page in Guide	Form No.	Other Baskets Using Same Form
page 78	6000-R	None
page 122	unknown	None
page 122	unknown	
page 80	2900-RO	None
page 170	2900-RO	
page 170	2900-SO	
page 170	2900-TO	
page 34	3900-BRST/BGST	90 Bee, 7" Hanging, 7" Measuring, 92 Sponsor (Large), Maple Leaf, 97 Perfect Attendance, 7" Canister, Barn Raising
page 140	unknown	None
page 36	15156^R/15351^G	None
page 128	unknown	Lily of the Valley, Jelly Bean, JAM 2000
page 28	13000-AO	88-89 Recruit, 90 Employee Birthday, 93 Regional Sponsored Award, Sweet Basil, 93 Sweetheart, Shamrock
page 62	13000-	
page 148	13000-APS	
page 186	10456	Gourmet Picnic
page 162	19402	None
page 162	16039	None
page 162	16021	None
page 162	16012	None

Basket	Collection(Year)	Orig.Price	AVG	HIGH
Purse, Kiddie	Feature (Natrl) (98)	27.95	—	—
	Regular Line (79-P)	12.95	36	63
	Retired(Natrl) (94)	28.95	51	60
7^L x 5^W x 3.5^H				
Purse, Medium	Retired(1sw/h) (79-97)	16.95	58	75
	Retired(split lid) (82-86)	24.95	123	255
11^L x 8^W x 5.5^H				
Purse, Shoulder 9.5^L x 5.75^W x 7^H	Retired (96-99)	84.95	105	140
Purse, Small	Heartland (88-98)	36.95	52	80
	Mother's Day (91)	34.95	95	120
9.5^L x 6^W x 6^H	Retired (79-99)	14.95	47	54
Purse, Tall	Retired (79-89)	27.95	74	105
9.5^L x 5^W x 9.5^H				
Quilting 12RD x 5.75^H	All-American (89)	46.95	140	210
Reach for the Stars(Small) see **Star Bound** 4.75^L x 3.75^W x 2.25^H				
Reach for the Stars(Medium) see **Shining Star** 5.75^L x 3.75^W x 3^H				
Reach for the Stars(Large) see **Star Team** 7^L x 5^W x 3.5^H				
Recipe	Heartland (98-P)	39.00	40	40
	Regular Line (96-P)	29.95	34	45
	Regular Line (Natrl) (99-P)	25.00	34	45
	Shades of Autumn (94)	29.95	90	125
	Woven Tradition (98-P)	39.00	40	40
8^L x 5.5^W x 4.5^{FH} x 6^{BH}				

KEY:
Values listed are for BASKET ONLY, unless otherwised noted, (-P) = to present

Page in Guide	Form No.	Other Baskets Using Same Form
page 82 checklist page 170	10898 10731 / 700-EO 17019	Acorn, Basket of Thanks, Tea, Mini Berry, Mini Chore, Mistletoe, Mini Cradle, Baby Easter, Patriot, 91 Hostess Easter, 93 Small Easter, Small Key, 94 Employee Christmas, Star Team, 99 Branch Excellence
page 170 page 170	10901 / 900-E 900-QO	91-P Bee Speaker, Bob and Dolores Hope, Boo Basket, 91 Customer Easter, Red Pottery Thank You, Spring, 96 Statehouse, Sparkler
page 170	18210	None
page 94 page 148 page 270	10839/800-ECS 800-EPS 10821/800-EO	Season's Greetings, 94 Regional Sponsored, 99 Branch Sponsoring Excellence
page 170	1000-EO	91 Employee Christmas, MBA, Tall Key, Two-Quart, Growing Strong Together, Membership
page 16	54000-ABRS	Basket of Plenty, High Achiever
page 130	unknown	Business Card
page 130	unknown	All-Star Trio, 89 Employee Birthday, Keepsake, Paint the Town, 00 Branch Sales, Rosemary, Sugar and Spice, 90 Sweetheart, Treasure Chest, 95 Horizon of Hope, 98 H.Appreciation
page 130	unknown	Acorn, Basket of Thanks, Tea, Mini Berry, Mini Chore, Mistletoe, Mini Cradle, Baby Easter, Patriot, 91 Hostess Easter, 93 Small Easter, 94 Employee Christmas, Kiddie Purse, Small Key, 99 Branch Excellence
checklist, HL checklist, Hostess checklist page 176 checklist, WT	10596 17418 19542 17400 10499	None

Basket	Collection[(Year)]	Orig.Price	AVG	HIGH
Recruit (1999) 5.5[RD] x 4.5[H]	Incentive [(99)]	N/A	146	200
Recruit "All-Star" 8[L] x 4[W] x 2[H]	Incentive [(93)]	N/A	138	200
Recruit "Flying High with Longaberger" 5RD x 4.5[H]	Incentive [(92)]	N/A	119	125
Recruit "Pegged for Success" 5[L] x 5[W] x 4.5[H]	Incentive [(96)]	N/A	102	135
Recruit "Rising Star" 12[L] x 12.25[W] x 16.25[H]	Incentive [(90-91)]	N/A	175	175
Recruit "Share the Tradition" 5[L] x 5[W] x 2.5[H]	Incentive [(88-89)]	N/A	170	220
Recruit "Together–We're Growing" 5.75[L] x 3.75[W] x 3[H]	Incentive [(90)]	N/A	169	180
Red Pottery Thank You 11[L] x 8[W] x 5.5[H]	Feature [(93)]	N/A	126	150
Regional Basket 15.75[L] x 6.5[W] x 11[H]	Incentive [(88-P)]	N/A	250	250
Regional Sales (00) 9.25[L] x 5[W] x 6.5[H]	Incentive [(00)]	N/A	—	—

KEY:
Values listed are for **BASKET ONLY**, unless otherwised noted, **(-P)** = to present

Page in Guide	Form No.	Other Baskets Using Same Form
page 114	unknown	88 Employee Birthday, 89 Inaugural, Forget-Me-Not, 5" Measuring, 92 Employee Christmas, 5" Hanging, Resolution, 92 Sponsor (Small), 5" Canister, Watch Your Business Bloom, 92 Recruit (Flying High)
page 112	16101	94 Hostess Appreciation, Rose Bud 93 Sponsor (Small), Lavender
page 112	10154	88 Employee Birthday, 89 Inaugural Forget-Me-Not, 5" Measuring, 92 Employee Christmas, 5" Hanging, Resolution, 92 Sponsor (Small), 5" Canister, Watch Your Business Bloom, 99 Recruit
page 112	unknown	93 Inaugural, Candy Cane, Violet, Small Peg, Teaspoon
page 112	1700-DST	Medium Hamper, Small Hamper, 90-91 Sponsor (Superstar)
page 112	13000-BBRS	90 Employee Birthday, 93 Regional Sponsored Award, 93 Sweetheart, Potpourri, Shamrock, Sweet Basil, Tee
page 112	45000-ABRST	All-Star Trio, 89 Employee, Birthday, Keepsake, Paint the Town, Shining Star, Rosemary, Sugar and Spice, 90 Sweetheart, Treasure Chest, 95 Horizon of Hope, 00 Branch Sales
page 74	190xx	91- P Bee Speaker, Bob & Dolores Hope, Boo Basket, 91 Customer Easter, Medium Purse, Spring, 96 Statehouse, Sparkler
page 124	unknown	Branch Basket, Director Basket
page 128	unknown	None

Basket	Collection (Year)	Orig.Price	AVG	HIGH
Regional Sales Excellence (98) 8.5^L x 8.5^W x 5^H	Incentive (98)	N/A	150	170
Regional Sales Excellence (99) 15^L x 9.5^W x 5.5^H	Incentive (99)	N/A	—	150
Regional Sponsored (1991) 10^L x 6^W x 4^H	Incentive (91)	N/A	188	225
Regional Sponsored (1992) 8.5^L x 5^W x 3.5^H	Incentive (92)	N/A	195	275
Regional Sponsored (1993) 5^L x 5^W x 2.5^H	Incentive (93)	N/A	187	275
Regional Sponsored (1994) 9.5^L x 6^W x 6^H	Incentive (94)	N/A	226	250
Regional Sponsored (1995) 7.5^L x 7.5^W x 3.5^H	Incentive (95)	N/A	234	300
Regional Sponsored (1996) 10RD x 4^H	Incentive (96)	N/A	190	210
Regional Sponsoring (00) 9.25^L x 5^W x 6.5^H	Incentive (00)	N/A	—	—
Regional Sponsoring Excellence (98) 4.25^L x 4.25^W x 3^H	Incentive (98)	N/A	—	127
Regional Sponsoring Excellence (99) 15^L x 9.5^W x 5.5^H	Incentive (99)	N/A	—	—
Remembrance 10.5^L x 9^W x 8^H	Feature (96-97)	99.95	140	160
	Hostess (90-92)	79.95	150	200

KEY:
Values listed are for BASKET ONLY, unless otherwised noted, (-P) = to present

Page in Guide	Form No.	Other Baskets Using Same Form
page 126	unknown	Large Berry, 91 Bee, 88-89 Sponsor, 96 Bee
page 128	unknown	Welcome Home, Small Market, 99 Regional Sponsoring Excellence
page 126	3400-	Small Chore, 93 Lg Easter, 95 Bee 88 Sm Easter, Gingerbread, $500 Million, Woven Memories
page 126	33000-	Be Mine, Small Oval, 93 Sponsor (Large), 97 Small Easter, Rose Petal
page 126	11321	Sweet Basil, 90 Employee Birthday, Shamrock, 93 Sweetheart, 88-89 Recruit, Potpourri, Tee
page 126	800-	Season's Greetings, Small Purse, 99 Branch Sponsoring Excellence
page 126	1400-	Medium Berry
page 126	500-	Darning, Crisco Cookie, Daisy 89 Easter
page 128	unknown	None
page 126	unknown	Sweet Sentiments
page 128	unknown	Welcome Home, Small Market, 99 Regional Sales Excellence
page 76	16748^R/21^B/30^G	Weekender, Top Performer
page 108	200-YOS	Beachcomber

Basket	Collection (Year)	Orig.Price	AVG	HIGH
Renewal (1997) $9^L \times 5^W \times 5^H$	Collectors Club (97)	39.95	77	105
Renewal (1998) $8.5^{RD} \times 4^H$	Collectors Club (98)	44.95	68	95
Renewal (1999) $6.75^L \times 5.75^W \times 4.75^H$	Collectors Club (99)	42.00	50	57
Renewal (2000) $6.75^L \times 5.25^W \times 3.25^H$	Collectors Club (00)	44.00	—	—
Resolution $5^{RD} \times 4.5^H$	Feature (87)	16.95	90	135
Rings & Things $7^{RD} \times 3^H$	Mother's Day (97)	34.00	—	—
Rose $14.5^L \times 7.5^W \times 3.75^H$	May (91)	29.95	200	250
Rose Bud $8^L \times 4^W \times 2^H$	Incentive (97)	N/A	155	200
Rose Garden $12^L \times 7^W \times 4.5^H$	Incentive (97)	N/A	108	127
Rose Petal $8.5^L \times 5^W \times 3.5^H$	Incentive (97)	N/A	121	130
Rosemary $5.75^L \times 3.75^W \times 3^H$	Booking (90-92)	N/A	57	78

KEY:
Values listed are for BASKET ONLY, unless otherwised noted, (-P) = to presen

Page in Guide	Form No.	Other Baskets Using Same Form
page 40	105702	Candle, 89 Employee Christmas, 90 Sponsor, Medium Key, 96 Perfect Attendance
page 42	13340	Basket of Love, Best Supporting Role
page 42	12998	None
page 44	18783	None
page 74	3800-ABS	88 Employee Birthday, 89 Inaugural, 92 Employee Christmas, Forget-Me-Not, 5" Hanging, 5" Measuring, 92 Recruit, 92 Sponsor (Small), Watch Your Business Bloom, 99 Recruit
page 150	10383	Button, Stitching, Cookie, Show Star 93 Employee Christmas
page 144	4700-CSS	Bakery, Bread (new), Breakfast, Crisco Baking
page 130	unknown	Lavender, 94 Hostess Appreciation 93 Recruit, 93 Sponsor (Small)
page 126	unknown	97 Large Easter
page 130	unknown	Be Mine, 93 Sponsor (All-Star), 92 Regional Sponsored Award, 97 Small Easter, Small Oval
page 28	45000-JOS	All-Star Trio, 89 Employee Birthday, Keepsake, Paint the Town, 90 Recruit, Reach for the Stars (Med.), Sugar and Spice, 90 Sweetheart, Treasure Chest, 95 Horizon of Hope, 98 H.Appreciation, 00 Branch Sales

Basket	Collection (Year)	Orig.Price	AVG	HIGH
Santa's Little Helper 5.75^L x 3.75^W x 3.5^H	Feature (99)	30.00	—	—
Seashell 7.75^L x 5.75^W x 5^H	Good Ol' Summertime (99)	39.00	60	85
Season's Greetings 9.5^L x 6^W x 6^H	Christmas (92)	44.95	79	125
Senior Employee 16^L x 9^W x 6^H	Employee (xx-97)	N/A	92	125
Senior Employee2 6.5^{RD} x 5^H	Employee (97-P)	N/A	—	—
Senior Recognition 8.75^L x 4.75^W x 6.5^H	Employee (xx-97)	N/A	85	125
Serving Tray 20^L x 14^W x 3.75^H	All-American (00)	98.00	—	—
	Collectors Club (99)	99.00	—	—
	Regular Line, Hostess (95-P)	74.95	88	100
Serving Tray, Small 11.5^L x 15.5^W x 3.75^H	Collectors Club (96)	69.95	150	200
Sewing, Rectangular 16^L x 11^W x 9^H	Retired (78-83)	26.95	381	400
Sewing, Round 13RD x 8.5^H	Feature (no stand) (85, 87)	37.95	207	218
	Hostess (95-00)	89.95	—	—
	Retired, (no stand) (78-86)	29.95	194	240
	Retired, (stand) (78-86)	29.95	217	300
Shaker Taker 7.5^L x 3.75^W x 2.75^H	Good Ol' Summertime (00)	39.00	—	—
Shamrock 5^L x 5^W x 2.5^H	Feature (90)	19.95	125	185
Shining Star 5.75^L x 3.75^W x 3^H	Incentive (95)	N/A	185	300

KEY:
Values listed are for BASKET ONLY, unless otherwised noted, (-P) = to present

Page in Guide	Form No.	Other Baskets Using Same Form
page 76	19721	None
page 92	15296	None
page 34	10316^R / 10219^G	Small Purse, 94 Regional Sponsored, 99 Branch Sponsoring Excellence
page 62	unknown	Original Easter, Harvest, 90 Bee Speaker
page 62	unknown	Small Fruit, 94 Perfect Attendance
page 62	unknown	89 Bee, 92 Employee Birthday, Sophomore & Junior Recognition, Memory, 25th Anniversary (Sm), 20th Century, Tour
page 18	15849	None
page 42	18091	
checklist, Hostess	60011	
page 40	12629	None
page 172	600-F	Large Market, 99 Director Sales & Sponsoring Excellence
page 78	3200-EO	Planter (Large Fern)
page 110	13234	
page 172	3200-NO	
page 172	3200-NO	
page 92	17469	None
page 74	13000-HGS	90 Employee Birthday, Sweet Basil, 93 Sweetheart, Potpourri, 93 Regional Sponsored Award, 88-89 Recruit, Tee
page 130	unknown	All-Star Trio, 89 Employee Birthday, Keepsake, Paint the Town, 90 Recruit, Sugar & Spice, Treasure Chest, Rosemary, 90 Sweetheart, 95 Horizon of Hope, 98 H.Appreciation, 00 Branch Sales

KEY: In blue = Not pictured in the Guide. **S** = Stained, **U** = Unstained
HL = Heartland® Collection, **WT** = Woven Traditions®, **R** = Red, **G** = Green

Basket	Collection (Year)	Orig.Price	AVG	HIGH
Show Star 7RD x 3^H	Incentive (96)	N/A	118	160
Sleeve, Sunroom 24.5^L x 20^W x 14^H	Regular Line, Hostess (99-P)	210.00	210	210
Sleigh Bell 16.5^{RD} x 11.5^H	Holiday Hostess (94)	139.95	182	250
Small Oval 8.5^L x 5^W x 3.5^H	Mother's Day (90)	28.95	63	100
Snapdragon 7.5^{RD} x 9.25^H	May (98)	47.00	70	85
Snowflake, Large 14^L x 12.75^W x 11.5^H	Holiday Hostess (97)	129.95	140	185
Snowflake, Small 10^L x 9.25^W x 6.5^H	Christmas (97)	49.95	70	90
Sophomore Recognition 8.75^L x 4.75^W x 6.5^H	Employee (xx-97)	N/A	67	75
Spare Change 6.5^L x 6.5^W x 3^H	Father's Day (91)	21.95	105	140
Sparkler 11^L x 8^W x 5.5^H	All-American (00)	48.00	--	—
Sponsor, Large "All-Star" 8.5^L x 5^W x 3.5^H	Incentive (93)	N/A	130	175
Sponsor, Small "All-Star" 8^L x 4^W x 2^H	Incentive (93)	N/A	113	160
Sponsor, Large **"Flying High with Longaberger"** 7RD x 6.5^H	Incentive (92)	N/A	125	175

KEY:
Values listed are for BASKET ONLY, unless otherwised noted, (-P) = to present

Page in Guide	Form No.	Other Baskets Using Same Form
page 130	unknown	Button, Stitching, Rings & Things, Cookie, 93 Employee Christmas
checklist, Hostess	15261	None
page 100	14427^R / 14435^G	None
page 148	33000-JPS	Be Mine, 93 Sponsor (All-Star), 92 Regional Sponsored Award, 97 Small Easter, Rose Petal
page 144	10863	None
page 100	12661^R / 12653^G	None
page 36	12645^R / 12637^G	None
page 62	unknown	89 Bee, Dresden Basket, Tour, 92 Employee Birthday, Memory, Junior & Senior Recognition, 25th Anniversary, Hartville, 20th Century
page 70	1300-JCWS	Small Berry, 98 Branch Excellence
page 18	18694	Spring, Bob & Dolores Hope, 91 Customer Easter, 91-P Bee Speaker, Boo, Medium Purse, 98 Perfect Attendance, 96 Ohio Statehouse, Red Pottery Thank You
page 112	13323	Be Mine, 92 Regional Sponsored Award, Small Oval, 97 Small Easter, Rose Petal
page 112	unknown	94 Hostess Appreciation, Lavender, 93 Recruit, Rose Bud
page 112	10162	90 Bee, Poinsettia, 7" Hanging, Barn Raising, 7" Measuring, Maple Leaf, 97 Perfect Attendance, 7" Canister

KEY: In blue = Not pictured in the Guide.   **S** = Stained, **U** = Unstained
HL = Heartland® Collection, **WT** = Woven Traditions®, **R** = Red, **G** = Green

Basket	Collection (Year)	Orig.Price	AVG	HIGH
Sponsor, Small "Flying High with Longaberger" $5^{RD} \times 4.5^H$	Incentive (92)	N/A	118	175
Sponsor "Together–We're Growing" $9^L \times 5^W \times 5^H$	Incentive (90)	N/A	175	200
Sponsor "Pegged for Success" $6.5^L \times 6.5^W \times 8^H$	Incentive (96)	N/A	193	225
Sponsor "Rising Star" $16.5^L \times 16.5^W \times 21.5^H$	Incentive (90-91)	N/A	185	230
Sponsor, Superstar "Rising Star" $12^L \times 12.25^W \times 16.25^H$	Incentive (90-91)	N/A	155	200
Sponsor "Share the Tradition" $8.5^L \times 8.5^W \times 5^H$	Incentive (88-89)	N/A	207	325
Spoon, Large $7.5^L \times 7.5^W \times 10^H$	Regular Line (82-P)	16.95	45	65
	Regular Line (Natrl) (00-P)	45.00	45	45
Spoon, Medium	All-American (90)	27.95	100	140
	Feature (96-97)	36.95	53	60
	Feature (Natrl) (99)	28.00	—	—
	Regular Line (83-P)	14.95	34	55
$6.5^L \times 6.5^W \times 8^H$	Regular Line (Natrl) (00-P)	34.00	34	34
Spoon, Small	All-American (90)	23.95	93	135
	Booking (xx-84)	N/A	49	55
	Feature (Natrl) (98, 00)	19.95	—	—
	Heartland (88-99)	23.95	37	45
	Regular Line (87-P)	19.95	26	40
$5.5^L \times 5.5^W \times 6^H$	Regular Line (Natrl) (00-P)	26.00	26	26
Spring	Easter (87)	25.95	226	300
	Feature (Natrl) (98)	29.95	37	50
	Heartland (90-97)	34.95	48	60
	Mother's Day (88)	28.95	130	170
	Regular Line (83-P)	14.95	38	75
$11^L \times 8^W \times 5.5^H$	Woven Traditions (95-97)	41.95	60	65

KEY:
Values listed are for BASKET ONLY, unless otherwise noted, (-P) = to present

Page in Guide	Form No.	Other Baskets Using Same Form
page 112	unknown	88 Employee Birthday, 89 Inaugural, 92 Employee Christmas, 99 Recruit, 5" Hanging, Forget-Me-Not, 92 Recruit, Resolution, 5" Measuring, 5" Canister, Watch Your Business Bloom
page 112	1100-ABRST	89 Employee Christmas, Candle, Medium Key, Collectors Club 97 Renewal, 96 Perfect Attendance
page 112	unknown	Large Peg, Medium Spoon, 94 Bee, 98 Perfect Attendance
page 112	1600-DST	Large Hamper
page 112	1700-DST	Medium Hamper, Small Hamper, 90-91 Recruit
page 112	1500-BBRS	91 Bee, Large Berry, 96 Bee 98 Regional Sales Excellence
checklist	11258	Mini Waste/Extra Small Waste
checklist	17680	
page 16	11000-OBRS	94 Bee, Large Peg, 96 Sponsor,
page 74	$16349^R/22^B/31^G$	98 Perfect Attendance
page 84	19658	
checklist	11169/11000-OO	
checklist	19658	
page 16	10000-OBRS	Medium Peg, Bittersweet, Carry
page 28	10000-OO	Along, 97 Bee
page 82	10871	
page 94	11096/10000-OCS	
checklist	11088 /10000-OO	
checklist	10871	
page 56	900-AX	91-P Bee Speaker, Bob and Dolores
page 84	10880	Hope, Boo Basket, 91 Customer
page 94	10936/ 900-AC	Easter, Medium Purse, Red Pottery
page 148	900-APS	Thank You, 96 Statehouse, Sparkler
checklist	10928 / 900-AO	
page 206	10936	

Basket	Collection[Year]	Orig.Price	AVG	HIGH
Spring Meadow $16.25^L \times 10.75^W \times 4^H$	Collectors Club[00]	95.00	—	—
Star Bound $4.75^L \times 3.75^W \times 2.25^H$	Incentive [95]	N/A	**215**	**300**
Star Team $7^L \times 5^W \times 3.5^H$	Incentive [95]	N/A	**219**	**300**
Statehouse $11^L \times 8^W \times 5.5^H$	Special Event [96]	N/A	—	**80**
Stitching $7^{RD} \times 3^H$	All-American [89]	25.95	**106**	**160**
Sugar and Spice $5.75^L \times 3.75^W \times 3^H$	Booking [88]	N/A	**62**	**95**
Sunburst 22RD	Booking [80]	3.95	**140**	**165**
Summertime $7.75^L \times 4.5^W \times 2.25^{FH} \times 4.5^{BH}$	All-American [96]	34.95	**60**	**65**
Sweet Basil $5^L \times 5^W \times 2.5^H$	Booking [92-94]	22.95	**42**	**65**
Sweet Pea $8.25^{RD} \times 7^H$	May [96]	45.95	**78**	**110**
Sweet Sentiments $4.25^L \times 4.25^W \times 3^H$	Sweetheart [95]	28.95	**67**	**85**
Sweet Treats $8^L \times 5^W \times 3^H$	Sweetheart [97]	32.95	**53**	**88**

280

KEY:
Values listed are for BASKET ONLY, unless otherwised noted, (-P) = to present

Page in Guide	Form No.	Other Baskets Using Same Form
page 44	17655	None
page 130	unknown	Business Card
page 130	unknown	Acorn, Basket of Thanks, Tea, Mini Berry, Mini Chore, Mistletoe, Mini Cradle, Baby Easter, Patriot, 91 Hostess Easter, 93 Small Easter, 94 Employee Christmas, Kiddie Purse, Small Key, 99 Branch Excellence
page 182	900-	91-P Bee Speaker, Bob and Dolores Hope, Boo Basket, 91 Customer Easter, Medium Purse, Red Pottery Thank You, Spring, Sparkler
page 16	5400-ABRS	93 Employee Christmas, Button, Cookie, Rings & Things, Show Star
page 28	45000-AO	All-Star Trio, 89 Employee Birthday, Keepsake, Paint the Town, 90 Recruit, Reach for the Stars (Med), Rosemary, 90 Sweetheart, Treasure Chest, 95 Horizon of Hope, 98 H.Appreciation, 00 Branch Sales
page 28	7000-O	None
page 18	18911	Dash Away Sleigh
page 28	10146	90 Employee Birthday, Potpourri, 88-89 Recruit, 93 Regional Sponsored Award, Shamrock, 93 Sweetheart, Tee
page 144	14915	None
page 186	19046	98 Regional Sponsoring Excellence
page 186	15938^R/62^G/54^B/71^P	None

Basket	Collection(Year)	Orig.Price	AVG	HIGH
Sweetheart (1990)	Employee Birthday(89)	N/A	76	95
	Sweetheart (90)	24.95	116	180
5.75^L x 3.75^W x 3^H				
Sweetheart (1993)	Sweetheart (93)	25.95	74	160
5^L x 5^W x 2.5^H				
Tea	Employee Christmas(94)	N/A	95	125
	Feature (Natrl) (98)	19.95	27	33
	Regular Line (79-P)	7.95	25	85
	Regular Line (Natrl) (99-P)	25.00	25	25
	Woven Traditions (95-99)	28.95	31	85
7^L x 5^W x 3.5^H				
Tea for Two 7.75^L x 5.75^H x 3.25^H	Mother's Day (99)	39.00	55	60
Team Award 9.5^L x 4.5^H x 5^H	Incentive (00)	N/A	—	—
Team Excellence (1998) 8.25^L x 8.25^H x 3.5^H	Incentive (98)	N/A	111	119
Team Excellence (1999) 15^L x 10^H x 7.5^H	Incentive (99)	N/A	—	—
Teaspoon	Regular Line (97-P)	24.95	25	25
	Regular Line (Natrl) (00-P)	25.00	25	25
5^L x 5^H x 4.5^H				
Tee 5.25^L x 5^H x 3^H	Father's Day (99)	29.00	38	45
Tenth Anniversary (1977-87) 15^L x 10^W x 7.5^H	Incentive (87)	N/A	262	320
Thanks-A-Million 5.5^L x 4^H x 4^H	Incentive (99)	N/A	—	—

KEY:
Values listed are for BASKET ONLY, unless otherwised noted, (-P) = to present

Page in Guide	Form No.	Other Baskets Using Same Form
page 62 page 186	45000- 45000-ARS	All-Star Trio, Keepsake, Paint the Town, 90 Recruit, Shining Star, 95 Horizon of Hope, Rosemary, Sugar and Spice, Treasure Chest, 98 H.Appreciation, 00 Branch Sales
page 186	11347	90 Employee Birthday, Potpourri, Shamrock, Sweet Basil, 93 Regional Sponsored Award, 88-89 Recruit, Tee
page 66 page 84 checklist checklist page 206	700- 10847 10740 /700-JO 10847 10710	Acorn, Basket of Thanks, Mini Berry, Mini Chore, Mistletoe, Mini Cradle, Baby Easter, Patriot, 91 Hostess Easter, 93 Small Easter Kiddie Purse, Star Team, Small Key, 99 Branch Excellence
page 150	14931	None
page 132	unknown	None
page 132	unknown	None
page 132	unknown	88 Bee Speaker, Heirloom, 77-87 Tenth Anniversary, 87 Employee Christmas, 99 Team Excellence, Medium Market, Founder's
checklist checklist	11665 17868	Small Peg, 93 Inaugural, Candy Cane, Violet, 96 Recruit
page 70	14940	90 Employee Birthday, Sweet Basil, 93 Sweetheart, Potpourri, 93 Regional Sponsored, 88-89 Recruit, Shamrock
page 120	500-A	88 Bee Speaker, Heirloom, Medium Market, 87 Employee Christmas, 99 Team Excellence, Founder's
page 122	14940	Ambrosia, 97 Horizon of Hope

Basket	Collection (Year)	Orig. Price	AVG	HIGH
Thyme	Booking (95-98)	25.95	34	45
	Collectors Club (98)	N/A	51	71
4.5RD x 3^H				
Timeless Memory	Mother's Day (97)	49.95	83	95
11.25^L x 9.25^W x 5.75^H				
Tissue	Employee Christmas (99)	N/A	—	—
	Father's Day (94)	29.95	84	100
	Regular Line (97-P)	31.95	32	32
6.5^L x 6.5^W x 6.25^H	Regular Line (Natrl) (99-P)	32.00	32	32
Top Performer	Incentive (88-94)	N/A	**	**
10.5^L x 9^W x 8^H				
Tour	Employee Birthday (92)	N/A	62	85
	Tour Baskets (88-00)	**	**	**
8.75^L x 4.75^W x 6.5^H				
Tour II	Tour Baskets (96-00)	29.95	55	65
7^L x 3.5^W x 4.75^H				
Tray	Holiday Hostess (87)	32.95	109	200
14^L x 9^W x 4.5^H				
Treasure	Regular Line, Hostess (98-P)	119.00	119	199
20.25^L x 13.75^W x 7.5^H				
Treasure Chest	Incentive (92)	N/A	200	280
5.75^L x 3.75^W x 3^H				
Tree-Trimming	Holiday Hostess (91)	79.95	150	200
12.5RD x 13.5^H				
Tulip	May (95)	42.95	100	105
14.25^L x 6.25^W x 3.25^H				
20th Century	Tour Baskets (97-P)	49.95	75	90
8.75^L x 4.75^W x 6.5^H				
25th Anniversary	Special Events (98)	49.95	119	125
8.75^L x 4.75^W x 6.5^H				

KEY:
Values listed are for **BASKET ONLY**, unless otherwised noted, **(-P)** = to present

Page in Guide	Form No.	Other Baskets Using Same Form
page 30	19003	Gold Nugget
page 42	19224	
page 148	13030	None
page 66	unknown	None
page 70	18490	
checklist	15831	
checklist	14184	
page 128	unknown	Weekender, Remembrance, Beachcomber
page 62	10022	89 Bee, Memory, Sophomore – Senior Recognition, Hartville, Dresden Basket, 20th Century, 25th Anniversay (Sm)
page 190	5600-BO	
page 190	15814	Hartville II, 98 Flag Sponsoring, 99 Bee
page 98	2300-JGRS	Advisor Recognition, Small Gathering, 92 Bee, 90 Employee Christmas, Pantry
checklist, Hostess	18716	Yuletide Treasures
page 128	45000-	All-Star Trio, 89 Employee Birthday, Keepsake, Paint the Town, 90 Recruit, Shining Star, Rosemary, Sugar and Spice, 90 Sweetheart, 95 Horizon of Hope, 98 Hostess Appreciation, 00 Branch Sales
page 98	1900-BRGS/BGRS	Banker's Waste, Master Employee, Waste (Inverted, Small Round)
page 144	14648	None
page 190	17575	Tour, 89 Bee, Junior, Sophomore & Senior Recognition, Memory, Hartville Basket, Dresden Basket, 25th Anniversary (Sm)
page 182	17612	Tour, 89 Bee, Junior, Sophomore & Senior Recognition, Memory, Hartville Basket, Dresden Basket, 20th Century

KEY: In blue = Not pictured in the Guide. S = Stained, U = Unstained
HL = Heartland® Collection, WT = Woven Traditions®, R = Red, G = Green

Basket	Collection (Year)	Orig.Price	AVG	HIGH
25th Anniversary Large $16^L \times 8^W \times 11^H$	Collectors Club (98)	115.00	194	250
Two-Pie $12^L \times 12^W \times 10^H$	Feature (G.Bonnie) (98) J.W. Collection (86)	95.00 34.95	130 480	150 650
Two-Pie Miniature $4.75^L \times 5^W \times 4^H$	Collectors Club (99)	130.00	—	—
Two-Quart $9.5^L \times 5^W \times 9.5^H$	All-American (91) Feature (85, 87)	36.95 28.95	110 74	150 85
Umbrella $10^{RD} \times 17.5^H$	J.W. Collection (94) Regular Line, Hostess (98-P) Retired (79-94)	74.95 100.00 18.95	177 100 110	250 155 150
Vanity $14.5^L \times 7.5^W \times 4.5^{FH} \times 6.5^{BH}$	Mother's Day (96) Regular Line (98-P)	44.95 50.00	86 50	105 50
Vegetable, Large $16^L \times 9^W \times 3.5^{FH} \times 9^{BH}$	Feature (96-97) Feature (Natrl) (99) Regular Line (87-P)	61.95 48.00 26.95	79 — 57	95 — 65
Vegetable, Medium $13^L \times 7.5^W \times 3^{FH} \times 8^{BH}$	Feature (Natrl) (00) Heartland (97-99) Regular Line (83-P) Retired(Natrl) (94)	37.00 50.95 14.95 38.95	— 54 47 60	— 75 65 75
Vegetable, Small $10.5^L \times 6.5^W \times 3^{FH} \times 7^{BH}$	Regular Line (83-P) Shades of Autumn (90) Woven Traditions (95-99)	12.95 35.95 35.95	32 229 44	45 325 50
Violet $5^L \times 5^W \times 4.5^H$	May (90)	24.95	229	355
VIP Baskets $12^L \times 7^W \times 10^H$	Incentive (86-P)	N/A	**	**

KEY:
Values listed are for **BASKET ONLY**, unless otherwised noted, **(-P)** = to preser

Page in Guide	Form No.	Other Baskets Using Same Form
page 42	12297	Magazine, Bread & Milk
page 84	19241	None
page 136	4800-BT	
page 42	19356	None
page 16	1000-CBRS	91 Employee Christmas, MBA,
page 78	1000-CO	Tall Key, Tall Purse, Membership, Growing Strong Together
page 136	11215	None
checklist, Hostess	11207	
page 172	11207 / 1200-OO	
page 148	14753	None
checklist	18449	
page 74	$16543^R/27^B/35^G$	Large Wine
page 84	19551	
checklist	15202 / 5200-CO	
page 86	18333	Yuletide Traditions
page 96	16713	
checklist	15105/5100-CO	
page 172	15113	
checklist	15008 / 5000-OO	None
page 176	5000-CGUBS	
page 206	15016	
page 144	14000-BVS	93 Inaugural, Candy Cane, Small Peg, Teaspoon
page 116, 118	unknown	None

Basket	Collection(Year)	Orig.Price	AVG	HIGH
Wash Day, Medium 18.75^L x 18.25^W x 9.5^H	Regular Line[00-P]	159.00	159	159
Wash Day, Small 16.25^L x 15.75^W x 8.5^H	Regular Line[00-P]	139.00	139	139
Waste, Inverted Large Round 14RD x 16^H	Feature [87]	59.95	124	150
	Retired(no/h) [79-84]	26.95	85	110
	Retired(1sw/h) [79-84]	28.95	114	120
Waste, Inverted Small Round 12.5^{RD} x 13.5^H	Retired(no/h) [79-84]	21.95	90	100
	Retired(1sw/h) [79-84]	23.95	—	125
Waste, Large Oval 16.25^L x 13^W x 16^H	Regular Line[00-P]	149.00	149	149
Waste, Medium (or Large Waste) 13.5^L x 13.5^L x 16^H	Feature (Natrl) [98]	71.95	—	—
	Retired [79-00]	21.95	92	105
Waste, Medium Oval 14.25^L x 11.5^W x 12.75^H	Regular Line[00-P]	104.00	104	104
Waste, Mini 7.5^L x 7.5^W x 10^H	All-American [90]	35.95	132	180
	Father's Day [95]	46.95	87	120
	Incentive [99-00]	N/A	--	—
	Regular Line [82-99]	16.95	45	65
Waste, Small 9.5^L x 9.5^W x 12^H	All-American [90]	45.95	138	210
	J.W. Collection [84]	34.95	1555	2100
	Retired [79-00]	16.95	56	75
Waste, Small Miniature 3.75^L x 3.75^W x 4.75^H	Collectors Club [97]	99.95	171	225
Waste, Small Oval 11.5^L x 9.25^W x 10.5^H	Regular Line[00-P]	79.00	79	79
Watch Your Business Bloom 5RD x 4.5^H	Incentive (97)	N/A	92	99

KEY:
Values listed are for **BASKET ONLY, unless otherwised noted, (-P)** = to prese

Page in Guide	Form No.	Other Baskets Using Same Form
checklist, Hostess	19372	None
checklist, Hostess	15695	None
page 80	2000-BO	None
page 166	2000-OO	
page 166	2000-BO	
page 166	1900-OO	Banker's Waste, Master Employee,
page 166	1900-BO	Tree Trimming
checklist	19666	None
page 84	11789	None
page 172	11703 / 1700-O	
checklist	19666	None
page 16	12000-OBRS	Also known as Extra Small Waste
page 70	11266	and renamed to Large Spoon in 1999
page 122	11258	
checklist	11258 / 12000-OO	
page 16	1800-OBRS	None
page 136	1800-OT	
page 172	11801 / 1800-OO	
page 40	17797	None
checklist	19461	None
page 112	unknown	5" Measuring, 89 Inaugural, Forget-Me-Not, 5" Hanging, 92 Recruit, Resolution, 92 Sponsor (Small), 5" Canister, 92 Employee Christmas, 88 Employee Birthday

Basket	Collection (Year)	Orig.Price	AVG	HIGH
Weekender	Feature (87-88)	54.95	**125**	**175**
10.5^L x 9^W x 8^H	Holiday Hostess (88)	65.95	**183**	**225**
Welcome Home 15^L x 9.5^W x 5.5^H	Collectors Club (97)	69.95	**133**	**145**
Wildflower 13.5RD x 8.5^H	Hostess (92-98)	64.95	**101**	**125**
Wine, Large 16^L x 9^W x 3.5^{FH} x 9^{BH}	Retired (83-86)	29.95	**95**	**120**
Winter Wishes 12.5^L x 8.25^W x 10.5^{FH} x 12^{BH}	Holiday Hostess (98)	95.00	**100**	**130**
Woven Memories 10^L x 6^W x 4^H	Tour (99-P)	39.95	**	**
Yuletide Traditions 13^L x 7.5^W x 3^{FH} x 8^{BH}	Christmas (91)	38.95	**93**	**140**
Yuletide Treasures 20.25^L x 13.75^W x 7.5^H	Holiday Hostess (96)	129.95	**149**	**200**

KEY:
Values listed are for **BASKET ONLY, unless otherwised noted**, **(-P)** = to present

Page in Guide	Form No.	Other Baskets Using Same Form
page 80 page 98	200-YO 200-YRGS	Remembrance, Top Performer, Beachcomber
page 40	10464	Small Market, 99 Regional Sales & Sponsoring Excellence
page 108	10111	None
page 172	5200-CO	Large Vegetable
page 100	12483^R / 12491^G	None
page 190	unknown	Small Chore, 93 Large Easter, 88 Small Easter, Gingerbread, 95 Bee, $500 Milliom, 91 Regional Sponsored
page 34	5100-CRST/CGST	Medium Vegetable
page 100	18619^R / 18627^G	Treasure

 # ★ Dimension Search ★ 

How To Use:

Many collectors are not always able to identify their baskets. This reference tool was designed to help you determine which basket you may have by looking at its dimensions. ****Note**** This tool can also be used to identify plastic protectors. Follow the same steps below, except add a 1/2" to an 1" to your protector's dimensions when referring to the basket dimensions.

Step 1 — Measure your basket. At the top, measure length and width. If round, measure the diameter across the basket. Next, measure its height. All measurements in this Guide are listed in standard form: **Length(L) x Width(W) x Height(H)**. Baskets that are sloped will have both its **Front Height(FH)** and its **Back Height(BH)** listed.

Step 2 — Go to the shape section that your basket most closely resembles. Octagonal baskets are listed as **Round**. The dimensions are in numerical order. Scan down the list to find your dimension. Because these baskets are individually hand-made, measurements may vary within a 1/2". Locate the measurement that is *closest* to your basket.

Step 3 — Once you have located your basket's dimensions, note the basket name and page number adjacent to it. Refer to that page number in the *"Quick Find"* section. The *"Quick Find"* will tell you:

(1) . . . the different collection in which your basket has been featured. Now is a good time to note distinguishing characteristics of your basket, such as color weaving or commemorative tags that may point you to a specific collection or series. . .

(2) . . . other baskets that use the same form. . .

(3) . . . its location in the Guide.

If you are still not able to determine which basket you have or have other questions, please feel free to contact us at 1-800-VERIFY IT, ext. 11

3.75^L x 3.75^W x 4.75^H	See J.W. Miniature Waste	pg. 288
4^L x 4^W x 4^H	See Chives	pg. 224
4^L x 4^W x 5.5^H	See Horizon of Hope (98)	pg. 244
4.25^L x 4.25^W x 3^H	See Sweet Sentiments	pg. 280
5 x 5^W x 2.5^H	See Sweet Basil	pg. 280
5^L x 5^W x 4.5^H	See Small Peg	pg. 258
5.25^L x 5.25^W x 4^H	See Bee (98)	pg. 216
5.5^L x 5.5^W x 2.5^H	See Ivy	pg. 246
5.5^L x 5.5^W x 6^H	See Small Spoon	pg. 278
6^L x 6^W x 3^H	See Easter, Small (98)	pg. 232
6^L x 6^W x 4.25^{FH} x 5.25^{BH}	See Finder's Keepers	pg. 234
6.5^L x 6.5^W x 3^H	See Small Berry	pg. 218
6.5^L x 6.5^W x 6.25^H	See Tissue	pg. 284
6.5^L x 6.5^W x 8^H	See Medium Spoon	pg. 278
7.5^L x 7.5^W x 3.5^H	See Medium Berry	pg. 216
7.5^L x 7.5^W x 10^H	See Mini Waste	pg. 288
8.25^L x 8.25^W x 3.5^H	See Team Excellence (98)	pg. 282
8.5^L x 8.5^W x 5^H	See Large Berry	pg. 216
8.5^L x 8.5^W x 7^H	See Cranberry	pg. 226
9^L x 9^W x 4.5^H	See Bayberry	pg. 212
9.5^L x 9.5^W x 2.75^H	See Picnic Pal	pg. 262
9.5^L x 9.5^W x 12^H	See Small Waste	pg. 288
10.25^L x 10.25^W x 4.5^H	See Bountiful Harvest	pg. 218
10.5^L x 10.5^W x 4.5^H	See Mother's Day (92)	pg. 254
12^L x 12^W x 4^H	See Pie	pg. 262
12^L x 12^W x 6^H	See Cake	pg. 222
12^L x 12^W x 10^H	See Two-Pie	pg. 286
12^L x 12.25^W x 16.25^H	See Medium Hamper	pg. 240
13.5^L x 13.5^W x 16^H	See Medium Waste	pg. 288
15^L x 15^W x 7.5^H	See Medium Picnic	pg. 266
15.5^L x 15.5^W x 12.25^H	See Evergreen	pg. 232
16^L x 16^W x 8^H	See Coverlet	pg. 224
16.5^L x 16.5^W x 21.5^H	See Large Hamper	pg. 240
17^L x 17^W x 22^H	See Large Hamper, 95	pg. 240

continued next page

10.5^L x 6.5^W x 3^{FH} x 7^{BH}	See Small Vegetable	pg. 286
10.5^L x 9^W x 8^H	See Weekender	pg. 290
10.75^L x 5.75^W x 7.5^H	See Flag	pg. 234
11^L x 7.25^W x 2.75^H	See Early Blossoms	pg. 228
11^L x 8^W x 5.5^H	See Spring	pg. 278
11.25^L x 9.25^W x 5.75^H	See Timeless Memory	pg. 284
11.5^L x 5^W x 3^H	See Cracker	pg. 226
11.5^L x 15.5^W x 3.75^H	See Small Serving Tray	pg. 274
12^L x 5.25^W x 3.75^{FH} x 5^{BH}	See Envelope	pg. 232
12^L x 7^W x 10^H	See VIP Baskets	pg. 286
12^L x 8^W x 4.25^H	See Holiday Cheer	pg. 244
12^L x 8^W x 11.5^H	See Mail	pg. 250
12^L x 11.75^W x 3^{FH} x 5.5^{BH}	See Small Basket Bin	pg. 212
12^L x 14.5^W x 3^H	See Paper Tray, Bottom	pg. 258
12^L x 14.5^W x 3^{FH} x 5.5^{BH}	See Paper Tray, Tapered	pg. 258
12.5^L x 8.25^W x 10.5^{FH} x 12^{BH}	See Winter Wishes	pg. 290
13^L x 7.5^W x 3^{FH} x 8^{BH}	See Medium Vegetable	pg. 286
13^L x 8^W x 5^H	See Medium Chore	pg. 224
13.25^L x 11.25^W x 9^H	See Gourmet Picnic	pg. 262
14^L x 6^W x 3^H	See Flower Pot Basket, Small	pg. 234
14^L x 7.75^W x 5.25^H	See Large Chore	pg. 224
14^L x 9^W x 4.5^H	See Small Gathering	pg. 238
14.25^L x 6.25^W x 3.25^H	See Tulip	pg. 284
14.25^L x 6.25^W x 9.5^H	See Cherished Memories	pg. 224
14.5^L x 5.5^W x 9.5^H	See Director Sponsored 2000	pg. 228
14.5^L x 7.5^W x 3.75^H	See Bread (new)	pg. 220
14.5^L x 7.5^W x 4.5^{FH} x 6.5^{BH}	See Vanity	pg. 286
15^L x 8^W x 2.25^H	See Bread (old)	pg. 220
15^L x 9.5^W x 5.5^H	See Small Market	pg. 252
15^L x 10^W x 7.5^H	See Medium Market	pg. 252
15.75^L x 6.5^W x 11^H	See Branch Basket	pg. 218
15.75^L x 10.5^W x 10.5^H	See Newspaper	pg. 256
16^L x 8^W x 11^H	See Magazine	pg. 250
16^L x 9^W x 3.5^{FH} x 9^{BH}	See Large Vegetable	pg. 286
16^L x 9^W x 6^H	See Harvest	pg. 242
16^L x 11^W x 9^H	See Large Market	pg. 250
16.25^L x 10.75^W x 4^H	See Spring Meadow	pg. 280
16.25^L x 15.75^W x 8.5^H	See Small Wash Day	pg. 288
16.5^L x 12.5^W x 5^{FH} x 7.75^{BH}	See Large Basket Bin	pg. 212
17^L x 7.5^W x 4.75^H	See Flower Pot Basket	pg. 234

continued next page

continued next page

Round

7RD x 5.5^{H}	See National Sales Level 1	pg. 254
7RD x 6.5^{H}	See 7" Measuring	pg. 252
7^{L} x 6.75^{W} x 3^{H}	See Generations, 7"	pg. 238
7.25RD x 2.25^{H}	See Catch-All	pg. 222
7.25RD x 5.25^{H}	See Small Pumpkin	pg. 264
7.5RD x 9.25^{H}	See Snapdragon	pg. 276
7.5^{L} x 7.5^{W} x 4.75^{H}	See Morning Glory	pg. 254
8RD x 4.5^{H}	See Med. Easter, 1990	pg. 232
8RD x 6^{H}	See Jingle Bell	pg. 246
8RD x 6.5^{H}	See Medium Fruit	pg. 236
8^{L} x 7.75^{W} x 3.5^{H}	See Generations, 8"	pg. 238
8RD x 9^{H}	See Tall Fruit	pg. 236
8.25RD x 7^{H}	See Sweet Pea	pg. 280
8.25RD x 7.75^{H}	See Hanging, Woven Bottom	pg. 242
8.5RD x 4^{H}	See Basket of Love	pg. 212
8.5RD x 7.5^{H}	See Planter, Small Fern	pg. 264
9RD x 8.5^{H}	See 9" Measuring	pg. 254
9.25RD x 7.25^{H}	See Pumpkin	pg. 264
9.5RD x 5^{H}	See Large Easter (90)	pg. 230
10RD x 4^{H}	See Darning	pg. 226
10RD x 5.5^{H}	See Planter, Patio	pg. 264
10RD x 6.25^{H}	See Homestead	pg. 244
10^{L} x 9.25^{W} x 4^{H}	See Generations, 10"	pg. 238
10^{L} x 9.25^{W} x 6.5^{H}	See Snowflake, Small	pg. 276
10RD x 17.5^{H}	See Umbrella	pg. 286
10.5RD x 5^{H}	See Popcorn	pg. 264
11RD x 10.5^{H}	See 11" Measuring	pg. 252
11.25RD x 9^{H}	See Pumpkin, Large	pg. 264
11.5^{L} x 9.25^{W} x 10.5^{H}	See Small Oval Waste	pg. 276
11.75RD x 6.5^{H}	See Hearthside	pg. 242
12RD x 5.75^{H}	See Quilting	pg. 266
12^{L} x 11^{W} x 4.5^{H}	See Generations, 12"	pg. 238
12.5RD x 6^{H}	See Large Easter 2000	pg. 232
12.5RD x 13.5^{H}	See Banker's Waste	pg. 212
13RD x 6.25^{H}	See Pinecone	pg. 262
13RD x 8.5^{H}	See Large Fruit	pg. 236
13RD x 12.5^{H}	See 13" Measuring	pg. 252
13.5RD x 8.5^{H}	See Wildflower	pg. 290
14^{L} x 12.75^{W} x 5^{H}	See Generations, 14"	pg. 238
14^{L} x 12.75^{W} x 11.5^{H}	See Snowflake, Large	pg. 276

continued next page

 # Additional Notes 

 # Additional Notes 

 # Additional Notes 

 # Additional Notes 

Additional Notes

 # Additional Notes